EGGPLANTS, ELEVATORS, ETC.

AN UNCOMMON HISTORY OF COMMON THINGS

JAMES MEYERS

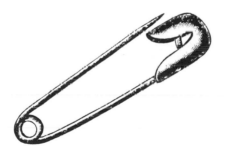

HART PUBLISHING COMPANY, INC. • NEW YORK CITY

HOW MANY TIMES have you said, "I don't know how people managed before they had zippers!"—or umbrellas, for that matter—or ice-cream.

Did you ever look at a common item you were using for the zillionth time and suddenly wonder, "What clever genius thought that up?"

EGGPLANTS, ELEVATORS, ETC. *An Uncommon History of Common Things* discusses all kinds of objects you'd really like to know about—whether they be truffles or typewriters or tulips or tobacco. Where did they come from? When and how were they discovered, or invented, or created? How did they develop? How many are used each year? What do they cost?

This fascinating book is chock full of facts, myths, and lore about the everyday items that mankind now finds indispensable to the good life. Here are hours of good reading, peppered with a few hundred rare and exciting pictures, and all kinds of data that will make you ooh and ah.

CONTENTS

PICTURE ACKNOWLEDGMENTS

COPYRIGHT ACKNOWLEDGMENTS

THANKS

We wish to thank the following organizations for their contributions of information for this book:

Baskin Robbins Ice Cream
The Greek National Tourist Organization

L.A. Dreyfus Co.
Sam Simon Umbrella Shop, New York
Schenley Affiliated Brands Corp
United Fresh Fruit and Vegetable Association
Virginia Dare Co.

EGGPLANTS, ELEVATORS, ETC.

AUTOMOBILES

Crushed-velour upholstery. Air conditioning. Power brakes and steering. Leather-padded dashboard. Quiet, cushioned ride. AM/FM radio, CB unit, and tape deck.

To the owner of an automobile fifty years ago, these features would probably seem fit only for the most expensive of limousines; today, we're apt to find them in many ordinary family cars. If we insist on comfort as much as speed and reliability in the automobiles we drive, it's not without good reason: in the age of the automobile, an American can spend up to 10 or 15 percent of his waking hours in the well-appointed confines of his home-away-from home, the car.

Without doubt, the automobile ranks among the two or three most important inventions of our age. The car has determined the shape of our cities and the routine of our lives, made almost every inch of our nation easily accessible to everybody, ribboned our country with highways, cluttered the landscape with interchanges, gas stations, parking lots, drive-ins, and auto junkyards, and covered over 50,000 square miles of green with asphalt and concrete! Considering that there is now one automobile in this country for every two persons (compared to, say, China, with over 14,500 persons per car), it's certainly easy to agree with a writer who described the American as a "creature on four wheels."

A taxi was creeping slowly through rush-hour traffic, and the passenger was already late.

"Please," he asked the driver, "can't you go any faster?"

"Sure I can," the hack replied. "But I'm not allowed to leave the cab."

The technological revolution that has produced our mobile, car-oriented society has taken place almost entirely in the last seventy or eighty years. But the idea of a self-propelled vehicle—with more modest accoutrements, indeed—had been on man's mind for centuries before the first automobile cranked into gear. As long ago as the thirteenth century, Roger Bacon predicted the use of vehicles propelled by combustion, and in 1472, a Frenchman named Robert Valturio described a vehicle combining wind power and a cogwheel system for propulsion.

If, in 1600, you happened to be walking along a Dutch canal, you might have been surprised to see a two-masted ship bearing down on you. Not in the canal—on the road. There was one such ship that was said to have reached a speed of twenty miles per hour while carrying twenty-eight fear-stricken passengers. In his notebooks, Leonardo da Vinci had envisioned some sort of self-propelled vehicle; and some Dutchman, quite naturally, had modeled such a vehicle after a sailing vessel.

About 1700, a Swiss inventor mounted a windmill on a wagon. It was hoped that as the windmill wound up a huge spring, the vehicle would lope along under its own power.

In the early eighteenth century, another Frenchman designed a machine run by a series of steel springs, similar to a clock movement, but the French Academy had the foresight to declare that a horseless vehicle "would never be able to travel the roads of any city."

No single man can be termed the inventor of the automobile.

The steam carriage was the precursor of the automobile.

Rather, advances on motor cars were made by many men working in various countries around the same time. But credit for the first mechanically propelled vehicle is generally given to the French engineer Nicholas Cugnot, who in 1769 built a three-wheeled steam-propelled tractor to transport military cannons. Cugnot's machine could travel at speeds of up to two-and-a-half miles per hour, but had to stop every hundred feet or so to make steam.

Through much of the eighteenth century, steam-driven passenger vehicles—both with and without tracks—were in regular operation in England. The early steam engine, however, was found to be impractical on ordinary roads, for it required great engineering skills on the part of the driver. Numerous fatal accidents stiffened resistance to the new machines, and beginning in 1830, Parliament passed a number of laws greatly restricting their use. One such regulation, called the Red Flag Law, stipulated that horseless cars must be preceded by a person on foot with a red flag in hand, or a red lantern at night, to warn of the car's approach. Another law limited the speed of horseless vehicles to a blinding four miles per hour. The limit was not raised until 1896, when English motor club members celebrated with an "emancipation run" from London to Brighton, initiating what was to become an annual event.

These early restrictions naturally limited interest in automotive research in England. Other sources of power were investigated elsewhere. Over the latter years of the nineteenth century, various electric cars were introduced with some frequency, but these never quite

The Benz Second Motor Tricycle Carriage (left), produced in 1886, ran at a maximum speed of 10 mph.

In 1900, the Benz "Duc" (right), was a popular automobile model.

Around the turn of the century, New York's equine helpmates were depositing some two-and-a-half million pounds of manure and 60,000 gallons of urine on the streets each day!

caught on with the public because they had to be recharged regularly. Most work on the internal-combustion engine was performed on the continent, especially in France and Germany. The internal-combustion engine, like the auto itself, had no single inventor. But in 1885, Gottlieb Daimler of Germany became the first to patent a high-speed four-stroke engine.

Around the same time, Karl Benz, another German, was building an internal-combustion tricycle that could reach a speed of ten miles per hour. The general public remained largely unimpressed. A German newspaper, reporting on Benz's work, asked the question: "Who is interested in such a contrivance so long as there are horses on sale?"

Daimler and Benz worked independently for years, but later joined to form what is now the Mercedes-Benz Company—the name Mercedes having been borrowed from the daughter of a Daimler associate.

The Landaulet Town Car was commonly used as a taxicab.

The first practical gasoline-powered car with a modern-type chassis and gears was the work of a Frenchman named Krebs, who designed the Panhard in 1894. In the early years of the industry, France led the world in automobile production. The still-flourishing Renault company was founded before 1900. But around the turn of the century, Americans began to take the lead in automotive innovation.

The first successful internal-combustion car in the United States was the work of the Duryea brothers, Charles and J. Frank, bike manufacturers from Springfield, Massachusetts. The Duryeas had read of Karl Benz's work in Germany, and built their first car in 1893. Two years later, the brothers formed the Duryea Motor Wagon Company, the first automobile manufacturing firm in the nation. They later went on to win one of the most important races in automobile history.

Racing and sport motoring were then considered the primary uses of the automobile. Few people could see the future of the car as a common means of practical transportation. The first automobile race ever held was won by a car that was powered by a steam engine. On June 22, 1894, Paris was bubbling with excitement as twenty horseless carriages lined up for the eighty-mile race from Paris to Rouen and back again to the big town.

Henry Ford began his motor company in 1903 with capital of only $28,000, 12 workers, and a plant only 50 feet wide.

Could these newfangled things run at all? And if they did, would they prove as fleet and as durable as a few changes of horses?

Less than five hours later, a De Dion Bouton lumbered down

By 1902, the year this advertisement appeared, Oldsmobile was producing 2,500 cars annually.

Price
$650,00
at Factory

Write Dept. P
for
Illustrated
Book

TWO of the nine Blue Ribbons (100 per cent.) for completing a strenuous 100 mile run without stop, at Chicago, August 2, 1902, were awarded

The Oldsmobile

The judges could not be shaken from their opinion that **The Oldsmobile is The Best Thing On Wheels**, for there is nothing to watch but the Road, and all roads are alike to the Oldsmobile, which is built to run *and does it.*

SELLING AGENTS

Oldsmobile Co., 138 W. 38th St., New York
Oldsmobile Co., 1124 Connecticut Ave., Washington
Quaker City Auto. Co., 138 N. Broad St., Philadelphia
H. B. Shattuck & Son, 239 Columbus Avenue, Boston
Banker Bros. Co., East End, Pittsburgh
Oldsmobile Company, 411 Euclid Ave., Cleveland, O.
William E. Metzger, 254 Jefferson Ave., Detroit
Ralph Temple & Austrian Co., 293 Wabash Ave., Chicago
Fisher Automobile Co., Indianapolis.
Rochester Automobile Co., 170 South Av., Rochester, N. Y.

Olds Gasoline Engine Works, Omaha
W. C. Jaynes Auto. Co., 573 Main St., Buffalo, N. Y.
Day Automobile Co., St. Louis and Kansas City, Mo.
George Hannan, 1455 California Street, Denver
Clark & Hawkins, 903 Texas Ave, Houston, Texas
The Manufacturers Co., 26 Fremont St. San Francisco.
A. F. Chase & Co., 215 So. Third St., Minneapolis
Oldsmobile Co., 728 National Ave., Milwaukee, Wis.
Abbott Cycle Co., 411 Baronne St., New Orleans, La.
F. E. Gilbert, Jacksonville, Fla.

OLDS MOTOR WORKS, Detroit, Mich., U. S. A.

the boulevards of gay Paree. The steamer had covered the distance at the daredevil rate of seventeen miles per hour.

The first auto race in America was held on Thanksgiving Day, 1895, over a snowy fifty-five mile course stretching from Chicago to Waukegan, Illinois. Sponsored by the *Chicago Times-Herald*, the event included about eighty entries. But only six vehicles managed to leave the starting line. Only two finished—the victorious Duryea, and a rebuilt electric Benz that had to be pushed over a considerable part of the route. The victory of the gasoline-powered Duryea did much to establish the internal-combustion vehicle as the car of the future.

At the time, American cities were certainly in desperate need of horseless carriages—and horseless streets. Around the turn of the century, New York City's equine helpmates were depositing some two-and-a-half million pounds of manure and 60,000 gallons of urine on the streets each day!

American engineers and inventors rose to meet the challenge with great advances in automotive technology in the later years of the nineteenth century; and in 1899, over 2,500 cars were produced by thirty different American companies. By 1904, there were over 54,500 cars on the roads here. But even then, poor roads and high costs made the automobile chiefly a sporting vehicle. It remained for American industrial genius to bring the car within reach of the average citizen.

Henry Ford is usually credited with introducing mass-production techniques to automobile manufacture, but Ford actually adapted innovations made earlier by Ransolm E. Olds. Olds was but thirty years old when he designed his first internal-combustion vehicle in 1897. Later, Olds was forced to seek financial help from a friend, a scrap merchant in Detroit, who agreed to advance the needed capital if Olds would locate his plant in Detroit, then a city of less than 300,000 people. By 1902, Olds was turning out 2,500 cars annually with assembly-line techniques, and the "Motor City" was born. Today, the Detroit-Flint corridor in Michigan produces about one-fourth of all American cars.

In the early 1900's, if you were lucky enough to own a sports model de luxe automobile, the chances were you had a chauffeur to drive you around.

Henry Ford began his motor company in 1903 with capital of only $28,000, twelve workers, and a plant only 50 feet wide. Additional funds were supplied by the Dodge brothers, themselves auto manufacturers, and the Dodges' initial $20,000 investment was eventually worth $25 million. Soon afterward, Ford improved on Olds's mass-production ideas and introduced the conveyor-belt assembly line. Ford's first successful mass-produced car was the Model N, brought out in 1906 for $500. (From the very beginning, Ford used letters of the alphabet to identify his models.) But the car that made Henry famous was the Model T.

Preparation for the Model T's production brought Ford so close to bankruptcy that he had to borrow $100 from a colleague's sister to pay for the car's launch. That $100, by the way, was eventually worth $260,000 to the generous donor. The first "Lizzie" rolled off the line in 1908, with a four-cylinder, 20-horsepower engine capable of speeds of forty miles per hour. It carried a price tag of $850.

Mass-production innovations continued to lower the price of the Lizzie. In 1916, a new model sold for just $360! Each vehicle finished its turn around the assembly line in just ninety minutes, compared to the earlier day-and-a-half assembly-line run.

Today, most plants can turn out fifty to sixty cars an hour, and the Chevrolet plant in Lordstown, Ohio, the nation's most modern, can produce over 100 vehicles an hour.

What is the most popular car in America? For years it's been the Chevrolet. In 1975, 1.6 million new Chevies left the assembly line, while the Ford ranked second with 1.3 million cars.

Sales of the Model T rose to 734,811 in 1916, accounting for half of all American-car production. Eventually some 15 million Lizzies were produced before the car was discontinued in 1927. From 1915 on, the Ford Company offered its prize automobiles in any color, "so long as it is black."

In 1908, there were over 500 car companies in the United States, but that year marked the beginning of General Motors' eventual dom-

ination of the automobile market. The corporation was largely the work of William Crapo Durant, the millionaire grandson of a Michigan governor. Durant gained control of his first car company, Buick, in 1904, and moved his plant to Flint, Michigan. In 1908, Durant took over the Olds Company—although Ransolm Olds himself had left the firm in 1905 to form the Reo Company. Durant now began to absorb a number of ailing car and accessory companies under the corporate umbrella of General Motors. The Cadillac Company—named for Antoine de la Mothe Cadillac, the founder of Detroit—joined GM in 1909. Durant even approached Ford with an offer to join General Motors, but Henry turned him down.

The roller coaster career of W.C. Durant took a turn for the worse shortly after General Motors was formed, and he eventually lost control of the corporation he had founded. Durant's new car firm, the Chevrolet Company, named after a race driver who had designed engines for Durant, was such a success that the new leaders of GM were forced to take Durant, and Chevrolet, into the firm. By 1918, Durant was again at the helm of the corporation. But the founder of what is

These vehicles were in vogue during the first decade of the 20th century.

Top left: The Extension-front Brougham.

Top right: The Electric Victoria-phaeton.

Bottom left: The Torpedo-type Touring Car.

Bottom right: The three-ton truck.

presently the largest manufacturing corporation in the world, with sales of $35 billion in 1975, declared bankruptcy in 1936, claiming over a million dollars in debts and assets of just $250—the clothes on his back!

The first decades of this century saw bankruptcy and merger greatly reduce the number of American car firms. In 1920, Walter Chrysler, a former vice-president at General Motors, joined the Willys-Overland company, once the number-two car producer after Ford, and laid the groundwork for the Chrysler Corporation. Chrysler absorbed Maxwell-Chalmers and the Dodge brothers' company, and introduced the Plymouth in 1929. The Lincoln Company became part of the Ford Corporation in 1921, and the Mercury was introduced in 1939.

The Studebaker and Packard, both introduced before 1902, eventually merged, and the Nash Company—founded by Charles Nash, who had replaced Durant at General Motors—joined the Hudson Company in the 1950's to form the American Motors Corporation. As early as 1914, 75 percent of all American cars were manufactured by the ten largest companies.

The Rolls-Royce Corporation was founded in 1904 by two Englishmen named—you guessed it, Rolls and Royce.

The familiar Volkswagen "beetle" was first produced in 1938. By the 1950's, Volkswagen was the largest car producer in Europe; and in 1972, the "beetle" surpassed the Model T in total sales for a single model, with over 15 million sold throughout the world.

The United States has been the leader in automobile production for many years. Over a million cars were produced here in 1916, and over 3 million in 1924, when there were some 15 million cars registered in America. In 1952, about 4 million American passenger cars rolled off the line, ten times the number produced by the second-ranking nation, Great Britain. At the time, there was a car on the road here for every 3.5 persons alive, compared to, for example, one car per 564 persons in Japan. The second-ranking nation in car use was, surprisingly, New Zealand, with six persons for each car.

American dominance of the automobile market has slipped somewhat in recent years, yet the United States still ranks first in total production, with 6.7 million passenger cars turned out in 1975. Japan ranked second that year with 4.5 million cars, followed by West Germany and France with just under three million each, Great Britain and Italy with about 1.4 million each, Canada with one million, and the Soviet Union with 670,000.

What is the most popular car in America? For years it's been the Chevrolet. In 1975, 1.6 million new Chevies left the assembly line, while the Ford ranked second with 1.3 million cars, followed in order by the Oldsmobile, Buick, Pontiac, Plymouth, Mercury, Dodge, and Cadillac. Among American auto manufacturers, General Motors was far and away the leader, with 3.6 million cars produced; Ford was second with 1.8 million, Chrysler third with 900,000, and American Motors fourth with 320,000.

There are now about 107 million passenger cars registered throughout this country, and 125 million licensed drivers. Car registration began here in 1901, in New York State. The first license plates appeared in France in 1893.

England's first license plate, A1, was purchased in 1903 by Lord Russell, after an overnight wait outside the license bureau office—and that plate was reportedly sold to a collector in 1973 for $35,000! As late as 1909, driving licenses were required in only twelve American states, when there were few traffic laws of any kind. The first modern traffic light, in fact, did not appear until 1914, on Euclid Avenue, Cleveland, Ohio. And in England driving tests were not required for would-be drivers until 1935!

Which should bring us to the subject of automobile accidents. The first traffic accident in the United States was recorded in 1896 when a

Duryea Motor Wagon collided with a bicycle in New York City, sending the cyclist to the hospital and the driver to jail. Three years later, a sixty-eight-year-old real estate broker named Henry Bliss became the first American to die as the result of an auto accident, when he was run over while stepping from a New York streetcar. By the early 1920's, traffic fatalities were already topping the 20,000 mark annually—not to mention an estimated 700,000 auto injuries each year.

In the mid-1950's, close to 3 million Americans were killed or injured each year in automobile accidents—about 570 deaths for every 10 billion miles driven, compared to fourteen deaths for every 10 bil-

Automobile races were attracting fans as early as 1907.

lion airplane miles, thirteen deaths for the bus, and just five for the train.

But Americans are far from the world's most reckless drivers. That honor belongs to the Austrians, who in a recent year suffered 386 auto deaths per one million population. That year, drivers in West Germany, Canada, and Australia also suffered more fatal accidents than their American counterparts, with the United States in fourth place with 272 deaths per million persons. The lowest rate among major car-using nations belonged to Mexico, with just 83 deaths per million persons.

Surprisingly enough, the death rate per vehicle mile has actually declined here since 1941, due in large part to the proliferation of divided highways. The Interstate Highway System, the largest single construction job ever undertaken by man, will, when complete, include about 42,500 miles of divided highway, accommodating an estimated 25 percent of all United States traffic. The system was 80 percent complete in the mid-70's.

Automobile design and usage have changed a great deal since the days of Daimler, Benz, and Duryea, but almost all cars, past and present, compact and luxury, have one thing in common: the internal-combustion engine. (A present exception is the Mazda, which operates with a rotary, or Wankel engine.) The internal-combustion engine converts heat generated by the burning of gasoline to the motive power required to turn the car wheels.

Basically, the internal-combustion engine works like this: fuel and air first mix in each cylinder of the engine. The piston in the cylinder, rebounding from its previous stroke, compresses the fuel and air mixture. At this point, a hot electric spark ignites the compressed mixture. The rapid combustion of the gasoline and air mixture speeds up the motion of their molecules, increasing the pressure they exert on the top of the piston. This pressure forces the piston down the cylinder.

The largest automobile ever constructed was a special Cadillac limousine built for King Khalid of Saudi Arabia in 1975, measuring 25 feet, 2 inches in length, and weighing 7,800 pounds.

Each downward stroke of the piston turns the crankshaft, which in turn spins the drive shaft. The drive shaft turns the gears in the differential, the gears turn the rear axle, and the axle rotates the rear wheels. Unless the car is equipped with four-wheel drive, the front wheels are not connected to the engine-driven mechanism.

A car runs more smoothly at night or in damp weather simply because the air is cooler, not because it contains more oxygen; the amount of oxygen in the air is constant. Cool air is more dense than

This restored Duryea automobile is now on display at the Smithsonian Institution in Washington, D.C.

warm air; and therefore, an engine takes in a greater weight of air when it is damp and chilly. This accounts for the increased power and the freedom from engine knock which so many motorists notice when they drive at night or in the rain.

A woman driving in Brooklyn stopped her car for a red light. However, when the light turned green again, she just stayed right where she was.

When the light had changed several times and she still hadn't moved, the traffic policeman finally went over to her and inquired politely, "What's the matter, lady, ain't we got no colors you like?"

Most cars today are equipped with either a four-, six-, or eight-cylinder engine—but a 1930 Cadillac was powered by a sixteen-cylinder engine! And speaking of Cadillacs, the largest automobile ever constructed was a special limousine built for King Khalid of Saudi Arabia in 1975, measuring twenty-five feet, two inches in length and weighing 7,800 pounds.

The largest car ever produced for regular road use was the 1927 "Golden Bugatti," which measured twenty-two feet from bumper to bumper. Only six of these cars were made, and some of these survive in excellent condition.

A proliferation of new items for the car trade are developed each year. Some of the latest are shown on these pages.

Portable Electric Vacuum

Has no cord, will travel! This portable cleaner goes anywhere, and weighs a mere 1½ pounds.

Back Supporter

Here's the answer to car-induced backache: an inflatable back supporter. This vinyl contraption folds flat, and can be inflated to render it firmer or softer.

Auto-Mate

This handy carry-all includes: tissue-dispenser, wastebasket, first-aid kit, map holder, flashlight, hand towel, and snack tray.

Auto Altimeter

Up, up, and away! This auto altimeter measures from zero to 15,000 feet, telling you how high you are as you motor along.

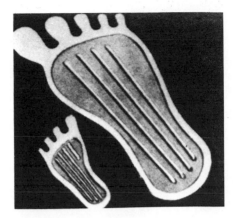

Phony Foot Pedals

*Do you like to drive barefoot?
These cast-aluminum phony
pedals clamp right over the
existing pedals.*

Wheel Cover

*With this textured-vinyl steering-
wheel cover, your hands will
cease to slip and slide while you
drive. The grip is warm in winter
and cool in summer.*

Fog-Proofing Stick

*For foggy or rainy nights, one
application of this fog-proofing
stick will clear your windshield
and windows. Smear a line every
couple of inches across the glass;
then buff with soft dry cloth.*

Key Holder

*Can't find your keys? With this
magnetic key holder, you'll never
have that problem again. Just put
a spare key inside, and slap the
case onto the side of your car.*

Automobiles over twenty feet in length are built more for comfort than speed, of course, but compared to the earliest automobiles even the most cumbersome of today's limos are virtual speed demons. The first auto race in Europe, held in France in 1895, was won by a car averaging but fifteen miles per hour. The Duryea brothers' car won the Chicago-to-Waukegan race that year with an average speed of only seven-and-a-half miles per hour. By 1898, the record automobile speed stood at a mere 39.3 miles per hour. A little over sixty-five years later, Craig Breedlove became the first person to drive a car over a mile course at an average speed in excess of 600 miles per hour. The record for the highest speed ever attained by a wheeled land vehicle was set on the Bonneville Salt Flats in Utah in 1970, when Gary Gabelich drove a rocket-engined car at an average speed of 631 miles per hour over a distance of one kilometer.

With the current fifty-five mile-an-hour limit on all American roads, you certainly won't need such horsepower. But if it's sheer velocity you're interested in, you might take a look at the Lamborghini Countach or the Ferrari BB Berlinetta Boxer, the fastest regularly produced cars now available, which can both reach speeds of 186 miles per hours.

If price is more important to you than speed, you might want to test-drive a Mercedes 600 Pullman, the most expensive standard car now on the market. One of these six-door beauties will set you back $90,000—less your trade-in, of course. And if used cars are your preference, you might be interested in a Rolls-Royce Phantom, once owned by the Queen of the Netherlands, that sold in 1974 for a record $280,000!

Speaking of used cars, the most durable car on record was a 1936 Ford two-door model that in 1956 logged its one-millionth mile—with the odometer showing zero miles for the eleventh time. Today, a car is considered well into old age by the time it reaches 75,000 miles.

But surely, the most incredible automobile record ever achieved belongs to Charles Creighton and James Hargis who, in 1930, drove a Ford Model A roadster from New York City to Los Angeles *without stopping the engine once.* The two men then promptly drove back to New York, completing the 7,180-mile round-trip in forty-two days.

Oh, one more thing: on both coast-to-coast journeys, the car was driven exclusively *in reverse!*

BREAKING 300

It wasn't enough for Sir Malcolm Campbell to be the first to drive a car faster than 250 miles an hour; his goal was 300!

And so on September 3, 1935, the flying Englishman and his mighty 2,500-horse-power *Blue Bird*, stood at the starting mark of the Bonneville Salt Flats at Great Salt Lake, Utah.

Adjusting his goggles, Sir Malcolm hopped aboard. He had six miles in which to pick up speed before hitting the timing tape. Screaming along at 280 with two miles to go, he closed his radiator front to streamline the car—and got into trouble.

Blotches of oil blacked out his windshield as the *Blue Bird* snapped the timing tape. In his rocketing prison, Campbell continued to torture the accelerator, and covered the required mile in 12 seconds. But as he slowed down to 280 miles, the left front tire blew and the *Blue Bird* went crazy. Campbell spun the wheel furiously in order to right the skidding car, and five miles later he stopped—with flames eating up the bad tire!

But Campbell had done only half a day's work. To establish a record he had to make the return trip.

Squirting out the fire, his mechanics threw on new wheels, and before he waved goodbye again the timers informed him he had run the course at a bit over 304 miles an hour. He could already see the newspaper headlines!

Only this time he had to let the car breathe. The radiator was left open, to push against a brick wall of wind; the speedometer read 290. Feeling his blood becoming a part of the car's circulation, he begged more speed out of it . . . and was timed at just under 296 for the return trip.

His average was 299.9—a tenth of a mile short!

He was already starting to think about next time as he walked unhappily away from the car. Suddenly an official shouted, "Wait, there's been a mistake!"

Sir Malcolm actually hit 298.013 on the second trip. His average speed was a neat 301.1291 miles per hour!

Famed British speed king, Sir Malcolm Campbell, was the first man to drive a car 300 miles an hour over a measured mile course.

BATHTUBS

This is a gullibility test. The bathtub was introduced in England in 1828. The first tub in America was used by a Cincinnati resident named Thompson in 1842. After an argument among medical authorities concerning the benefits and hazards of bathing, the bathtub was banned in Boston in 1845. Six years later, the first bathtub was installed in the White House for Millard Fillmore.

Believe it? Well, this capsulized history of the bathtub appeared in the *New York Evening Mail* in 1917, and was immediately accepted as fact by many readers. But the article was actually the devious work of humorist H.L. Mencken, and was—as Mencken readily admitted—a "tissue of absurdities, all of them deliberate and most of them obvious." Yet, much to Mencken's amazement, more than one lazy writer subsequently published the information as the gospel truth, leading to a plague of misinformation often called the Great Bathtub Hoax!

The institution of bathing is much older than Mancken facetiously suggested; although the porcelain tub, now indispensable in every home, is a rather recent innovation. The fact is, regular bathing has periodically gone in and out of fashion over the centuries.

Considering what we now know about hygiene, it's likely that the tub is here to stay.

From time immemorial, the act of bathing has been regarded as a sacred rite in many cultures. The ancient Egyptians bathed before worship, in the belief that both the body and soul should be pure in the presence of the gods. Christian baptism is a bathing rite, symbolizing the washing away of original sin. To the devout Hindu, a bath is a once-yearly rite, taken only in the water of the sacred Ganges.

The ancient Greeks are thought to have introduced the bathtub, or at least the wash basin. The Greek vessels were used to hold water for rinsing, but were too small to accommodate a bather. The ruins of the palace at Knossos, Crete, reveal a number of bathrooms that were apparently supplied by a relatively advanced plumbing system. Vase paintings suggest that the Greeks used some form of shower as well. Most early Greeks, by the way, washed only with cold water—warm water was considered effeminate.

In later periods, the Greeks built public baths; but it was the Romans who made the bathhouse the center of their social lives. In the early days of the Roman Republic, wealthy citizens often installed private baths in their homes, similar to the modern Turkish bath.

This is the type of tub that was used in ancient Rome, where bathing was considered an honorific pastime.

Later, the public bath came into vogue in almost all cities and
towns of the Empire. Huge baths, or *thermae*, became the recreation
centers of the Imperial City itself, providing not only bathing facilities
but gyms, libraries, theaters, gardens, and assembly halls.

The Roman baths were masterpieces of architecture and engineering, and the epitome of imperial luxury. The walls were usually covered with marble; the high, vaulted ceilings were decorated with colorful mosaics. The water taps were made of silver. Statues were every-

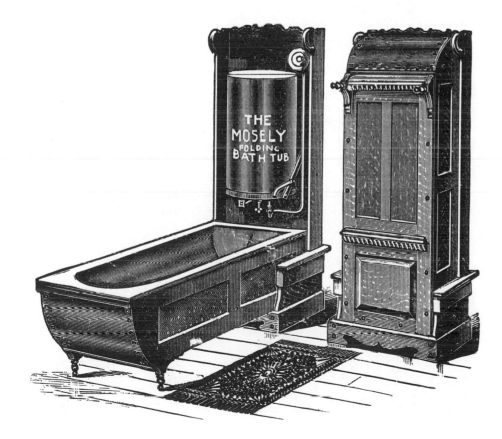

*This zinc-lined folding
bathtub with panel front,
oval top, and antique finish
was in vogue in 1893.*

where, with small cubical lockers set in the niches between them. Hot water was provided by furnaces and piped into the bath. The rooms were kept warm by smoke and hot air circulating under the floors and in the hollow walls.

The first large Roman public bath was built by Agrippa in 27 B.C. Others were constructed by Nero (65 A.D.), Titus (81 A.D), Domitian (95 A.D.), Trajan (100 A.D.), Commodus (185 A.D.). Diocletian built baths in the year 302 that were large enough to accommodate 3,200 bathers at one time!

The Baths of Caracalla, constructed in 217, could accommodate

In the 19th century, many Londoners visited the Turkish baths on Jermyn Street, in the heart of fashionable Mayfair.

1,600 bathers in an area of more than a million square feet—an area which included a stadium. Extensive remains of many Roman baths still stand today.

The Roman's bathing ritual consisted of a series of baths, each taken in a different room. The bather began in the undressing room, then moved to another room where he was anointed with oil, then to the gym for exercise. After the gym came the *calidarium*, or hot bath; then the steam room, the *tepidarium*, or lukewarm bath; and finally, the *frigidarium*, or cold bath which was usually a sort of swimming pool. Sounds much like our modern health spa, doesn't it?

The Meshlakh, or cooling room, was one of the features of the Jermyn Street baths.

Until the second century, men and women bathed together in Rome. Then emperor Hadrian ordered segregated bathing. However, Hadrian's decree was frequently overlooked during the more decadent eras of the Empire. In most cities outside Rome, men and women used the bathing facilities at different hours, but it was always considered immoral for a woman to bathe at night.

The Roman baths were the social centers of the time, combining the modern barroom, health spa, and community center. They were open continually except for religious holidays and times of national crisis. Customarily a Roman would bathe before the principal meal of the day, but some of the more idle—and cleaner—citizens went through the entire bathing ritual as many as six or seven times a day.

As the Empire waned and barbarian invaders destroyed the Roman aqueduct systems, most baths were shut down. But the public bath lived on in the Eastern Empire, and was eventually adopted by the Arabs, who liked vapor baths. The Turkish bath is a direct descendant of the Roman bath, via Constantinople.

The Teutonic tribesmen who overran Europe bathed for the most part in cold rivers or streams. During the Middle Ages, among some communities, bathing was considered a sin, an act of pride and an overt concern for the sensual. Probably, the Church's opposition to bathing stemmed from the excesses of the Roman public bath.

Among the medieval landed classes, the lack of a need to bathe was considered a sign of wealth and leisure. Many an aristocrat bragged of never having taken a bath. Consequently, the demand for perfume and aromatic oils was very high, and the need for spices helped spur the explorations of the fifteenth century which led to the discovery of America. By the way, Queen Elizabeth of England reportedly bathed once a month, "whether she needed it or not."

Turkish baths were popular in 19th-century New York.

Photo courtesy of Sherle Wagner.

After the institution of bathing was revived by the Crusaders' contact with Eastern bathhouses, the common people took frequent public baths. Public baths were common in France as early as the twelfth century, and were reputedly as notorious for their promiscuous activities as had been their Roman precursors. By the seventeenth century, no decent citizen would consider entering a public bath, and the Church frequently decried the excesses of the institution.

Because of the aristocracy's aversion to bathing, many of the more famous palaces surviving today are completely without sanitation fa-

The ultimate in modern bathtub luxury is this translucent oval-shaped white tub designed by Robert Gottfried of Palm Beach. The fixtures are made of rose quartz and 24-carat gold. This tub is produced by Sherle Wagner of New York.

This vinyl fold-up steam bath is billed as the "poor girl's sauna."

cilities. Although many people dispute it—and other refuse to believe it—there were evidently no toilets of any kind in either the Louvre or in the palace at Versailles. Members of the court were expected to relieve themselves before they entered the palace; the rows of statues that lined the garden promenades provided convenient niches for an undisturbed tinkle.

In Europe, the medicinal spring bath has been popular for centuries. During the eighteenth century, the English city of Bath—so named after an ancient Roman spa built there—became the most fashionable resort in all Europe, thanks chiefly to the restorative work

This turn-of-the-century bath scene was used in advertising Pears' soap.

of Beau Nash. Such luminaries as Pitt, Nelson, Gainsborough, Garrick, Gay, Pope, Steele, and Fielding came to enjoy the social life and the hot, radioactive waters of the natural spring. Like earlier baths, however, the resort at Bath eventually became associated with debauchery and the spread of disease.

The word "spa," incidentally, comes to us from the Belgian town of Spa. A mineral spring discovered in 1326 helped make the town a very fashionable resort during the eighteenth century. Today, the most famous spas in the world are at Baden-Baden in Germany (*bad* means "bath" in German), Carlsbad in Czechoslovakia, Vichy in France, and Hot Springs in Arkansas.

The earliest bathtubs in America were simple wooden tubs, lined with metal and the water was poured in by hand. The first public bath was opened here in 1852. An 1895 law ordered all municipalities in New York State to provide free public baths for their citizens, many of whom had no other means of washing.

In the early decades of this century, many apartments in American cities were equipped with a bathtub in the kitchen. When European immigrants arrived here many considered the bathtub an unnecessary luxury, and used the tub as a planter for flowers and vegetables.

Traditionally, in Japan, the bath was a large wooden tub placed outside in the garden and filled with very hot water. The entire family bathed together at the same time. In Japanese baths, both public and private, there is rarely an attempt to achieve privacy. Public baths often have large unprotected openings through which people passing in the street can observe the bathers. But nowadays, bathing in Japan—especially in the cities—is becoming westernized.

America easily leads the world today in bathtubs per capita. Many American homes are equipped with two or three or even four tubs. The shower has recently replaced the bath as the preferred washing ritual. A shower, by the way, uses up only about half as much water as a tub bath.

Some clever individuals have put the bathtub to a rather strange inventive use: bathtub racing. Tubs filled with outboard motors annually race over a thirty-six-mile course near Vancouver, British Columbia. Reportedly, the record distance achieved by a hand-propelled bathtub in twenty-four hours is an impressive 36.6 miles.

The Aztecs were accustomed to taking steam baths in these igloo-type saunas.

CATS

An old cat laps as much milk as a young.
—William Camden,
Remains

Are you an ailurophile or an ailurophobe? In plain English: Do you love or hate our feline fellow mammals? Either way, you're in large company.

Ever since the domestication of the feline, the cat has been variously regarded as a representation of the gods or an embodiment of the devil. Even today, there seems to be no middle ground. The dog may be loved, hated, or tolerated, but the cat—well, choose your side.

Dogs and cats are far and away the most popular pets in the world today. But the dog has been a friend of man for much longer, having been domesticated some 50,000 years ago. On the other hand, the cat was not tamed to any extent until just 5,000 years ago. Yet the dog, as we know it today, is in evolutionary terms a rather recent development. The cat family, on the other hand, evolved into its present form some 7 million years ago, long before most surviving mammals. During the intervening ages, it has undergone little change.

Paleontologists believe that the cat family descended from the Miacis, a weasel-like carnivore that lived about 50 million years ago. The Miacis evolved in many directions, one of them producing animals such as the mongoose and the civet that are thought to be ancestors of both the great cats and the smaller felines.

Over the ages, the feline species spread to all parts of the earth, with the exception of Australia and a few islands. The original ancestors of the cat evolved into two general families. One family, called the Hoplophoneus, included the Smiladon, or saber-toothed tiger, and other extinct animals. The second group, the Dinictis, produced all our modern cats.

There are many ways of classifying the members of the cat family, but the most commonly accepted divides the felines into three genera. The *Panthera* genus includes the great cats, such as the lion, tiger, leopard, and jaguar. The lion is the only gregarious member of the cat family. Its nickname "king of the jungle" is something of a misnomer. The tiger is generally larger and stronger than his unstriped cousin. Fortunately, the two creatures rarely meet—there are no tigers in Africa, and few lions anywhere else.

"Ligers and Tigons" may sound like a classic spoonerism, but these animals actually exist. They are the hybrid offspring of the

This appealing calico puss seems, in Shakespeare's phrase, "a harmless necessary cat" (Merchant of Venice).

lion and tiger, and there are about a dozen of these creatures in captivity today. When the father is a lion, the cub is called a liger; when the sire is a tiger, the cub is a tigon. And if a liger and tigon mate—well, you figure it out.

In Egypt, where the cat was a sacred beast, mummy cases were sculpted for the animals.

Metropolitan Museum of Art, Dick Fund, 1956.

The *Acinonyx* genus includes only, since ancient times, the cheetah, a sleek, spotted cat that has been domesticated and used in hunting in Egypt, India, and other Asian lands. The cheetah has been called the fastest animal on earth, and can race along at speeds of sixty miles per hour—though some claim to have clocked this quick-footed cat at close to seventy-five miles!

The third genus, *Felis*, includes the puma, ocelot, bobcat, serval, lynx, and, of course, the common house cat, known rather plausibly in zoological circles as *Felis catus*.

Paleontologists believe that the cat family descended from the Miacis, a weasel-like carnivore that lived about 50 million years ago.

There is no record of domesticated cats before 3,000 B.C., though by that time the kitty was already regarded as sacred in some Near Eastern cultures. The domestication of the cat either originated in the Nile area and spread elsewhere, or developed independently in various places. In any case, the Egyptians tamed a species of wild African cat, *Felis lybica*, an animal about the size of the modern house cat, and put him to work protecting grain supplies from rodents. Egyptian artwork also depicts small cats killing snakes in the royal household.

Rodent-hunting cats proved so valuable that the Egyptians considered them representations of the gods—a designation that conveniently helped protect the cat from ancient ailurophobes. The Egyptian cat-god *Bast*, was a symbol of the kindly powers of the sun, as opposed to *Sekmet*, the lion-god, who represented the destructive forces of nature. The cat was also worshipped or in some way connected with religious observance in Babylonia, Burma, Siam, Japan, and China, where the domesticated cat first appeared around 500 B.C.

The Egyptians went so far in their ailurophilia as to embalm cats, as they would a member of the royal household. Thousands of cat mummies have been found in Egyptian ruins—along with even

A good cat
deserves a good rat.
—*French proverb*

more mouse mummies, presumably entombed to provide food for the resurrected cats. In the 1890's, 180,000 mummified cats found near Cairo were auctioned off in England, where many were used as fuel. The auctioneer used a mummified cat as a gavel to peddle the cats in ton lots.

Legend has it that cats led to the defeat of the Egyptian army in 525 B.C., through a stratagem of the Persian invader Cambyses. The Persian king placed a row of cats in front of his troops, and the Egyptian archers refused to shoot their arrows across the sacred animals.

The domesticated African cat spread from Egypt to Europe, where it interbred with a European wild cat known as *Felis silvestris*, literally "forest cat." The Greeks kept few cats, but did use them as household mousers. Phoenician traders brought the domesticated cat to Italy long before the days of the Roman Empire, and cats were not uncommon as household pets among aristocratic Romans. The Romans had a saying that still—well, holds water: "Cats love fish, but won't touch the water."

The first record of domesticated cats in Britain dates from around 936, when a law was enacted in Wales for their protection. Throughout the Middle Ages, in most countries, cats—especially black cats—were suspected of sorcery, perhaps due to their stealth, independence, and nocturnal habits. Even today, you find an occasional individual who's convinced the cat has some supernatural powers. As Sir Walter Scott wrote, "Cats are a mysterious kind of folk. There is more passing in their minds than we are aware of."

Today, some ailurophiles entertain the idea that mass cat slaughter during the Middle Ages led directly to the spread of the Black Death, because of the consequent rise in the rat population. Actually, considering the sanitary conditions of the day, rats, fleas, and the plague would have flourished with or without the intervention of the feline.

Speaking of mousers, you've no doubt heard the one about the traveler who came sadly to the front door of a farmhouse to report an unfortunate accident. "I hate to tell you this, ma'am," he said, "but I just ran over your cat on the road. I'm terribly sorry. Of course, I'll replace him."

The cat would eat fish, but would not wet her feet.
—John Heywood, *Proverbs*

Let take a cat, and foster him well with milk
And tender flesh, and make his couch of silk,
And let him see a mouse go by the wall,
Anon he waveth milk, and flesh, and all,
And every dainty which is in that house,
Such appetite hath he to eat a mouse.
—Chaucer, *Canterbury Tales*

The oldest domestic cat on record, a tabby owned by a woman in England, died on November 29, 1939, at the ripe old age of 36 years!

"Well, don't just stand there!" the woman snapped. "There's a mouse in the kitchen!"

Domesticated house cats fall into two broad groups: short-haired and long-haired. The long-haired variety developed in Persia and Afghanistan, and the two prevalent types of long-haired cat are now called the Persian and the Angora. As a pet, the Persian has replaced the Angora in most Western countries.

The Abyssinian cat, a beautiful short-haired feline, developed entirely from the African wild cat, through Egypt.

The Manx cat.

The Angora cat.

The tailless Manx cat is common in the Far East, where few long-tailed cats are found. The name comes from the Isle of Man off England, though it is unknown whether the cat was brought there or developed there by mutation.

The Siamese cat, a much favored pet, first reached the United States in 1895 and has flourished ever since. Incidentally, almost all Siamese cats are cross-eyed.

The number of cats extant throughout the world today is anybody's guess. The United States ranks first among ailurophilic nations. There are an estimated 20 to 25 million cats in American households today, but with the inclusion of all alley cats and other strays, the total cat population could well top the 40 million mark, which is the population figure estimated for American dogs. The popularity of cats in this country continues to grow. The cat-care business is now a multimillion-dollar industry, providing cat food

---

There are an estimated 20 to 25 million cats in American households today.

---

and accessories, cat hospitals, kennels, and even kitty cemeteries. Pedigreed cats sell for upwards of $200.

The precise origin of our word "cat" is uncertain, but similar words designate the feline in many unrelated languages. One Latin word for the feline was *catus*, and the Ango-Saxons dubbed the creature *catt* or *cat*. In French, we find *chat*, in Italian *gatto*, in Spanish *gato*, and in German *Katze*.

The origin of "puss" is unknown, but "kitty" comes from *chaton*, a diminutive of the French *chat*. Since at least 1450, "Tom" has been used to designate a male. A polecat, by the way, is not a cat at all—in the United States, the term designates a skunk.

According to some accounts, the expression "to fight like Kilkenny cats" dates back to a somewhat ailurophobic custom among Hessian soldiers stationed in Ireland: tying two cats together by the tails and hanging them over a fence or clothesline. One day, the story goes, an officer approached a group of soldiers thus occupied. To hide their deed, one soldier cut off the tails of both tormented animals. The officer was then told that the cats had fought so hard that they'd devoured each other, leaving only the tails.

The notion that a cat can fall from a great height and survive is not an old wives' tale, and may have contributed to the idea that a cat has nine lives. One cat fell from the twentieth floor of a Montreal apartment building in 1973 and suffered only a pelvic fracture.

The story of a cat that fell from the Washington Monument and survived has been batted about for years. According to some, the facts are these: during construction of the Monument, workers came across a cat lurking in the framework near the top of the structure. The cat panicked, and leaped from the scaffolding. Incredibly enough, the cat survived the 500-foot-plus fall—but, even more amazingly, the stunned creature was pounced on and killed almost immediately by a wandering dog.

We have no idea how old that unfortunate feline was when it lost its ninth life, but on the average, a house cat can be expected to live from eight to twelve years, with one year in a cat's life equivalent to about seven years in a man's life. However, many cats have survived for considerably longer, and life spans of over twenty years are not at all uncommon. The oldest domestic cat on record, a tabby owned by a woman in England, died on November 29, 1939, at the ripe old age of 36 years!

The average household kitty weighs from eight to twelve pounds, but the largest puss on record, a tom from Connecticut, weighed in at a hefty forty-three pounds. And the most valuable cat on record is, depending upon how you look at it, either a tabby inappropri-

Who is to bell the Cat?
It is easy to propose
impossible remedies.
　　　　　—Aesop

ately named "Mickey" who killed more than 22,000 mice during a twenty-three-year career with an English firm, or a pair of house cats which, in 1963, inherited the entire estate of their ailurophilic owner, a California doctor. The estate was valued at $415,000!

A serval wildcat trots off with his prey.

CAVIAR

Synonymous with opulence is that salty, lumpy marine delicacy known as caviar. The word is rich with princely connotations for almost everyone—including those with no idea what caviar actually is. For it has been said that those who respect caviar's place in the elite of epicurean treats far outnumber those who have actually tasted it. Many who do have a chance to sample the delicacy can only wonder why it is so prized. But, as any connoisseur can testify, caviar is an acquired taste that for reasons of the pocketbook is best not acquired.

Caviar is the prepared roe, or eggs, of the *acipenser*, a fish found in the Caspian and Black Seas, and the Girond River in France. At one time, the acipenser could be found in many European rivers, and even in some North American lakes; but since the onset of the industrial age the fish's habitat has been reduced to portions of Russia, Iran, and Rumania. Today, virtually all caviar is produced in those three countries.

There are three kinds of *acipenser* that most graciously donate their eggs for the benefit of man's palate, and thus there are three kinds of "true" caviar. The Beluga is the largest fish of the three, growing up to twelve feet in length and weighing up to a ton—the Beluga is obviously no sardine! One Beluga can produce up to 130 pounds of caviar. Another species, the Sevruga, is much smaller; four feet long and weighing sixty pounds, the Sevruga can produce only about eight pounds of caviar.

The Ocietrova, or sturgeon, may weigh up to 400 pounds and will produce about forty pounds of caviar. The term "sturgeon" is often applied to all three kinds of caviar-producing fish, but the Ocietrova is, in fact, the only true sturgeon.

The taste for caviar flourished in the Middle Ages, when sturgeon roe was prepared as a feast for kings. The Cossacks of Russia organized massive caviar-hunting expeditions twice each year, with every member of the community taking part in the two-week campaigns. Among other things, the Cossacks used cannons to stun the fish in the water!

Today, the gathering of roe is somewhat more scientific. The fish live in the salt water of the Caspian and Black Seas but spawn in fresh water, depositing their roe at the bottom of river beds. The fish are caught as they prepare to spawn: the roe, at that time, is barely edible.

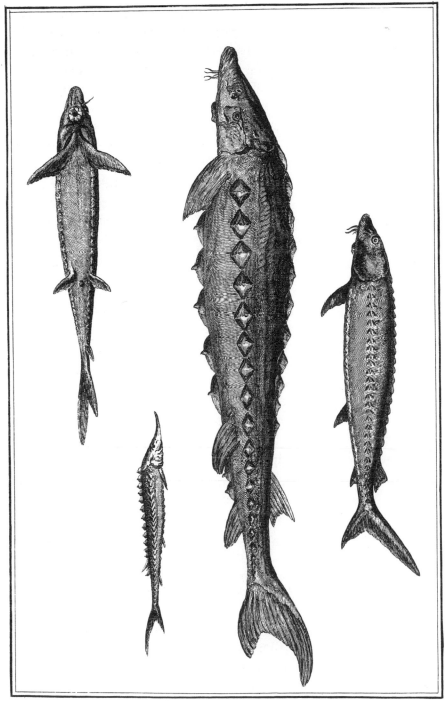

Caviar is produced from the roe of the sturgeon fish.

Drawing courtesy of Romanoff Caviar.

Caviar is often served as an hors d'oeuvre at sumptuous banquets.

Photo courtesy of Romanoff Caviar

□ The captured fish are placed in submerged floating cages, where due to the lack of food, they are forced to use up the reserve nourishment stored in their roe. When the roe is fit for consumption, the fish are killed and the eggs extracted.

The roe is then pressed through a sieve to remove membranes from the eggs, and then steeped in a brine solution. The production of caviar requires only fifteen minutes, but must be carried out with great skill.

The best caviar is sold by weight. Some caviar is poured into linen bags and hung to drain after steeping, then sold in tubes as "pressed caviar."

The best caviar is slightly salted, and extremely nourishing. Malossol caviar contains up to 30 percent protein. Due to its salt content, caviar will remain fresh for a long time. But never place it in a freezer or you'll end up with a worthless lumpy broth!

The roe of various fish have been enjoyed as a delicacy by the rich for thousands of years. "Red caviar," however, is a cheap imitation made from salmon roe. The Roman emperor Heliogabalus maintained a fleet of fishing boats exclusively for obtaining eel roe. The captured eels were placed in tugs and fattened on the meat of Christians slain in the Coliseum.

The French have been connoisseurs of caviar from medieval times on. Rabelais speaks of the delicacy in *Pantagruel*, calling it *caviat*. He also mentions *bourtargue*, a kind of caviar made with red mullet roe.

In Shakespeare's day, caviar was recognized as a food for the more discerning, as Hamlet suggested when he said: "The play, I remember, pleas'd not the million; 't was caviare to the general." In other words, the play, like caviar, was pleasant only to a trained palate.

The Czar Alexander I is often credited with introducing caviar to the social elite of Paris. The word "caviar," however, is not Russian in origin (the Russians call it *ikra*), but comes from the Italian *caviola*, derived from the Turkish word *khavyah*.

Sixty-five long tons of caviar are imported into the United States from Iran each year, and the total American retail market for caviar is $6 million annually.

Today, you can expect to pay anywhere from four to ten dollars for an ounce of the prized delicacy—and an ounce is considered scarcely a portion.

Until recently, about 35,000 pounds of fresh caviar were consumed yearly in the United States; a current caviar shortage has reduced American consumption to 20,000 pounds. Sixty-five long tons of caviar are imported into the United States from Iran each year, and the total American retail market for caviar is $6 million annually. But if the treat is beyond your pocketbook, or if you've already tried caviar and have been ashamed to admit that you can't stomach it, take heart. The epicurean chronicler Thomas Mouffet had this to say about the costly treat: "As for caviar, or their eggs being poudred, let Turks, Grecians, Venetians, and Spaniards celebrate them ever so much, yet the Italian proverb will ever be true: *Who eats caviar eats flies, dung, and salt.*"

CHEWING GUM

No one knows for sure how many people chew gum, but some 35 billion sticks will find their way into American mouths this year. That's about 5 billion packets, or 25 packets for each man, woman, and child in the United States.

"Does your chewing gum lose its flavor
On the bedpost overnight?"

The title of this 1960's song may not tickle your funny bone if you don't chew gum, but those who do indulge will certainly get the picture. The sight of a dried up, mouldering piece of chewed gum stuck to the underside of a desk won't strike the non-chewer as very appetizing, but to the gum-chewer—well, a piece of gum is a piece of gum.

And there are gum-chewers galore in this country, male and female, young and old, from every stratum of society. No one knows for sure how many people chew gum, but some 35 *billion* sticks will find their way into American mouths this year. That's about five billion packets, or twenty-five packets for each man, woman, and child in the United States. At, say, ten cents a throw, Americans will spend this year some $500 million on gum. And you thought gum-chewing was on the wane?

The urge to masticate seems to be quite strong in the human animal, for gum-chewing has been popular in many cultures over the last two thousand years. The ancient Greeks chewed a gum obtained from the resin of the mastic tree. Our words "mastic" and "masticate" are both derived from the Greek word for "chew."

Over a thousand years ago, the Mayans and other American Indians chewed chicle-based gums. But the first gums American colonists encountered were spruce gums introduced to the Pilgrims by the Wampanoog Indians in the early seventeenth century. Made from wads of resin the Indians found stuck to the bark of spruce trees, spruce gums were waxy and tough, more cordial to the teeth than to the taste buds.

Yet spruce gums were to remain the only chews available in the United States for close to 200 years, until the introduction, in the nineteenth century, of paraffin gums. The first spruce chewing gum to be commercially manufactured in this country was the "State of Maine Pure Spruce Gum," brought out in 1848 by a Bangor, Maine entrepreneur named John Curtis. Curtis later sold spruce gums under such names as "American Flag" and "200 Lump Spruce." He also sold paraffin gums dubbed "Licorice Lulu," "Sugar Cream," and "Biggest and Best."

Pioneers settling the American West found the Osage Indians chewing a chicle-based gum made from the hardened sap of the sapodilla tree. The Osage, who'd been chewing chicle for thousands of years, had apparently obtained their first chaws from Indian tribes living south of the Mexican border, where the sapodilla grows.

The Mexican General Antonio Lopez de Santa Anna—yes, the same Santa Anna of Alamo notoriety—thought that chicle could be used in the manufacture of rubber. So in 1839, he brought some sapodilla sap to the American inventor Thomas Adams. Attempts to manufacture rubber from the tree sap failed, but by the 1870's, Adams's company was marketing the nation's first commercial chicle-based chewing gums.

Chicle, Adams found, lasted much longer than paraffin or spruce, and carried flavors better than the earlier gums. Adams was soon selling such treats as *Peppermint*, *Spearmint*, *Black Jack* (licorice, of course, still popular), *Clove*, *Pepsin*, and *Cinnamon*. Today, the Adams Company and the William Wrigley, Jr. Company are the nation's largest manufacturers of chewing gums.

Thirty-year-old William Wrigley, Jr. moved to Chicago in 1891 and set up the Wrigley Company with just thirty-two dollars of his own money and a $5,000 loan. The firm initially sold soap, then branched out into baking powder. In 1892, Wrigley ordered some chewing gum from the Zeno Manufacturing Company to offer jobbers as an inducement to buy his baking powder. Wrigley's salesmen dispensed two packs of gum with each ten-cent package of baking powder, and the jobbers soon reported that they found it much easier to sell the gum than peddle the powder. It didn't take Wrigley long to see the possibilities.

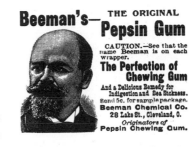

In the days of unregulated advertising, chewing gum manufacturers often made extravagant claims for their product.

A typical Wrigley's chewing gum ad.

By the turn of the century, Wrigley's gum was being sold coast to coast in stores and vending machines. Chewing gum factories were soon springing up in a number of foreign countries, including Canada, England, Germany, Australia, and New Zealand. By the end of World War II, the taste for Wrigley's product in America, Europe, and Asia was so great that his factories could barely keep pace with the demand.

Today, most chicle comes from Mexico. Sapodilla trees are tapped with grooved cuts and the latex is collected in small receptacles, as in the gathering of maple syrup. Most productive sapodilla trees are over seventy years old. For best results, each tree is tapped only once every six to eight years. The collected sap is then boiled, coagulated, and molded into blocks.

At the manufacturing plant, the chicle is kneaded into a hot sugar and corn syrup mixture, then flavored and rolled into thin strips. Most modern gums contain 20 percent chicle, 60 percent sugar, 19 percent corn syrup, and one percent flavoring. Of course, after a few hours of chewing, the wad in your mouth isn't likely to contain anything but the gum itself. Some gum manufacturers now use synthetic products to give their gum its chewiness.

Gumdrops are made not from chicle, but from gum arabic, a substance obtained from exudations of certain types of acacia tree. Gum arabic products were used as medicaments for many years, since the slow solution of gum in the mouth allowed a steady release of the active ingredients.

Many gum specialties have come and gone over the 100-year history of chewing gum marketing. For decades, the Adams Company has been selling Chiclets—pellets of gum wrapped in a sugar candy. The 1970's saw the introduction of "squirt" gum, wads of chewing gum with liquid centers that "explode" into the mouth upon the first chew. And the sweet, pink chew known as bubble gum needs little identification.

Bubble gum first appeared in 1933. But it wasn't until 1947, when the Topps Chewing Gum Co. began to offer the familiar Bazooka penny piece. Later, Topps included baseball cards with slabs of gum,

The largest collection of baseball cards in the world—200,000 cards—belongs to the Metropolitan Museum of Art in New York, and the most prized Topps card in existence is the 1952 Mickey Mantle, valued as high as $100.

that bubble gum became the ubiquitous source of oral gratification it is today.

The earliest baseball cards appeared during the 1880's in packets of cigarettes and tobacco. Candy companies began to issue cards in 1913, and bubble gum manufacturers included cards with their product beginning in 1933. Topps entered the baseball card field in 1951, and has since become the giant of both the bubble gum and baseball card industries, distributing some 250 million cards each year.

The Topps company estimates that there are now more than 100,000 serious baseball card collectors in the United States. Enthusiasts will pay surprisingly high sums for a valuable specimen. The largest collection of baseball cards in the world—200,000 cards—belongs to the Metropolitan Museum of Art in New York, and the most prized Topps card in existence is the 1952 Mickey Mantle, valued as high as $100.

During baseball's spring training period, Topps signs and photographs all rookies and established players whom they believe have a chance to make the major league rosters in the upcoming season. Each player is photographed both wearing a cap and bareheaded. If the player is traded to another club after his picture is taken, the bareheaded photo is used on the player's card. In case you were wondering, a players *is* paid for the use of his picture—$250 each year a new card appears.

The baseball card trade is not without its lighter side. A number of right-handed practical jokers have posed for the Topps photographer wearing a left-handed glove, or vice versa, and more than one player has appeared on a card bearing another player's name. In 1969, California Angels' third baseman Aurelio Rodriguez duped Topps into photographing the team batboy in his place, and thousands of cards bearing the batboy's image over Rodriguez' name were distributed before Topps caught the error.

A stick of sugarless gum contains but 6 or 7 calories—while a regular stick contains a whopping 8 calories!

In 1975, Kurt Bevacqua of the Milwaukee Brewers won the Topps World Series Bubble-Blowing Contest with this 18" bubble. The prizes were a $1,000 donation to the charity of the winner's choice, a giant-sized baseball card of the player, and a year's supply of Bazooka bubblegum.

Few people buy Topps baseball cards for the slab of bubble gum included in each package. Bubble gum addicts are more likely to get their fix from a piece of Topps Bazooka gum. Bazooka was introduced in 1947, and owes its name to the resemblance between the early five-cent size and the bazookas used in World War II.

Each piece of Bazooka gum comes with a premium of sorts—a Bazooka Joe comic. Topps first included the comics with their gums in 1953, and in the years since, the firm has developed a repertory of close to 700 different comics. The company tries not to repeat a joke for about seven years so that the comics are fresh for each new generation of bubble gum chewers.

Sugarless gums have been with us since the 1940's, and now account for 10 percent of all chewing gum sales. A stick of sugarless gum contains but six or seven calories—while a regular stick contains a whopping eight calories!

Gum makers have also developed gums that won't stick to dentures, and they are presently working on such earth-shattering innovations as a bubble gum whose bubbles glow in the dark.

In the early days of chewing gum marketing, gum companies tried to sell their products by stressing their value to dental health. Advertisements pointed out that primitive races whose diets demand a great deal of chewing usually have excellent teeth. When the Wrigley Company began to market its chewing gum in England around 1911, the firm's ads pointed up the values of gum to dental *and* mental health,

Early chewing gum advertising stressed the —er, good taste of the product.

IN GOOD TASTE

The use of WRIGLEY'S shows consideration for those about you, which is one of the evidences of refinement.

Your friends prefer a sweet breath.

After every meal

THE FLAVOR LASTS

claiming that gum eased tension and thereby improved concentration.

Wrigley faced an additional challenge in convincing the Englishman to chew gum: to rid gum-chewing of its lower-class connotations. When Wrigley began to advertise heavily in English magazines, he surprisingly chose those publications most read by the social elite. Sure, the ads read, gum may be out of place at the opera or in Buckingham Palace, but gum-chewing can be both proper and highly beneficial at most other times. The results of the ad campaign? Sales of Wrigley's products in England doubled over the next twenty years.

In the Soviet Union, where the manufacture of chewing gum is prohibited by the State, foreign tourists are frequently accosted by young Russian boys clamoring for "tchewing gum! tchewing gum."

Few people today chew gum for dental health. Ask the average gum-chewer why he uses gum and you'll most likely receive in response, a shrug of the shoulders. But the answer is simple: gum-chewing uses up excess nervous energy.

The use of chewing gum rises in periods of social tension, and falls in more tranquil times.

Studies have shown that the use of gum rises in periods of social tension, and falls in more tranquil times. For instance, the use of gum in this country soared from a per capita 98 sticks in 1939 to 165 sticks by the early 50's, duplicating a similar rise during World War I. Today's per capita consumption of chewing gum stands at 175 sticks per year. So, as if you needed any further confirmation, the chewing gum barometer suggests that we once again live in troubled times.

CHRISTMAS CARDS

The big Christmas miracle is how everyone receives more Christmas cards than he sends.

No one could fail to notice that most Christmas cards today have nothing whatsoever to do with Christ or Christianity—but did you know that Yuletide greeting cards were secular from their inception? Sanctimonious individuals may annually decry the deluge of cards and bewail the "loss of religious spirit" but the fact is that few of the customs we now associate with Christmas have anything at all to do with religious commemoration—and some of these customs are a good deal older than Christianity itself!

The date of Christ's birth is purely conjectural—there is no historical evidence that Christ was born on December 25. Mention of a December 25 celebration of Christ's birth first appeared around the year 353, but it wasn't until 440—more than four centuries after his actual birth—that the Church proclaimed that day as the official date for the festival. Conveniently, December 25 already marked a holiday among many Europeans—the celebratory rite of the winter solstice, marking the beginning of lengthening days and the expectation of spring and rebirth. Due to changes in the calendar, Christmas no longer falls exactly on the solstice.

As the celebration of a midwinter Christmas spread with Christianity, people in various cultures retained many of their pagan solstice customs and incorporated them in the Christmas rite. At that time of year, the ancient Romans had exchanged gifts to mark the feast of Saturnalia. Celtic and Teutonic tribes kept many customs of their twelve-day Yule celebration. Mistletoe, for instance, was prominent in midwinter Druid rites, and holly was similarly used by the Anglo-Saxons. The evergreen tree had long been regarded as a symbol of survival by Scandinavian peoples—though the Christmas tree proper did not find its way to England until 1840, introduced by Queen Victoria's German-born husband, Albert.

By the middle of the nineteenth century, Christmas was being observed throughout the Christian world very much as it is today— with the notable absence of the Christmas card. The idea, if not the custom, of pictorial representations of seasonal greetings dates back to the Middle Ages. An engraving by one "Master E.S." depicting the infant Christ stepping from a flower has been dated to around 1466, and is thought to be a copy of an even earlier design. Similar works from the fifteenth century refer to both Christmas and New Year. Calendars in

the seventeenth and eighteenth centuries often carried Yuletide greetings, with domestic winter scenes, sailing ships, and red-cheeked goddesses among the favored motifs.

As to the first legitimate "Christmas card," there is some controversy. According to many accounts, the idea of a Christmas greeting card sprang from the fertile brain of Sir Henry Cole, the first director of the Victoria and Albert Museum in London. In 1843, Cole commissioned John Collcott Horsley, a fashionable artist of the time, to design his first card. Horsley was well known not only for his artwork, but for leadership of a campaign against the use of nude models by artists—work that earned him the nickname "Clothes-Horsley"

This 19th-century Christmas card is one of the 70,000 unusual cards in the Hallmark Historical Collection.

The artist's first card consisted of one unfolded sheet, oblong in shape, with a rustic bower forming a frame for three illustrations. The central scene depicted a typical middle-class Victorian family gathered around a sumptuously laden table, drinking to the health of an absent friend—the card's recipient. The card also showed a moralistic scene depicting a charitable soul feeding the hungry at Christmas. The card also contained a representation of another good Samaritan clothing the naked—though Horsley, true to form, depicted the naked indigent as fully clothed. Above the tableau, appeared the word "To" followed by a space for an inscription; on the bottom of the card, the word "From" followed by a picture of an artist with a palette and the

The first Christmas card was designed by John Horsely in 1843.

date "Xmasse 1843." A banner stretching across the bottom of the central scene carried the greeting "A Merry Christmas and a Happy New Year to you." Christmas cards haven't changed much, have they?

Horsley became the world's first Christmas-card sender when he presented Cole with a signed copy of his original design, bearing the brilliantly original inscription:

> *"To his good friend Cole*
> *Who's a merry young soul*
> *And a merry young soul is he:*
> *And may he be for many years to come! Hooray!"*

The Christmas card first appeared in the United States in 1874, brought out by Bavarian-born Boston lithographer Louis Prang.

Cole had a thousand copies of the original card printed and issued by Summerby's Home Treasury Office. Only a dozen are known to exist today. Two of these can be found in the 70,000-card Hallmark Historical Collection, the largest and most representative museum of greeting card art in existence.

Other accounts credit sixteen-year-old William Maw Egley with engraving the maiden Christmas card one year before Cole and Horsley's collaboration. Egley's card, which still exists, was remarkably similar to Horsley's, depicting a Christmas dinner party, skaters, dancers, and a moralistic scene showing the poor receiving Christmas gifts. Egley's message was "A Merry Christmas and a Happy New Year to you."

Initial reaction to the distribution of Christmas cards was hardly favorable. Some critics claimed Horsley's card was too secular, and accused him of encouraging intemperance and alcoholism. Others criticized the idea of cards as a foolish extravagance. In fact, certain

Protestant sects refused to condone the Christmas card until the turn of the century.

But Yuletide cards caught on quickly among the general population, and within twenty years were well entrenched in Victorian Christmas celebrations. At first, cards were generally not mailed or signed, but delivered by messenger with a calling card. The penny post, introduced in England in 1840, did much to popularize Yuletide greetings by mail; and by the 1850's, Christmas cards began to appear on the European continent as well.

Victorian Christmas cards were considerably more elaborate than today's, often adorned with layers of lace, silk fringes, tassels, ribbons,

---

In 1954, Americans sent about 2 billion Christmas cards; now the yearly figure stands at close to 4 billion, for an average of 20 cards for every man, woman, and child in the country.

This card was published by the Obpacher Brothers of Munich, 1870-1890.

dried flowers, satin, or mother-of-pearl. Some were glass frosted. One surviving Victorian card consisted of 750 pieces of material stitched together.

The favored motifs were, from the very beginning, secular. Dolls and little girls were popular; so were courting couples, feasts, animals, flowers, winter scenes, and moralistic drawings, with an occasional angel thrown in for a bit of religious spice. In a sense, many cards were actually collages— for a drawing of a girl, for instance, a piece of satin might serve as a dress. And the inscriptions were no less banal than most of the modern ilk. Witness, for example, this gem: "When snow lies at Christmas and Granpa shivers—the children are bright; they look forward to feeding the chickens in spring."

The Christmas card first appeared in the United States in 1874, brought out by Bavarian-born Boston lithographer Louis Prang. Prang's card was designed by Mrs. O.E. Whitney, and based on an English card signed *Charles Dickens* that Prang had brought back from Europe. At first, the cards were produced for export to England, since the custom of sending greeting cards at Christmas had yet to appear in America. But Prang's cards—among the first to depict religious scenes—went on sale here the following year. Christmas-card fever soon became a permanent American ailment.

Through the years, Christmas-card design has often changed to reflect the feeling of the times. During the Depression, many cards spoofed poverty to make light of temporary hard times. Santas carrying flags were popular during World War II, as were inscriptions such as "Missing You" and "Across the Miles." The Cold War years saw an increased demand for humorous cards.

Today, Christmas cards are a multimillion-dollar industry in most English-speaking countries. Hallmark Cards, the largest American greeting card company, boasts annual sales of $400 million. In 1954, Americans sent about 2 billion Christmas cards; now, the yearly figure stands at close to 4 billion, for an average of twenty cards per person.

Of course, many Americans send considerably more than twenty cards. One Werner Erhard of San Francisco sent 62,824 cards in a single year. This is believed to be the largest outpouring of Christmas-card generosity in history.

Critics continue to lay the blame for an outlandish waste of time, money, and paper at the feet of overzealous Christmas-card senders.

This card was published by Raphael Tuck of London, 1880–1890.

Christmas cards prove that if there is much sentiment in business, there is even more business in sentiment.

One surviving Victorian Christmas card consists of 750 pieces of material stitched together.

The English magazine *Punch* hit it on the head when, in a 1900 editorial, it declared: "We deprecate the absurd habit of Christmas cards and presents—I refer, of course, to those we have to *give!*"

COCKTAILS

The ancient Greeks had a cocktail hour in the late afternoon or evening, complete with hors d'oeuvres.

A recent joke has it that a man strolled into a crowded bar, examined the array of aperitifs, liquors, cordials, and mixers on the shelves, glanced up and down the bar at the rickeys, fizzes, gimlets, tonics, sours, and slings the patrons held in hand, then leaned forward and told the bartender: "I've got a tough one for you: ever heard of a whiskey?"

Hardly the funniest joke in the world, but it does make a point. Walk into any American bar today and you'll find dozens of different kinds of spirits lining the shelves. You'll also notice that very few of the patrons are imbibing their favored spirit straight from the bottle. To Americans, the mixed drink may seem quite a universal, time-worn tradition—but the fact is, the cocktail as such is an American invention, and a fairly recent one at that.

In America, the word "cocktail" may mean either a mixed drink, as opposed to straight spirits, or any alcoholic beverage sipped before lunch or dinner. In the second sense, the cocktail has been with us for thousands of years. The ancient Greeks had a cocktail hour in the late afternoon or evening, complete with hors d'oeuvres. An Athenian gentleman would drop by a neighbor's house during the "happy hour" with a goatskin of wine, and expect to be treated to an outlay of appetizers—the Greeks called them "provocatives to drinking"—that might include caviar, oysters, nuts, olives, shrimp, and paté. Compare that spread to today's barfare of peanuts, cheese, and crackers and you'll agree that in some ways we haven't come very far in the last 2,500 years.

The cocktail in the sense of a mixed drink is a much more recent invention. In the past, not only wine and beer but hard liquor, too, was usually drunk straight, or at most diluted with water. As for tomato juice, tonic water, ginger ale, club soda, orange juice, and other mixers, few of these had yet made the trip from the grocery store to the barroom as recently as 200 years ago.

Alcohol itself, of course, has been with us since well before recorded history began. Alcohol still ranks as the oldest and most widely used drug on earth. Primitive man probably discovered the first alcoholic drinks by accident, since any sugar-containing mishmash left exposed to warm air will eventually ferment. Studies of alcohol use among various preliterate societies suggest that alcohol was used by prehistoric man primarily in conjunction with war, religious worship, and various rites of passage—births, marriages, funerals, and feasts.

The Babylonian Code of Hammurabi, dating around 1750 B.C., set down regulations for drinking houses. Egyptian doctors frequently prescribed alcohol as a medicine. By studying the remains of the Egyptian and Babylonian cultures, we can conclude that alcoholism has been a problem for well over 4,000 years.

The Chinese have been distilling an alcoholic beverage from rice since at least 800 B.C., and the Arabs have swilled alcohol from palm sap for many, many centuries. The earliest alcoholic beverage in the West was wine, brewed either from grapes or honey. Mead, a sweet wine made from honey, was widely enjoyed in Poland as recently as the nineteenth century.

The Greeks made their wine from grapes, but usually drank it diluted with water. Thus, the wine Athenians quaffed during their cocktail hour was probably less than 8 percent alcohol, a weak beverage by modern standards. In fact, most of the wine the Greeks and Romans enjoyed would probably taste rather crude to the modern palate. After all, we live in an age when an avid oenologist paid over $14,000 for a single bottle of 1806 Chateau Lafite-Rothschild!

Hard liquor is a newer arrival in the West. Around the year 300, the Irish brewed up *usquebaugh* from oat and barley beer. Tenth-century Italians began distilling brandy from wine, and sixteenth-century Scots first made whiskey from malted barley. The first cognac was distilled by the French around 1750. But it wasn't until Louis Pasteur's research in the 1850's into the action of yeasts and molds that Western man developed the controlled fermentation that makes for a consistently good alcoholic product.

Over the years, there were probably scattered incidents of man

I drink on every occasion, and betimes on no occasion.
—*Cervantes, Don Quixote*

The only fishing through
the ice some men ever do
is for the olive.

mixing hard liquor with a sweet beverage, but the cocktail did not become a popular drink until early in the nineteenth century. The origin of the word *cocktail* is uncertain. One claim maintains that it comes from a French drink served in New Orleans in the 1800's, called a *coquetier*, named for the tiny egg-cup in which the drink was usually served to women.

There are, however, dozens of other theories. According to some, the first cocktail in this country was served in a tavern in Elmsford, New York, where cockfights were often held. The story has it that Betsy Flanagan, a barmaid, decorated the bar with the tail feathers of some of the deceased combatants, and inserted one in a mixed drink when an inebriate requested "one of those cocktails." Another story tells us that as a publicity stunt, the proprietor of the tavern regularly inserted the tail feathers of fighting cocks in his mixed drinks, the feathers to be used as swizzle sticks.

Still another claim traces the name of the beverage to England, where in the Yorkshire dialect the word "cocktail" referred to foam spilling over a glass of ale. By the way, another word for beer froth was "barm," which gave us the term "barmy" (in America, "balmy") for tipsy or feeble-minded.

Washington Irving maintained that the cocktail was a Dutch drink popular in New Amsterdam in the seventeenth century.

An etymologist with a sense of humor proposed that the word came to us from Mexico, taken from the inventor of the drink, a daughter of King Axolotl VIII whose name was Xochitl or Coctel!

In any case, the first mention of the cocktail in print appeared in an 1809 issue of the Hudson, New York, *Balance*, which described the concoction as a "stimulating liquor composed of spirits of any kind, sugar, water, and bitters."

Speaking of bitters, angostura, the most popular modern variety, have been with us since 1824, when a German doctor living in Venezuela prepared them as a tonic for his ailing wife. He reportedly learned the recipe from sailors, who frequently added bitters to rum as a cure for seasickness. When angostura bitters became part of the Manhattan cocktail, their place behind the bar was established forevermore.

Enters the wine,
comes out the secret.
—*Hebrew Proverb*

The cocktail party is thought to have originated as an outgrowth of the aperitif hour before dinner. As the "hour" gradually lengthened, a buffet of some kind became necessary to allay the appetites of the imbibers. Psychologists attribute the popularity of the cocktail party, and the before-dinner cocktail itself, to their function as a separation between the working day and the evening relaxation. In recent years, many other countries have followed the American example and have adopted both the cocktail hour and the cocktail party.

According to one story, the flat champagne glass is designed after a cast of Marie Antoinette's breast, from which French courtiers drank the queen's health.

In the United States, a well-stocked cocktail bar must include dozens of different spirits to provide for the varying tastes of American drinkers. But as a rule, tipplers in most other countries prefer a beverage produced from a native product—in effect, the "national drink" of that nation. For instance vodka, an unaged spirit obtained from potatoes or grain and filtered through vegetable charcoal, is the overwhelming favorite in Poland and the Soviet Union, where the raw materials are plentiful. Vodka, by the way, has recently replaced bourbon as the most popular liquor in America.

Bourbon, America's contribution to the whiskey world, accounted for about one-fourth of all distilled spirits consumed in this country during the 1960's. But that figure has now decreased to about 15 percent, while vodka consumption has doubled over the same period. Vodka drinking now accounts for about 20 percent of the total American alcohol intake. Consumption of scotch whiskey, meanwhile, has held steady at about 12 percent.

Named after the county in Kentucky which may have been its birthplace, bourbon is distilled from a mash that by law must contain at least 51 percent corn. But Jack Daniel's whiskey, which many people consider bourbon, is technically a sour mash whiskey, or a Tennessee whiskey, and not a bourbon at all. Jack Daniel's, produced for over a century in the small Tennessee town of Lynchburg, is filtered through ten feet of sugar maple charcoal to remove some of the harsh esters. The Federal government decided that this filtering process changed the whiskey's character so much that the drink could not be called bourbon.

Whiskey is usually distilled from the fermented mash of grain usually oats, barley, rye, or corn. Whiskey is produced primarily in Scotland, Ireland, Canada, and the United States. Rum is obtained from fermented sugar cane or molasses, and produced primarily in the Caribbean.

Brandy is distilled from wine or the fermented mash of fruit—grapes, cherries, apples, plums, apricots, peaches, blackberries, or whatever. Tequila is distilled from the sap of an agave plant indigenous to Mexico, not from the mescal cactus, as so many people believe. Flavored spirits like gin, aquavit, and absinthe are produced by redistilling alcohol with a flavoring agent. Juniper is used to flavor gin; caraway seeds to flavor aquavit.

Cheers!

In the Orient, millet and rice are most commonly used for distilling spirits. *Ng ka py* is how you order a shot in Peking. It's made from millet, with various aromatics added. Saké, a beverage made from rice, is the favorite in Japan.

Spirits differ greatly in alcoholic content. Most wines contain from 8 to 12 percent alcohol, with certain aperitif and dessert wines, like vermouth and sherry, as high as 18 percent. The strength of beer ranges from a weak 2 percent brew produced in Scandinavia to about 8 percent. Four or 5 percent is the average in the United States. Most hard liquors contain from 40 to 50 percent alcohol, with cognac as high as 70 percent. Cordials and liqueurs contain from 25 to 40 percent alcohol.

The strongest spirits that can be produced are raw rum and certain vodkas, which contain up to 97 percent alcohol. Polish White Spirit Vodka is the strongest liquor sold commercially, packing a wallop of 80 percent alcohol.

Most liquor bottlers identify the alcoholic content of their product by "proof." The term dates back to the earliest days of liquor distilling when dealers would test the strength of an alcoholic product by soaking gunpowder in the beverage, and then igniting it. Spirits with enough alcohol to permit the ignition of gunpowder were considered to be 100 proof—the idea being that the gunpowder test was "proof" that the juice was strong. In England, 100 proof was established as eleven parts of alcohol by volume to ten parts of water. In the United States, the proof figure was set as double the alcoholic percentage. Thus, 86 proof whiskey is 43 percent alcohol, and pure alcohol is 200 proof.

Just as nations have their favored beverage, most have a favored toast as well. The term originated in the custom of dunking a slice of toast in a glass of wine, for reasons unknown. Englishmen like to toast with *Cheerio, Cheers,* or *Down the hatch.* Scandinavians say *Skoal. Prosit* is a German favorite, though the word is Latin. Italians clink glasses to the tune of *Cin cin.* The Spanish favors *Salud,* and the French *Culs secs.* Americans have coined the likes of *Bottoms up, Here's mud in your eye,* and *Here's looking at you*—as well as some more indelicate expressions from the frontier West.

While we're on the subject of word origins: the word *booze* does not, as widely believed, come from a liquor bottler named E.C. Booz. The word is quite old, originating perhaps in the Dutch word *buyzen,* to tipple, or the Middle English *bouse,* to drink deep.

America has nevertheless contributed quite a number of terms to the barfly's dictionary. In the Old West, rotgut whiskey was referred to by such affectionate terms as *old pine top, skull varnish, tarantula juice, Taos lightning, snake water, bug juice,* and *redeye.*

Today, the names of popular cocktails are somewhat more flattering. The origins of some are obvious; others, lost in history. The *Rickey,* for example, is said to be named after a certain Colonel Rickey. The word *Julep* comes from the Arabic *julab*. The *Black Russian* is named for its primary ingredient, vodka. (It's not black, but it's certainly Russian.) The *Grasshopper*, consisting of green creme de menthe, with creme de cacao, and cream, owes its name to its green color. The *Martini*, *Tom Collins*, and *Alexander* are named after individuals. The origins of the *Fizz*, *Sour*, and *Stinger* shouldn't be hard to imagine. As for the *Zombie*, you won't need three guesses—the talk is that three Zombies will turn you into one.

But the names of modern cocktails are certainly not lacking in color. Witness the *Red Devil*, *Sitz Mark*, *Bourbon Fog*, *Hurricane*, *Barbed Wire Fence*, *Rhett Butler*, *Cable Car*, *Sombrero*, *Tequila Sunrise*, *Pink Lady*, *Pink Elephant*, *Godfather*, *Harvey Wallbanger*, and a warm wine-and-brandy concoction billed as the *Instant Cold Cure*.

Among the less exotic—and more popular—cocktails we find the *Old Fashioned*, a mixture of whiskey, sugar, bitters, and club soda. The *Screwdriver* combines vodka and orange juice; the *Bloody Mary*, vodka and tomato juice. A *Daiquiri* includes rum, lime juice, and sugar. A *Mint Julep* usually includes bourbon, mint leaves, sugar, and water. A *Margarita* combines tequila, salt, lime juice, and Triple Sec. A *Manhattan* is made with whiskey, vermouth, and bitters. And the ever popular *Martini* includes gin, a dash of vermouth, and an olive.

For those who are all thumbs when it comes to cocktail craftsmanship, the Schenley company offers 6.8-ounce bottles of premixed drinks called "Cocktails for Two." The sixteen cocktails now available include the *Black Russian*, *Apricot Sour*, *Strawberry Margarita*, and *Extra Dry Martini*.

Speaking of the Martini, there's the tale about the South Seas explorer whose friend gave him a bon voyage packet containing bottles of gin and vermouth and a jar of olives. A tag attached to the gift said, *for insurance against loneliness*. When on the high seas, the explorer opened the present. Inside the package, a card contained the following: "I have never yet seen anyone start to

45 WAYS TO SAY DRUNK

Addled	In one's cups	Seeing double
Bagged	Jug-bitten	Shellacked
Balmy	Loaded	Smashed
Besotted	Listing to	Soaked
Bibulous	starboard	Sodden
Blotto	Muzzy	Soused
Boozy	Nappy	Stiff
Canned	Oiled	Stinko
Corned	Plastered	Stoned
Crocked	Pickled	Swacked
Decks-awash	Pie-eyed	Tanked
Drunk as a lord	Polluted	Three sheets to
Flying the ensign	Potted	the wind
Fuddled	Pot-valiant	Tipsy
Half-seas over	Raddled	Under the affluence
Hopped up	Reeling	of incohol

make a Martini without someone else coming along and telling him how to do it."

And then there's the one about the man who ordered a Martini in a bar, drank down the cocktail in one gulp, and then began biting the glass. When he'd nibbled the glass down to the top of the stem, he left it on the counter and walked off.

"Did you see that?," a man who had been standing next to the Martini drinker exclaimed aghast to the bartender. "He's nuts!"

"Yeah, he must be," the bartender responded. "He left the best part!"

The production of alcoholic beverages in the United States now stands at over 100 million proof gallons per year, with an estimated half-billion proof gallons in stock. Not bad for a nation in which about one-third of the population are teetotalers.

Today, about 77 percent of adult men and 60 percent of women are regular consumers of alcoholic beverages. Studies have shown

Bacchus was the ancient Greek god of wine.

that the wealthy and better educated are more likely to be numbered among the drinkers. But in France, where there are few abstainers, those who do swear off the grape are more likely to come from the well-educated, monied classes.

France is the nation with the highest per capita consumption of alcohol: 22.66 liters of pure juice per year, more than twice the American figure. Italians are the highest per capita consumers of wine, downing on the average 153 liters to the American's mere 8. West Germans are the number one swillers of hard spirits—barely beating out the Americans in that category. The Germans are also far and away the leading drinkers of beer and ale, with the average German consuming 182 liters of brew per year. There is a claim, however, that the residents of Australia's Northern Territory far outpace the Germans.

Most wines contain from 8 to 12 percent alcohol, with certain aperitif and dessert wines, like vermouth and sherry, as high as 18 percent.

We have no reliable figures for the communist nations, but vodka consumption in the Soviet Union is thought to be extremely high, and Czechoslovakia is said by some to surpass all nations in per capita beer consumption. At the other end of the scale, the citizens of Iceland and Israel rank as the smallest consumers of alcohol.

The above figures may surprise those who think that "light wine" countries such as France and Italy consume less alcohol than "hard liquor" nations like Great Britain and the United States. Great Britain, famous for its whiskies, is often thought to be high on the list of alcohol imbibers, but Britons actually consume less alcohol per capita than the citizens of any country in the West.

That hasn't stopped jokesters from commenting on the soft spot the Scotch have for their famous export. Perhaps you've heard the one about the elderly Scotsman who, while carrying a bottle of whiskey on his hip, slipped and fell on a path of ice. Climbing to

The production of alcoholic beverages in the United States now stands at over 100 million proof gallons per year, with an estimated half-billion proof gallons in stock.

his feet and feeling something wet trickling down his leg, he murmured: "I hope it's blood."

Dewar's, incidentally, is the best-selling non-premium scotch in America, Chivas Regal the best-selling premium. In Scotland, Bell's is the most popular domestic scotch whiskey.

With all that drinking going on, it's no surprise that alcoholism is a major problem in many societies. In the United States, an estimated five million people are alcoholics, and perhaps another four million are problem drinkers. In France, estimates of alcoholism put the figure as high as 9 to 15 percent of the total population!

> **If all be true that I do think,**
> **There are five reasons we should drink:**
> **Good wine—a friend—or being dry—**
> **Or lest we should be by and by—**
> **Or any other reason why.**
> **—Henry Aldrich, Five Reasons for Drinking**

Religious proscription has done little to thin the ranks of the dipsomaniacs. The Koran forbids alcohol use. Devout Buddhists and Hindu Brahmins also spurn the grape. And many Christian sects have forbidden drinking—with mixed results.

As for legal prohibition, the longest on record is a wee twenty-six years, in Iceland, from 1908 to 1934. Russia tried to illegalize the grape early in this century, but the attempt lasted a mere ten years. Our own "noble experiment" lasted only thirteen years—much too long in the many minds of many people.

For our point of view regarding man's oldest and most popular intoxicant, we may turn to the Bible. The Good Book mentions two drinks: "wine which gladdeneth the heart of man, and water, which quencheth the thirst of jackasses " (Psalm 104).

COFFEE

Coffee has two virtues: it is wet and it is warm.

No one need be told that human beings are lovers of the grape. But did you realize that the brew of the coffee bean is drunk by more people than any other beverage on earth?

Coffee is regularly consumed by about one-third of the world's population, and consumption continues to rise steadily. At the turn of the century, world imports totaled about one million tons. But by 1950, that figure had doubled. Today, the total stands at about three-and-a-half million tons—making coffee the second largest item of international commerce after petroleum!

Americans presently put away about one-and-a-quarter million tons of coffee each year, more than the entire world drank just a half-century ago. Coffee is, to say the least, an institution in this country, with the average American gulping down two-and-a-half cups daily.

Americans are not the world's heaviest coffee consumers—the average Swede consumes close to 30 pounds of coffee each year!

You won't have to look far to find someone who insists he couldn't live without it. And speaking of institutions, in many states, the coffee break is not only a fixture in almost all offices and factories, it's dictated by law.

Still, Americans are not the world's heaviest coffee consumers—the average Swede consumes close to thirty pounds of coffee each year! In fact, in much of Western Europe, the word for coffee, *café*, has come to be synonymous with an eating place. Even in this country, we prefer to call our beanery a coffee shop, a coffee house, or a cafeteria—which literally means "coffee store" in American Spanish.

Americans and Europeans may be avid consumers of the brew, but it's likely that most Western coffee addicts go through their lives without once laying eyes on a coffee bush. The reason: coffee simply won't grow in the climate of Europe or the United States. The coffee plant is a tropical evergreen shrub indigenous to the eastern hemisphere; twenty-five species grow wild in Africa, Asia, and the Near

Next time your guest asks for "just half a cup" of coffee, trot out this 3½" ceramic mug, which holds just four liquid ounces.

Coffee was served at the Russian Café in the park of the 1867 Paris Industrial Exposition.

East. Oh, there is some coffee grown in the United States—but only in Hawaii.

Most coffee shrubs flourish best in year-round temperatures of from seventy-seven to eighty-eight degrees; a temperature dip to around thirty-two degrees will kill most coffee plants. And many species require more than sixty inches of rain each year.

Two species of the coffee plant are far and away the most common. *Coffea arabica*, the oldest known variety, hails originally from Arabia or Ethiopia, and is now grown extensively in South America. *Coffea robusta* originated in East and Central Africa and is still the major coffee plant of that continent. *Robusta* is not— well, "robuster" than *arabica*. Actually, it's milder in taste and aroma, and is less favored by Westerners; but in recent years, Africa has become increasingly important as a coffee exporter.

The average coffee shrub grows to a height of about thirty feet, with white flowers and red, fleshy fruits. Each fruit contains pulp and two seeds, and it is the seeds—not "beans"—that are used to make the brew. Why? Caffeine, of course.

Caffeine is an alkaloid that mildly stimulates cerebral and cardiac

Sweetening one's coffee is generally the first stirring event of the day.

activity—in short, it's a pick-me-up. Try to imagine the difference in American offices and factories if the drug were suddenly to disappear, for caffeine is often the oil that makes the American brain run smoothly. And not without its price: caffeine causes gastric acidity and nervousness as well as heightened cardiac action. But coffee-swillers, take heart. Though theoretically the drug can be fatal in large doses, there is no case on record of a caffeine overdose.

Oddly enough, though coffee is today a fixture from Titicaca to Timbuktu, the beverage was virtually unknown in most of the world just a few centuries ago. For years on end, the tribesmen of Ethiopia and Central Africa crushed coffee berries and mixed them with animal fat to form balls they devoured before their war parties. The Africans also made a wine from the coffee fruit, though they never brewed a hot coffee beverage.

According to some historians, the *arabica* shrub was taken to Southern Arabia for cultivation sometime before the year 600, though the Arabs didn't learn how to brew the hot beverage until the tenth or eleventh century. The word *coffee*, by the way, comes to us either from the Arabic *qahwah*, or from Kaffa, a province in Ethiopia that is reputedly the birthplace of the *arabica* plant.

Arab legend maintains that the coffee bean was actually discovered by goats. According to the tale, a goatherd named Kaldi living around the year 850 was puzzled one day by the queer antics of his flock. After watching them cavort around the fields on their hind legs, the goatherd discovered that the animals had been nibbling on the berries of a wild shrub, and decided to sample the fruit himself. The snack produced a delightful sense of exhilaration, and Kaldi went on to loudly proclaim his find.

Once the Arabs had learned to brew a hot beverage from the fruit, coffee became very popular on the Arabian peninsula, especially in connection with long Moslem religious services. Orthodox priests soon pronounced the beverage intoxicating and banned its use, but still the dark brew spread throughout the Near East.

Venetian traders were probably the first to bring coffee to Europe. During the sixteenth and seventeenth centuries,

The coffee plant produces delicate blossoms and rich berries.

Coffee became widely popular in London during the 17th century. The first coffee house opened its doors in 1652. Soon, coffee houses became the centers of political, social, literary, and business life in the city.

the beverage reached one European country after another. In many places, coffee was banned for a while because of religious, political, or medicinal objections. The Italian clergy at first opposed the drink as the beverage of the infidel, but after Pope Clement VIII tasted the brew, he proclaimed it fit for Christians.

Coffee became widely popular in London during the seventeenth century. The first coffee house opened its doors in 1652. Soon coffee houses became the centers of political, social, literary, and business life in the city. In America, the first popular coffee houses opened as early as the 1680's—and the *Mayflower* listed among its cargo a mortar and pestle to be used for grinding coffee beans.

At that time, almost all European coffee was imported from Yemen and Arabia, since the Arabs had jealously guarded their coffee monopoly by forbidding the export of fertile seeds on pain of death. But around 1700, Dutch traders managed to smuggle some coffee shrubs out of Arabia, sending the embezzled botanica to the island of Java, then a Dutch possession. The growth of coffee plants in Java soon became so prolific that the island's name became synonymous with the brew.

The French, too, managed to get their hands on the coveted shrub, and established coffee plantations in many of their colonies. One coffee plant brought to the *Jardin des Plantes* in Paris is reputed to be the father of all Latin American coffee.

The Dutch and French both founded huge coffee plantations in the Guianas of South America; and like the Arabs, tried their best to guard their prize crop. But according to some accounts, a dashing Brazilian officer won the heart of the wife of the governor of French Guiana. As a token of her affection, she gave him some of the precious

Coffee should be black as Hell, strong as death, and sweet as love.
—Turkish proverb

Coffee beans being ground to powder in the Dutch colony of Surinam.

beans and cuttings. Brazil began coffee cultivation in 1727, and was to become the largest coffee growing nation on earth.

From its introduction there in 1658, coffee was the major crop of Ceylon (now Sri Lanka). In 1869, a terrible blight wiped out the entire Ceylonese crop. Forced to start again from scratch, the Ceylonese decided to give up on coffee and plant tea instead. Today, tea is the principal crop of the island.

Coffee is the major export crop of many of the countries between the two tropics. A price drop in coffee can throw the economy of many nations into complete turmoil, as happened in Brazil in the decade between 1925 and 1935.

After Brazil, Colombia is the world's second largest coffee exporter. In 1973, the Ivory Coast ranked third.

Brazil once accounted for 66 percent of all coffee exports, but as

The rarest coffee in the world is Jamaica Blue Mountain. That particular coffee is sold in only a few stores in the U.S.

African production has continued to rise, that figure has dropped to 40 percent. Today, about 30 percent of all coffee comes from Africa.

The rarest coffee in the world is Jamaica Blue Mountain. That particular coffee is sold in only a few stores in the United States. Only 800 bags, or 100,000 pounds, are produced each year.

Roasted coffee beans can be brewed into a beverage in dozens of ways, but basically, there are two methods: decoction and infusion. In decoction, the brew is produced by boiling the coffee until its flavor is extracted. In an infusion, water near the boiling point flows over unheated coffee grounds.

Americans prefer their java brewed by infusion with either a drip pot or a percolator. The brew is then mixed with milk and sugar. The French prefer *café au lait*, an equal mixture of strong coffee and warm milk. Many Europeans prefer *espresso*, a strong infusion drunk without milk.

Cappucino is a combination of coffee and frothy milk with nutmeg or cinnamon added. Turkish coffee is a heady, usually bitter decoction made from a strong, aromatic bean. Viennese coffee is usually served with a large dollop of whipped cream. And Irish coffee, a mix-

---

A customer in the cafe called the waiter to his table and asked, "Is this tea or coffee? It tastes like cough medicine."

Well, if it tastes like cough medicine, it must be tea," the waiter replied. "Our coffee tastes like turpentine."

---

ture of coffee, whiskey, and whipped cream, can be good to the very last drop—even if you don't like coffee.

Many urban Americans, especially Easterners, are fond of iced coffee, a beverage that is just now being introduced to some areas of the country. And speaking of ice, there's coffee ice cream. Coffee is also used in some chocolates, and caffeine is an important ingredient in another American institution, Coca-Cola.

For those who don't care for caffeine, there's de-caffeinated cof-

A person has the right to complain of the coffee when he finds grounds for it in his cup.

fee, a brew made from ground coffee with all but about two percent of its caffeine removed. And for the real caffeine-hater, there are coffee substitutes made from chicory and other herbs. Postum, a popu-

Photo courtesy of General Foods Corp.

Maxwell House coffee, with its famous motto, "Good to the Very Last Drop," is one of the most popular American coffees.

lar American drink for more than seventy-five years, is made from bran, wheat, and molasses.

While we're on the subject of caffeine: the oft-heard idea that caffeine is an effective antidote to inebriation is simply—er, without grounds. Time is the only remedy for excess alcohol in the bloodstream, so coffee is an aid to the intoxicated only insofar as it takes time to drink it.

Instant coffee is actually brewed in the factory and reconstituted in the home. In the spray-drying method of manufacture, a concentrated brew is sprayed into a chamber and mixed with hot dry air. The air carries off the moisture, leaving behind the particles you find in your jar of instant.

In the freeze-drying method, a coffee extract is frozen and introduced into a vacuum chamber, where the moisture is sublimed and a solid mass left behind. The mass is then reduced to granules and packaged for those coffee lovers for whom time is more important than taste.

The debate between the instant-coffee connoisseur and the fresh-brewed fancier will probably go on forever. Which makes sense, since among Americans today, there seems to be no middle ground: you either love coffee or you hate it. If you number yourself among the coffee-crazy, drink hearty—and the next time you pour yourself a cup of java, give silent thanks to an Arabian goatherd and his errant flock.

Good coffee keeps more people awake than a bad conscience.

PRIME COFFEE EMPORIA

If you're interested in unusual coffees, here's a list of fine stores. Mail orders are welcome.

The House of Yemen, 370 Third Avenue, New York, New York 10016, is noted for Amahara Ethiopian and Bedouin Arabica.

McNulty's Tea and Coffee Co., 109 Christopher Street, New York, New York 10014, is where afficionados buy Colombian Supremo, Mocha-Java, Mocha-Colombian Supremo, and Toltec.

The Vermont Country Store, Weston, Vermont 05161, is the place to stock up on Guatemala Antiqua and Santos Coffees.

H. Roth and Son, 1577 First Avenue, New York, New York 10028, supplies Hawaiian Kona to devotees of this unique brew.

COMICS

In the first century B.C., Romans chuckled over tablets with satiric inscriptions sold in the market places of the Eternal City.

ZOWIE! SOCKO! GLUG! WHAP! POW! Place those words before an American of any age and, without fail, the reaction will be: comics!

In terms of longevity, complexity, and influence, those innocent little cartoon panels certainly are no joke. In fact, the comic strip and comic book together form perhaps the largest and most influential iconographic field in the history of man.

The newspaper comic strip is a relatively new development, of course, but its forerunners are ancient. In the first century B.C., Romans chuckled over tablets with satiric inscriptions sold in the market places of the Eternal City. Chances are, they weren't much different from the editorial cartoons we enjoy today.

Before the invention of the printing press, German artists produced woodcuts arranged in panel form like the comic strip, dealing chiefly with religious history and current politics. After the printing press came into use, the illustrations took the form of small images printed together on one piece of paper, or a series of several sheets that could be hung on the wall to form a narrative frieze.

In the seventeenth century, the Protestant Reformation and the consequent religious wars led to propagandist strips based on political events. A limner by the name of Romeyn de Hooghe was the first artist to devote himself consistently to the narrative strip, producing pictorial indictments of the persecution of the Huguenots under Louis XIV, and accounts of the accession of William III to power in Holland and England.

Today, detective-comic buffs might be amused to learn that German artists began producing crime strips as early as the sixteenth century. Most strips illustrated heinous crimes and the punishment the perpetrators could expect to receive—in gory detail.

The father of the modern comic strip was Rodolphe Töpffer, a Swiss illustrator and schoolmaster. Töpffer observed that more people can read pictures than can read words—hardly a deduction worthy of Dick Tracy. He went on to produce picture-story books and collections of small drawings that were the forerunners of the modern newspaper strip. Töpffer also put out collections of his drawings in oblong

During the 1930's, Little Orphan Annie *achieved superlative heights of popularity. Created by Harold Gray, the character of Annie captured the American imagination, and has been reproduced in everything from dolls to a Broadway hit.*

albums of about 100 pages. These were the precursors of the comic book.

The dominant comic illustrator in the nineteenth century was the German Wilhelm Busch. Beginning with comic illustrations which he drew for a variety of periodicals, Busch was the first truly professional comic-strip artist. His tales of naughty children and pesky animals wouldn't be out of place on today's funny pages. Two infant pranksters named Max and Moritz, his most memorable characters, were to

---

Yellow Kid *was the first continuous comic character in the United States, and standardized the use of speech balloons for comic strip dialogue.*

---

form the models for the later *Katzenjammer Kids*. Busch's use of oscillations to suggest movement and his use of conventional signs to suggest emotions provided a vocabulary for the comic strip artist that is still in use today.

The newspaper comic strip in this country was born out of the rivalry between two giants of the American press. In 1893, the *New York World* published the first full-color comic page in the nation, depicting a set of humorous characters under the title *Hogan's Alley*. Soon afterward, publisher William Randolph Hearst countered with the first weekly full-color comic supplement, eight pages in the *Morning Journal*.

Hearst's supplement featured *Yellow Kid*, a strip by Richard Outcault, whom Hearst had lured away from the *World*. *Yellow Kid* was the first continuous comic character in the United States, and standardized the use of speech balloons for comic strip dialogue. Incidentally, the Italian word for comic strip is *fumetto*, "little puff of smoke," so-named after the speech balloon.

Later, Hearst put out Rudolph Dirks's *Katzenjammer Kids*, the first strip fully developed in form and the most durable comic strip in history. Dirks's strip used speech balloons and a continuous cast of characters, and was divided into panels—unlike *Yellow Kid*, which employed full panoramic scenes.

With the advent of newspaper syndication, comic strips spread rapidly. In 1904, the first daily black-and-white strip, *A. Piker Clerk*, appeared in the *Chicago American*. Actually, the strip was a horse race tip sheet, as was *M.A. Mutt*—later *Mutt and Jeff*—which eventually dropped its racing connections and developed into a general interest strip.

The period between 1907 and 1920 was the golden age for comics. This era saw the birth of dozens of long-running strips and the development of the genres that predominate today. There was the gag strip, *Bringing Up Father*, in 1913, the first American strip to gain international renown; the family saga strip, *Gasoline Alley*, in 1919; the career girl strip, *Winnie Winkle*, was started in 1920; the fantasy and parody strips, *Krazy Kat* came into being in 1911 and *Popeye* was inaugurated in 1919. *Krazy Kat* was the first newspaper strip aimed at the intelligent adult.

In the late 20's and 30's, adventure, detective, and sci-fi strips became popular. *Tarzan* began in 1929, followed by *Dick Tracy* and *Flash Gordon*. Nineteen-thirty saw the birth of *Blondie*, perhaps the most successful strip of all time. The comic strips that have since become household words in American life are too numerous to name.

The first true comic *book* was marketed in 1933 as an advertising giveaway. The size, glossy cover, and panel format of that first comic book have remained the same right up to today.

Comic strips are popular throughout the world, and China is no exception.

At first, comic books were basically reprints of newspaper strips. In 1938, *Action Comics* appeared; *Superman* and the other superheroes were not long to follow. By 1943, comics accounted for one-third of all domestic magazine sales. *Superman* alone had a circulation of 1,500,000 copies per month! By the way, the first issue of *Action Comics* now sells among collectors for close to $5,000!

Early comic books were for the most part brutal, sadistic, blood-and-guts affairs that most parents tried to keep out of the hands of their children. In 1951 and again in 1954, Congress investigated the comic-book industry and—simplistically enough— blamed the rise of juvenile delinquency on sadistic comic books. The industry was forced to adopt a code of self-censorship that still exists. But comics contin-

Copyright 1960, The Chicago Tribune

Chester Gould's Dick Tracy *first appeared in 1931. The name has become a synonym for a cagey cop.*

ued to suffer criticism, especially for their racist, militarist, and fascist values.

Partly as a rebellion against this type of politically neanderthal comic—*Steve Canyon*, for example—a number of newspaper strips appeared in the late 50's that were heavy with sociological and philosophical overtones. Most took their cue from the earlier *Pogo* (1946) and *Peanuts* (1950). Today, the funnies page is a conglomeration of science fiction, fantasy, adventure, slapstick, and subtle humor—something for every taste.

Without doubt, the comic is the dominant graphic mythology of the twentieth century. It's the comic strip—not film nor television—that reaches one-third of humanity each day. In the last seventy years, an estimated 8 to 12 million comic strip pictures have been produced throughout the world.

Today, over 100 million Americans—virtually half the population—read one or more comic strips regularly. About 300 strips are presently published in American newspapers—*Blondie* alone can be found in 1,200 papers across the country, and *Dick Tracy* reaches 50 million readers daily in 500 papers. When Chic Young asked for suggestions for a name for Blondie's second baby, he received 400,000 replies. Al Capp's offer of a prize for the "most gruesome face" for a new *Lil' Abner* character generated over a million replies!

American comics are now read worldwide. *Peanuts*, incidentally, is called *Radishes* in Denmark. In England, a large chain of hamburger stands, the Wimpy Bar, owes its name to a *Popeye* character with a weakness for the burger. Not to be outdone, Texans in a spinach-growing area in the eastern part of the state have erected a statue of Popeye in tribute to his appetite for the vegetable.

Surprisingly enough, studies have shown that the more educated a person is, the more likely he is to follow a comic strip. The peak age for Sunday comic strip readers is—no, you'd never guess—thirty to thirty-nine years old!

By the time any American has learned to read, he's likely to have his favorite strips. According to a 1960's survey, the most popular strips countrywide, are in order, *Blondie, Dick Tracy, Little Orphan Annie, Peanuts,* and *Rex Morgan, M.D.*

Little Orphan Annie began a run as a successful Broadway show ("Annie") in 1977. *Bringing Up Father* has been made into a movie eleven times!

Today, most syndicated strips are the work of an entire staff of writers, calligraphers, artists, and editors. In no other art form is the creator so much the prisoner of his creation, for the characters he invents frequently assume lives independent of their creator—and continue to live on, even after the artist's death!

It would be hard to think of a place in which different periods of history are so intermingled as on the funny page. You'll find *Moon Mullins, Dick Tracy, Gasoline Alley,* and other ancient works side by side with new strips like *B.C.* and *Doonesbury.* But they all have a few things in common: Zowie! Socko! Glug! Whap! Pow!

DICE

Comparing the vast, electrified skyline of a modern city with the stark simplicity suggested by an ancient ruin, it's easy to see that man has changed his environment a great deal over the past millennia. But has man's nature changed along with his environment? Not really. Take the institution of dice gambling, for instance. We know that prehistoric man used dice much like ours, played dice games similar to our own, and—to seal the argument—cheated his opponents with loaded dice!

For his dice ancient man used, among other things, plum and peach pits, stones, seeds, bones, horn, pottery, shells, and beaver teeth.

The best throw of the dice is to throw them away.

The card catalogue of any large library will illustrate the age-old controversy over dice gambling. Almost as soon as man had developed the printing press, he began to publish treatises for or against the innocuous little cubes—mostly against. The flavor of those early works, is suggested by one sixteenth-century treatise published in England and entitled: "A Manifest Detection of the Most Vyle and Detestable Use of Dice Play." A bit heavy-handed, perhaps, but you get the idea.

Dice are the oldest gaming implements known to man. Before dice became gaming pieces, numbered cubes were used as magical devices for divining the future. The next time you're searching for a word to stump a self-proclaimed vocabulary know-it-all, try "astragalomancy"—that's the practice of divination by means of dice!

Primitive man probably used cubical knucklebones or the anklebones of sheep for his gaming pieces. The Arabic word for knucklebone, in fact, is the same as for dice. Even today, experienced elbow shakers often call dice "bones" or "devil's bones".

This Greek vase in the Vatican Museum depicts Ajax and Ulysses playing at dice.

A bone die, spotted like a modern die.

A strip of bone marked malest *(bad luck).*

A crystal die.

A strip of ivory marked victor *(winner).*

A 14-faceted stone, marked with Roman numerals.

Archaeologists have shown that dice predate the written word, and can be found in almost every culture in the world, including the American Indian, Eskimo, and African. Excavations in Egypt have turned up stone dice dating from 2,000 B.C. Archaeologists in China have discovered gaming cubes from 600 B.C. that look remarkably similar to the modern thing.

For his dice ancient man used, among other things, plum and peach pits, stones, seeds, bones, horn, pottery, pebbles, shells, and beaver teeth.

The Greeks and Romans were heavy gamers, favoring dice of bone or ivory and occasionally of semiprecious stone. Even Plato was not wont to take the art lightly, writing that "nobody can become a skilled dice-player if he has not devoted himself to it from his childhood, but only plays for pleasure."

The Bible mentions that Roman soldiers cast lots for Christ's robe after the Crucifixion. The Emperor Claudius went so far as to publish a book on dice games. And Julius Caesar, at the Rubicon, uttered the famous words: *Jacta alea est*—"the die is cast."

To mark the spots or "pips" of his dice, early man either bored holes in the cubes or carved circular marks on the faces. He was also quite adept at loading dice. The earliest written records of man mention both dice and crooked dice. Dice especially made for cheating have been found in the tombs of Egypt, of the Orient, and of the Americas.

Modern man has improved both the manufacture of dice and the methods of loading them. Today's galloping ivories are usually made of cellulose or plastic. There are basically two varieties: "casino" dice and "drugstore" dice.

Casino dice are handmade, sawed from plastic rods, and perfectly cubical to within one five-thousandth of an inch. Casino dice three-quarters of an inch on a side are most often used for casino games of craps.

The drugstore die is smaller, machine made, and seldom as perfectly cubical as the casino die.

"Peewee" dice are only a quarter-inch on a side.

At various times, dice have been fashioned in the shape of a pyramid, pentagon, and octagon.

In the manufacture of casino dice, each spot is drilled precisely 17/1000 of an inch into the face, then filled with paint weighing exactly the same as the plastic removed for the hole. Thus the die remains balanced on all sides.

So much for honest dice. Through the ages, man has devised a number of ways to improve his odds at "indoor golf." The most familiar way is "loading" the dice—a weight of some kind is placed inside the die against one face, thereby assuring that the opposite face will come up more often than one might mathematically expect.

There are more subtle methods, however. "Shapes" are dice with one slightly sawed-off edge. The longer faces are more likely to come up than the shortened faces—imagine rolling a brick and trying to leave one of the narrow sides up.

"Tops" or "bottoms" are dice with incorrectly numbered faces. Instead of the numbers one through six, a "tops" die might show the numbers three, four, and five, each repeated on two faces. When used in conjunction with a die reading one, five and six, the pair cannot produce a seven.

You're not likely to be fooled by such a crass trick, you say? Keep in mind that only three faces of the die are visible to you at any one time; a good dice cheat can slip in his "tops" by sleight of hand and withdraw them from play before you can say "Rip-off!"

A good dice cheat can bilk you even with honest dice. There are ways to "spin" the dice to improve the chances of certain combinations. Your best bet is to immediately suspect anyone who suggests a game of craps and just happens to have his own ivories on hand.

That brings us to the subject of craps. The game is American in origin, a variant of an old European game known as "hazard" that was popular in London in the seventeenth and eighteenth centuries. In fact, the 1-1 and 1-2 combinations in hazard have been known as "crabs" since the sixteenth century.

According to some accounts, the origin of craps can be traced to Bernard de Mandeville, a Frenchman who brought the game of hazard to New Orleans in 1813. Since the nickname for Creoles was Johnny Crapauds, the game became known as Crapaud's game, and later, simply craps. Mandeville, himself, lost a fortune at the game, and was forced to sell his New Orleans property to pay his debts. A street cut

Death and the dice level all distinctions.
—*Samuel Foote,*
The Minor

Backgammon is much older than craps, ranking as the oldest dice game still widely played.

through his land was called Craps Street; it later changed to Burgundy Street.

American blacks around New Orleans are often credited with developing the game of craps as it is played today. They also left us with a wealth of dice slang. There's hardly any need to tell you what "Mississippi marbles" or "Memphis dominoes" are. Or "snake eyes," or "boxcars." How about "Little Joe from Kokomo?" Fours, my friend. And let's not forget that time-worn exhortation: "Come on, mama, baby needs a new pair of shoes!"

A New York dicemaker by the name of John H. Winn—that's right, Winn—has been called the first craps banker in history, and is credited with the invention of open craps, that variety of elbow athletics you're most likely to find in an alley or pool hall. Craps was spread by American soldiers during the two World Wars. Today a variant known as "bank craps" is played in casinos throughout the world.

Most experienced casino gamblers consider bank craps the casino game which offers the player the greatest chance to walk away a winner. Some also nominate craps as the most exciting of all casino games. It's certainly the most colorful to watch.

Earlier in this century, many American drugstores and soda fountains offered counter dice games to their patrons. Counter games are still legal in some parts of the country. Some of the more descriptively named games still enjoyed by Americans include Drop Dead, Pig, Heaven and Nine, and Hooligan. When you think of it, craps isn't bad either!

Today, backgammon is rapidly becoming one of the most popular games in America. The fact is, backgammon is much older than craps, ranking as the oldest dice game still widely played. The ancient Romans played a variety of backgammon. And as for the name, etymologists trace it either to the Saxon expression *bac gamen*—"back game"—or the Welsh *back gammon*—"little battle."

There are literally thousands of other games that employ the time-less cubes. Despite the use of cards and spinners, dice remain, quite simply, the best way of introducing the element of chance into any game, no matter how complex. As Mallarme suggested in the title of one of his most famous poems, "A Throw of the Dice Never Will Abolish Chance."

In some things, then, there is simply no room, or need, for improvement. Long before man had perfected the way he would build or find his home, his food, his weapons, his clothes, or his power, he'd just about perfected the way he would gamble.

In the late 19th century, dice games drew crowds at the gambling saloon in Wiesbaden, Germany.

DICTIONARIES

The dictionary is the only place where success comes before work.

"Everything that coruscates with effulgence is not ipso facto aurous" is a rather highfalutin way of saying "All that glitters is not gold," but without a dictionary you'd never guess it.

"Look it up in the dictionary" is a piece of advice foreign to few ears, but did you realize that until the eighteenth century speakers of English had no lexicographic authority to consult for the meaning of the thousands of English words now nestled between *aardvark* and *zymurgy*?

The first English work to bear the title "dictionary" (in its Latin form, *dictionarius*, from *dictis*, "saying" or "word" and *dicere*, "to say") appeared around the year 1225. But that first manuscript actually listed Latin words to be learned by rote by students, with only a few English words inserted, here and there, for explanation. Words were not grouped alphabetically, but were arranged according to subject.

English words began to appear regularly in fifteenth-century dictionaries, but still served only as aids to the study of Latin. One noted dictionary of this era was the charmingly titled *Storehouse for the Little Ones*, or *Promptorium Parvulorum,* brought out around 1440 by a Dominican friar aptly named Galfridus Grammaticus— Geoffrey the Grammarian. The work contained about 12,000 English words and their Latin equivalents. It did not appear in print until 1499 for one rather compelling reason—the printing press hadn't yet been invented.

The *Storehouse* was not the only fifteenth- and sixteenth-century dictionary with a colorful title—metaphoric titles were the custom for many years. A work dating from 1500 was dubbed *Ortus Vocabulorum, The Garden of Words*, and a 1573 student's dictionary was somewhat presumptuously named *Alvearie,* or "Beehive."

The first real English dictionary was the *Abcedarium Anglico-Latinum pro Tyrunculis*, a Latin-English work completed by Richard Huloet in 1552. This compendium contained some 26,000 words with their Latin translations. Each word was defined in English. Thus, the *Abcedarium*, though designed as a Latin aid, can be considered a bona fide English dictionary.

The *Abcedarium* was popular in its time, but relatively expensive. So in 1570, a physician named Peter Levins brought out what was basically a cheaper version of Huloet's work, entitled *Manipulus Vocabulorum—A Handful of Words*. The entries were arranged—not alphabetically—but according to the spelling of their *final* syllables, making the book, in effect, the first rhyming dictionary in the English language.

Early dictionaries made no attempt to include all English or Latin words, only those that were considered troublesome to students. The title of a 1604 work by Robert Cawdrey explains it best: *A Table Alphabeticall, conteyning and teaching the true writing and understanding of hard usuall English wordes . . . gathered for the benefit and helpe of Ladies, Gentlewomen, or any other unskillful persons.* As for the difference between "Ladies" and "Gentlewomen," you'll have to consult a dictionary.

The more tersely titled *The English Dictionarie* appeared in 1623, compiled by Henry Cockeram, but based to a great extent on Cawdrey's work. Cockeram's dictionary was hardly the last word in lexicographic precision, as is readily apparent in a definition such as "Hyena: A subtil beast, conterfeiting the voice of a man . . . He is sometimes male and sometimes female."

Until the 18th century, speakers of English had no lexicographic authority to consult for the meaning of the thousands of English words now nestled between aardvark and zymurgy.

In 1702, John Kersey—alias "J.K. Philobibl."—issued a wordbook entitled *New English Dictionary* that was the first volume to define words in everday usage. And in 1721, a schoolteacher named Nathaniel Bailey published the *Universal Etymological English Dictionary*, containing "more words than any English Dictionary before extant."

Another of Bailey's works, *Dictionarium Britannicum*, appeared in 1730, displaying "not only the Words, and their Explications, but the Etymologies." Bailey was also among the first to indicate the pronounciation of words along with their definitions.

In 1791 came the *Critical Pronouncing Dictionary and Expositer of the English Language*, compiled by an elderly actor named John Walker. Walker's book is still considered valuable for its treatment of pronunciation.

The phonetician, Isaac Pitman, based his popular shorthand system on Walker's principles.

Perhaps the most remarkable dictionary of the eighteenth century was the accomplishment of the legendary Samuel Johnson. Johnson's prodigious work—which was completed single-handedly—was brought out in 1755 as *A Dictionary of the English Language*. As Johnson's renowned biographer James Boswell noted: "The world contemplated with wonder so stupendous a work achieved by one man, while other countries had thought such undertakings fit only for whole academies."

From Samuel Johnson's dictionary of the English Language (1755):

Lexicographer: A writer of dictionaries; a harmless drudge, that busies himself in tracing the original, and detailing the signification of words.

Oats: A grain, which in England is generally given to horses, but in Scotland supports the people.

Most earlier lexicographers sought to lay down rules for usage and spelling, but Johnson sought more to reflect current usage—to reflect rather than dictate the accepted meaning—explaining in his *Preface* that no scholar "can embalm his language and secure it from corruption."

Said Johnson: "No dictionary of a living tongue can ever be perfect, since while it is hastening to publication some words are budding, and some falling away."

Today's dictionaries, likewise, make little attempt to dictate, only to reflect the ever-changing meaning of words.

Johnson was the first to use illustrations of word usage gleaned from "the best writers," as do many modern lexicographers. Because of the extensive research involved in gathering the illustrations, Johnson's work—planned to take three years—eventually required eight.

In 1755, Dr. Samuel Johnson published a dictionary that was a landmark in lexicography.

After his long years of toil, Johnson was piqued by an article written by Lord Chesterfield, the statesman and author, in which the Earl claimed undue credit as the patron of Johnson's dictionary. (Chesterfield had actually sent Johnson a ten pound subscription for the dictionary in 1747.) "I have been pushing on my work through difficulties, of which it is useless to complain," Johnson wrote in his now-famous letter to Chesterfield, "and have brought it, at last, to the verge of publication, without one wit of assistance, one word of encouragement, or one smile of favour . . . Is not a Patron, my Lord, one who looks with unconcern on a man struggling for life in the water, and, when he has reached ground, encumbers him with help?"

Although English dictionaries had been published in America as early as 1788, the first English dictionary compiled by an American was *A School Dictionary*, brought out in 1798 by a Connecticut teacher named—appropriately enough—Samuel Johnson, Jr.

In 1806, another Connecticut resident, Noah Webster of New Haven, issued *A Compendious Dictionary of the English Language* with some 40,000 words. But the most important milestone in American lexicography came in 1828, when Webster published his masterpiece, *An American Dictionary of the English Language*, with about 70,000 entries. Webster's work was the first American dictionary to gain wide acceptance in both the United States and England.

You may be confused by the plethora of dictionaries on the market bearing the name "Webster's." The fact is none of these books—or at least, very few—are directly derived from the work of Noah Webster. The word "Webster's" has become merely an identifying title, like the word "dictionary" itself, and cannot be copyrighted. Anyone at all

Noah Webster compiled An American Dictionary of the English Language *in 1828. Revised versions of this monumental work are still widely used in the United States today.*

can publish a book and call it "Webster's Dictionary," although the G.&C. Merriam Company of Springfield, Massachusetts, claims that their dictionaries are the legitimate successors to Webster's works.

Many stories have been told about the famed American lexicographer—most of them apocryphal. Witness, for example, this droll tale:

One day Mrs. Webster entered the parlor to find her husband locked in an embrace with the maidservant. "Noah!" she sputtered, "I *am* surprised!"

Noah disentangled himself and quickly regained his professional composure. "No, my dear," he told his wife, "It is *I* who am surprised. *You* are merely astonished."

Many other dictionaries have come and gone since the days of Webster and Johnson, but the greatest English dictionary on either side of the Atlantic remains the *Oxford English Dictionary*, conceived in the mid-nineteenth century but not completed until 1928. The *Oxford* lists all recorded English words, and their varying usages from the seventh century through the twentieth. Thus, a simple word such as "place," due to its many uses and its long history of change, might occupy twenty or twenty-five small-print pages. Compiled with the aid of hundreds of research assistants in both England and America, the *Oxford* remains the largest dictionary in the world. Its twelve volumes contain about 415,000 words, almost two million illustrative quotations, and close to 228 million letters and figures!

The last words of Noah Webster were probably zyme, zymosis, and zymurgy.

Schoolboy wisdom holds that "antidisestablishmentarianism" (28 letters) is the longest word in the language, but the Oxford English Dictionary *includes the word "floccipaucinihilipilification" (29 letters).*

A glance at a card catalogue in any large library will suggest the tremendous range of dictionaries now available, covering almost every specialized vocabulary imaginable. Witness, for example, *A Dictionary of the Stitches Used in Art Needlework,* or *Dictionary of*

the *Underworld: the vocabulary of crooks, criminals, racketeers, beggars and tramps, convicts, the commercial underworld, the drug traffic, and the white slave traffic.*

And then there's the *Dictionary of Waste Disposal and Public Cleansing*—published, *natürlich* in Germany.

The number of dictionaries in existence today is difficult to calculate, but in English, there is a dictionary for most of the 5,000 foreign languages spoken throughout the world today.

By the way, the first Bohemian-English dictionary—626 pages long—was brought out in 1876, and the long-awaited Mongolian-English dictionary was published in 1953.

How many words are there in the dictionary? First of all, no English dictionary but the *Oxford* claims to include anywhere near all the words in the language.

The word "unabridged" in a dictionary title does not mean the work contains all the words in the language, but merely that the book includes all entries appearing in earlier editions of the work.

English, the second most commonly spoken language in the world after Mandarin Chinese, contains the largest vocabulary of any language on earth, an estimated 800,000 words—of which the average person uses only about 60,000. *Webster's Third International Dictionary* contains about 450,000 entries.

You'll find more dictionary entries under the letter *T* than under any other, for *T* is the most common initial letter in our language. The most common letter in English is *E*, and the most common words are *the, of, and,* and *to,* in that order.

Schoolboy wisdom holds that *antidisestablishmentarianism* (28 letters) is the longest word in the language, but the *Oxford English Dictionary* includes the word *floccipaucinihilipilification* (29 letters). The word means "the action of estimating as worthless."

Webster's Third International Dictionary, meanwhile, lists *pneumonoultramicroscopicsilicovolcanoconiosis* a lung disease common to miners.

The longest word in common use is generally thought to be *disproportionableness* (21 letters). And the longest chemical term ever used, the name of an amino acid compound, contains some 3,600 letters.

In the 19th century, Montgomery Ward featured a number of dictionary stands. The styles pictured above are the Harvard model (top) and the Noyes model (bottom).

However, as any lexicographer with a sense of humor will point out, the longest word in our language is actually *smiles*—because there's a mile between the first and the last letters!

Incidentally, excluding proper names, the oldest word in the English language still in use in a comparable form is *land*, derived from the Old Celtic *landa*, "heath." This word is thought to have been in use on the European continent well before the beginning of the Roman Empire.

The dictionary is easily the most useful reference work ever created—competing perhaps with the Yellow Pages. But there are a number of languages in existence today that are not likely to be recorded in a new dictionary. Why? Well, there are now about twenty languages in which no one can converse, for the simple reason that there is only one speaker of the tongue still alive. Eyak, an Alaskan Indian language, is certainly one of the most moribund "living" languages on earth—spoken only by two aged sisters when they chance to meet!

Worcester's Unabridged Dictionary *was a popular 19th century American dictionary.*

The word "unabridged" in a dictionary title does not mean the work contains all the words in the language, but merely that the book includes all entries appearing in earlier editions of the work.

The first edition of Webster's Unabridged Dictionary *used much the same format as today's* Webster's Third International Dictionary.

DOGS

Americans will spend some one-and-a-half billion dollars this year on pet food, close to four times the sum spent on baby food.

"He cannot be a gentleman that loveth not a dog," reads an old proverb, and there can be no doubt that the American loveth all things canine. There are now about 1.1 million pedigreed dogs registered in this country—about one pedigreed pooch for every 200 Americans. The number of mongrels extant is anybody's guess. One knowledgeable estimate puts the total number of dogs in the United States as over 40 million!

Americans will spend some one-and-a-half *billion* dollars this year on pet food, close to four times the sum spent on baby food! And there are at present over 400 pet cemeteries in this country!

When did this long and happy relationship between man and dog begin? Far too long ago to estimate a date, for man had domesticated the dog well before recorded history began. The bond between man and his best friend was—and still is—a symbiotic relationship, with both parties benefitting from the alliance.

The word *dog* originally referred to a particular English breed of canine, but is now used generally to refer to all members of the *Canus familiaris*. Other species in the *Canus* genus are the *aureus* (the jackal) and the *lupus* (the wolf). Anthropologists aren't quite sure which species was the first to join forces with his upright fellow hunters.

Most likely jackals and primitive dogs, originally independent hunters and scavengers, found it advantageous to follow nomadic human hunters for the bones and food scraps left behind when they broke camp. Gradually, prehistoric man came to realize that the presence of these beasts surrounding the camp at night could benefit him as well, since the howling canines would warn of the approach of deadly predators. The more the hunter went out of his way to feed his watchguards, the more dependent upon him they became.

Slowly, dog and man began to join forces in hunting, the dog contributing his scent to flushing out game, and man returning the favor by providing the dog with a steady diet of meat. We know that abo-

The probable view of the fox terrier or dachshund which lies upon our hearthrug is that he is one of a pack, the other members of which are the human inhabitants of the house. . . . From the dog's point of view, his master is an elongated and abnormally cunning dog.
—Louise Robinson

rigines of Ireland, Switzerland, and the Baltic lands used dogs for hunting—and occasionally partook of dog flesh—long before farming was introduced in Europe. Cave paintings 50,000 years old depict hunters with dogs at their side.

The original domesticated canines—wolf, dog, and jackal—were probably interbred to evolve the modern *familiaris* species. Subsequent breeding by man gradually produced distinct breeds. The oldest records of Mesopotamia and Egypt show that distinct breeds of domesticated dogs had been developed by the year 3000 B.C., including animals much like the modern greyhound and terrier. The ancient Greeks and Romans kept dogs. The breed classifications of the Romans were quite like our own, distinguishing between scent-hunting and sight-hunting dogs, and between *Canes villatici* (housedogs), and *pastorales* (sheep or herding dogs).

Depiction of a dog from a Boeotian amphora, 750 B.C.

In the fourteenth century, attack dogs with spears and buckets of fire harnessed to their backs were used to upset cavalry horses. But for the most part, throughout the Middle Ages, dogs were used for hunting and herding. Yet over the centuries, man has come to rely on the dog more for companionship than for anything else. By the seventeenth century, the dog was a ranking member of the household as a note by Samuel Pepys might suggest: *At night my wife and I did fall out about the dog's being put down in the cellar . . . because of his fouling the house . . . and so we went to bed and lay all night in a quarrel.* Today, the dog is valued as a guard, a shepherd, a guide, a hunter, a retriever, a soldier, a policeman, and a friend.

Dogs skilled at sniffing out caches of concealed drugs are becoming increasingly popular among many police forces. Recently, a Florida policeman demonstrated his dog's sleuthing talents to a group of students. He hid packets of drugs around the room, and then loosed his keen-nosed sidekick to find them. The policeman hid ten packets; the dog brought back eleven.

At last glance, there were 163 recognized dog breeds in the United States. All canines can be broken down into six main groups according to their original use by man.

The Sporting Group includes dogs that hunt by air scent, such as the *pointer*, the *retriever*, the *Labrador*, the *Irish setter*, the *Weimaraner*, and the *cocker spaniel*. These dogs serve primarily as hunters' assistants, finding and retrieving small game.

Retriever.

Originally from Spain, the spaniel was used by the Irish in the first century for hunting. On the other hand, the pointer (or "bird dog,") is of a more recent origin, first appearing in Britain some time during the seventeenth century. The development of pointing breeds paralleled the increasing use of sporting firearms.

The dachshund.

The Hound Group is made up of those dogs that hunt by ground scent. This group includes the *Afghan*, the *beagle*, the *basset hound*, the *bloodhound*, the *dachshund*, the *foxhound*, the *saluki*, and the *greyhound*. Dogs similar to the dachshund can be found in Egyptian carvings dated around the fifteenth century B.C. Most English hound breeds are thought to be descendants of hounds brought from Normandy during the invasion of William the Conqueror. The bloodhound probably owns the keenest sense of smell of all dogs.

But the most spectacular canine tracking feat on record was not the work of a bloodhound. In 1925, a Doberman pinscher named

A turn-of-the-century Dutch milk dealer prepares for a trip to the market with his 3-dog team.

The Bettmann Archive, Inc.

"Brandy"—a short-haired St. Bernard of the King Kong strain, was bred to have a white mask rather than the usual black facial markings.

"Sauer" tracked a thief 100 miles across the Great Karoo, an arid plateau in South Africa, by scent alone. And a fox terrier lost by a truck driver in Hayes Creek, Australia, rejoined his master eight months later in Mambray Creek—a distance of 1,700 barren miles from Hayes Creek!

The Working Group includes dogs that serve primarily as guides, guards, and herders, such as the *Doberman pinscher*, *German shepherd*, the *collie*, the *great Dane*, the *Newfoundland*, the *St. Bernard*, the *Shetland sheep dog*, and the *Siberian husky*. These dogs probably constitute the most useful group of canines. Eskimos use them for draught animals. In this country, they're valuable as "seeing-eye" and "police" dogs—a term not restricted to German shepherds. The Newfoundland has been used to rescue swimmers, while for centuries the

Two mountain climbers, trapped in a snow storm in the Alps, had just about given up hope of surviving when one of them spotted a St. Bernard equipped with a brandy keg. "Look!" he shouted joyously to his companion. "Here comes a dog with man's best friend."

The smooth fox terrier.

St. Bernard has served as a rescue dog for the monks of the Alpine Hospice of St. Bernard.

The Terrier Group—dogs that hunt by digging and flushing out burrowing animals—includes, not surprisingly, most terriers, along with the *schnauzer*. The word "terrier" comes from the Latin *terra*, "earth." Most terrier breeds were developed in the British Isles. The *Airedale terrier*, for instance, was first bred in the Aire valley of England.

The Pekinese has existed in China for over 5,000 years.

The pomeranian.

The Toy Group consists of dogs that serve primarily as human companions, and includes such favorites as the *Pekinese*, the *Maltese*, the *Chihuahua*, the *toy poodle*, the *Yorkshire terrier*, the *pug*, and the *pomeranian*. Most toys are miniature versions of older larger breeds. The Pekinese has existed in China for over 5,000 years.

The smallest dog on earth, the *Chihuahua*, usually weighs in somewhere between two and four pounds, although some specimens have tipped the scales at a mere sixteen ounces.

Small toy dogs became popular in the British Isles when laws were enacted to control poaching pooches. The eleventh-century King Canute, for instance, decreed that all dogs kept within ten miles of the king's forest preserve must have their knee joints cut to hinder them from chasing his game. But exceptions were made for any dog that could fit through a "dog gauge," a ring seven inches wide and five inches high.

The water spaniel.

The sixth group of dogs is known as the Nonsporting Group, a miscellaneous class consisting chiefly of dogs with muscular necks and strong jaws. The *bulldog*, the *Boston terrier*, the *chowchow*, the *Dalmatian*, and the *poodle* are listed among this group. The chowchow is most likely the oldest member, dating at least from 150 B.C. in China. The Boston terrier is one of the few breeds originating in the United States. It was developed by a Bostonian named Robert Hooper in the

Poodles—the most popular breed of dog in America.

mid-nineteenth century. Despite its modern association with the French, the poodle is probably of German origin.

Which breed of dog is most favored by Americans? Beagle? Collie? German shepherd? Surprisingly, it's the poodle. With some 200,000 registered dogs, there are more than twice as many poodles as there are German shepherds, the second most popular breed. In fact, almost one in every five pedigreed dogs registered in the United States is a poodle!

A list of registered dogs by breed offers a few other surprises. The

Today, the most popular up-and-coming dog breed In America is the Yorkshire terrier. The Yorky led all breeds in new registrations in 1975, with 14,640.

"You'll just have to choose between us, Edward..."

large numbers of registered dachshunds, Labrador retrievers, and St. Bernards would startle those who consider these breeds to be mere curiosity pieces. Yet such supposedly populous breeds as the bulldog and bloodhound rank pitifully low in actual registration.

Today, the most popular up-and-coming dog breed in America is the Yorkshire terrier. The Yorky led all breeds in new registrations in 1975, with 14,640. At the other end of the scale, the *Chinese fighting dog* is now the rarest dog breed on earth, with only twenty-three specimens known to exist in 1976—all of them, oddly enough, in California. And if you are the proud owner of a *Belgian Malinois*, you own almost 10 percent of all the Malinois in this country.

Only eight breeds of purebred dogs originated in the United States: the *American foxhound*, the *American water spaniel*, the *Boston terrier*, the *Chesapeake Bay retriever*, the *coonhound*, the *Amertoy*, the *spitz*, and the *Staffordshire terrier*.

The British Isles holds the pedigreed pooch title: Of the world's 163 recognized breeds, 47 originated in Great Britain.

Few dogs today perform any service aside from friendship, though originally the canine was valuable to man because his senses were strongest where man's were weakest. The dog's sense of smell is among the keenest in the animal kingdom. A trained dog can select an item touched only by his master's finger from among dozens of other objects; a bloodhound can pick up one scent from among hundreds. Some dogs can reputedly pick up a scent that is ten days old!

The canine's sense of hearing is likewise extremely acute. Dogs have responded from seventy-five feet to orders unintelligible to men only ten feet away. The range of sound a dog can hear is much wider than man's: "dog whistles"—too high-pitched to be heard by the human ear—can be picked up by dogs 100 yards away.

Most dogs, alas, have poor vision. As a rule, they're nearsighted, yet they can be particularly sensitive to movement. All dogs are colorblind—their visual world is a drab panorama of black, white, and gray. On the other hand, dogs have "eyeshine," and like cats, can see quite well in the dark.

But it is not the dog's keen smell or hearing that has endeared him to modern man, it's his uncomplaining readiness to obey and lavish affection on his human friends. "To his dog," an old saying goes, "every man is Napoleon—hence the popularity of dogs." A dog is loyal, loving, and lovable, even if his master can boast none of these qualities. The Prussian monarch Frederick the Great hit it on the head: "The more I see of men, the better I like my dog."

Another saying—reportedly a Turkish proverb—has it that "if dogs' prayers were answered, bones would rain from the sky." But most American canines enjoy a diet considerably better than bones—-considerably better than the diet of many impoverished peoples, in fact. Many dog owners will argue as to the correct amount of food a dog requires each day, but most authorities agree that dogs over six months of age should be fed one large meal daily, with perhaps one smaller snack. A half-pound of food will suffice for a toy dog, a pound of chow for a dog weighing from ten to twenty pounds, and two to four pounds for a dog weighing above fifty pounds.

The dog commends himself to our favor by affording play to our propensity for mastery, and as he is also an item of expense, and commonly serves no industrial purpose, he holds a well-assured place in men's regard as a thing of good repute.

—Thorstein Veblen

Photo courtesy of Twentieth-Century-Fox.

Buck stole the limelight from Clark Gable in the movie "Call of the Wild."

Speaking of heavier members of the canine set, the largest dog on record tipped the scales at a colossal 295 pounds. And larger unverified claims have been heard.

The largest litter ever born consisted of 23 pups. It was thrown by a foxhound in Pennsylvania in 1944.

The most prolific dog on record, a greyhound in London, sired an amazing 2,414 registered puppies, along with at least 600 other unregistered whelps.

Like baseball fans, dog lovers have been known to argue over obscure items of canine trivia. To clear up a few disputes: the country dog does not live longer than the city dog. The city dog may get less exercise, but as a rule he's more pampered, and survives on the average three years longer than his country cousin. Of course, these urban figures don't take into account stray mongrels roaming the streets.

Municipal licensing of dogs, by the way, was instituted in England in 1735 to reduce the number of strays. The first dog licensing in the United States began in New York State in 1894.

To dispel another myth, the mongrel is not generally any smarter than the purebred dog. Individual dogs differ in intellectual capacity and disposition much the same as individual human beings differ: there are smart as well as stupid dogs in both classes. And finally, the dog does *not* sweat through his tongue—the dog's most important sweat glands are actually on the soles of his feet!

There are many words and phrases based on the name of man's best friend. *Dog-eared, dogleg,* and *doggone* are among them, but *dogma* is not.

The expression "raining cats and dogs" has many reputed origins. The most gruesome holds that during the seventeenth and eighteenth centuries in England, a heavy cloudburst would fill the gutters with a torrent of refuse not unlikely to include a number of dead dogs and cats. A poem by Jonathan Swift describing a city rainstorm ends with the lines:

> *Drown'd Puppies, stinking Sprats, all drench'd in Mud,*
> *Dead cats and Turnep-Tops come tumbling down the Flood.*

Our word *cynic* actually comes from *kynos,* the Greek word for dog, and owes its use either to a former dog kennel that served as the

The Bettmann Archive, Inc.

first school of the Greek Cynics, or from the uncouth, belligerent manners adopted by adherents of that philosophy. The word *cynosure*, in Greek, literally means "dog's tail!"

As Robert Benchley wrote, "There is no doubt that every healthy, normal boy . . . should own a dog at some time in his life, preferably between the ages of forty-five and fifty."

These tombstones at the Hartsdale (N.Y.) Canine Cemetery testify to man's love for his best friend.

EGGPLANTS

Botanists in northern Europe dubbed the eggplant mala insana, *or "mad apple," because they thought that eating the fruit could result in insanity.*

The eggplant is neither oval in shape nor white, and certainly bears no relation to the egg in taste or in usage. "Eggplant," then, is a misnomer? Well, almost.

The first eggplants to reach Europe during the Middle Ages were actually a rare white species, with oval fruits that closely resemble a hen's egg. The name *eggplant* was a natural, and stuck to the plant even when the more common purple varieties made their appearance in Europe.

The eggplant was once known as the "love apple" in England because it was thought to possess aphrodisiac properties. Botanists in northern Europe dubbed the eggplant *mala insana*, or "mad apple," because they thought that eating the fruit could result in insanity. Curiously, the French call the eggplant *aubergine*, related to the word *auberge*, or "inn."

Fruit? Yes—the eggplant is botanically a fruit, although the plant is used almost exclusively as a vegetable. The eggplant is, to be exact, the *Solanum melongena*, a member of the nightshade family closely related to the tomato and potato. Specimens range in size from the large fruit eaten in America to tiny Near Eastern varieties which happen to be more strongly flavored than the eggplants we customarily enjoy.

In addition to the familiar purple variety, there are white and yellow varieties, and a dwarf species whose fruits grow only three or four inches long.

A peculiar variety called the snake eggplant produces narrow, elongated fruits up to a foot in length with their ends curled up like a serpent's tongue.

The eggplant originated in India and eastern Asia, and has been cultivated since remotest history. One of the oldest references to the

The type of eggplant most commonly used in cooking is the long purple variety.

The pile of eggplants at the lower right corner of this amorous scene testifies to the former belief that "love apples" possessed aphrodisiac qualities.

fruit appears in a fifth-century Chinese book, which describes how fashionable Oriental ladies used a black dye made from eggplants to stain and polish their teeth. The "mad apple" has been a particular favorite in the Near East since Biblical times. The ancient Persians stuffed eggplants, and the Arabs scorched them over charcoal and crushed the flesh into a puree.

During the early Middle Ages, the Arabs brought the eggplant to Spain and Greece. The fruit was first mentioned in northern Europe by Albert of Cologne in the thirteenth century, but it was not well known there until the sixteenth century. The first eggplants began appearing on English dinner plates around 1587. Initially, the English called the fruit "Guinea squash," since it was brought to London by traders in West Africa. The Spaniards brought the eggplant to America during the seventeenth century. But most of the eggplants grown here until this century, were used exclusively for ornament. The eggplant, incidentally, is one of the few items of produce grown in the United States that also thrives in the tropics.

Eggplants are now extensively cultivated in east and southern

The New York Improved Purple Eggplant.

The eggplant is botanically a fruit, although it is used almost exclusively as a vegetable.

Asia, as well as in Africa, South America, southern Europe, and the United States. Requiring strong, steady sunshine, the plant is rarely grown outdoors in England or northern Europe.

Most American eggplants come from Florida, Texas, and New Jersey. About a million and a half bushels of eggplants are produced here each year, and smaller quantities are imported, chiefly from Mexico. But the average American, by and large, shuns the eggplant, consuming but four ounces of the fruit per year.

Eggplants are edible from the time they are one-third grown, and are usually picked before they reach maturity. Plants are often started in protected beds, then transplanted to the garden or field. Ripe eggplants are eaten raw, pickled, or cooked. The cooked fruit is favored for its similarity in texture to meat, and many dishes—the Italian Eggplant *Parmigiana*, for instance—are prepared like meat dishes, with cheese, sauce, and spices.

The versatile eggplant can be baked, broiled, scalloped, fried, sautéed, stuffed, or marinated. Italy, Greece, France, and several eastern countries all have their favorite eggplant dishes. In the Near East, large eggplants are stuffed with meat, or pureed into a dip, or diced and mixed with onions, tomatoes, and garlic.

The Italians like to slice the fruit and sauté it in olive oil, with plenty of tomato sauce. A Sicilian specialty is *melanza caponata*.

The French enjoy *ratatouille*, a baked vegetable casserole with tomatoes, peppers, onions, and zucchini.

Many Japanese dishes call for eggplant. In fact, the eggplant is the fourth most important "vegetable" in Japan, after the sweet potato, radish, and Chinese cabbage.

The popular Greek dish *moussaka*, made from eggplant, lamb, onions, and spices, originated in the early Middle Ages.

Another eggplant dish, *Imam Bayaldi*, owes its name to sixteenth century Ottoman Turks. Acccording to a legend, a holy man, or

The round purple eggplant blooms later than other varieties, and for that reason is grown principally in southern regions.

CHILLED PICNIC RATATOUILLE

Makes: 6 servings.

¼ cup salad or olive oil

2 cloves garlic, minced

1 onion, sliced

1 green pepper, seeded and cut in strips

3 medium unpared zucchini, cut into ¼-inch slices

1 medium eggplant, pared and cut into cubes

2 teaspoons dried leaf basil

1 teaspoon dried leaf oregano

1½ teaspoons salt

⅛ teaspoon pepper

3 tomatoes, peeled and cut in wedges

Heat oil in large skillet, add garlic, onion, green pepper and zucchini; cook about 3 minutes or until onion is tender, stirring frequently. Add eggplant, basil, oregano, salt and pepper; cover and cook over medium heat 15 minutes, stirring occasionally. Add tomato wedges, cover and cook 5 minutes longer or just until tomatoes are heated. Refrigerate several hours or overnight. Pack in container with a tight lid to carry to picnic.

Imam, was served a particular eggplant dish by a beautiful woman. When she bent over to present the dish, her veil slipped from her face for a moment. The holy man, captivated by this brief glimpse of her beauty, and overwhelmed by the aroma of the succulent food, simply passed out. The dish *Imam Bayaldi* was then christened "the priest has fainted."

When you shop for eggplants, look for firm fruits of uniform color. The best eggplants are heavy in relation to their size. Avoid wilted or soft eggplants, or fruits marked with brown spots which may indicate decay.

"Mad apples" are also excellent plants for a kitchen garden, so you might test your purple thumb with a small crop. Experts advise that you start the seeds indoors and transplant them to the garden only when the daily temperatures reach the seventy-degree range. They say you can serve eggplants with any dish. How about eggplant and eggs?

The Dwarf Very Early Eggplant is usually ripe for cooking a month before other varieties of the fruit.

ELEVATORS

During the 1977 power blackout in New York City, the business and commercial life of the world's busiest metropolis came to a complete halt for an entire day. Though buses were still running to take people to work and many offices had sufficient natural lighting to make some work possible, the blackout shut off one electrical device without which the modern city is completely helpless: the elevator.

With thousands of offices vacant for the lack of a means of reaching them and hundreds of thousands of people stranded in high-rise apartment buildings, the importance of the elevator in today's city was drawn sharply into focus. There can be no doubt that the invention of the elevator has had a great deal to do with shaping our urban geography. But the question arises, did the need for taller buildings spur the invention of the elevator, or did the invention of the elevator produce higher office and apartment buildings?

No one can prove that the paucity of high buildings before the modern era was due solely to the lack of a means to reach the upper floors. It could more easily be argued that the demands for utilizing urban space were never so great as to make the high-rise a necessity, and that once the demand was there, human ingenuity rose to the job of inventing an efficient elevator. But one thing is certain: the idea of vertical transportation, if not the means, has been with us for well over 2,000 years.

Ruins from a number of ancient civilizations contain shafts; some archaeologists believe that these shafts were actually hoistways in which goods and perhaps people were lifted. But no mention of an elevator-like device appears in any ancient writings until the first century B.C., when the Roman architect-engineer Vitruvius described lifting platforms that utilized pulleys and human, animal, or water power. The Roman Coliseum, built in 80 A.D., used crude lifting platforms to raise gladiators and wild animals to the arena level.

In 17th-century France, a device known as the "flying chair" occasionally brought passengers to the upper floors of higher buildings.

Many medieval monasteries were built atop steep cliffs or surrounded by high walls, and some of the more unsociable cloisters depended upon a device known as the basket elevator for entry and exit. A basket elevator was just that—a basket in which the passenger was lifted or lowered by rope along the outside of the monastery walls. Not the most gracious entry, perhaps, but unwanted guests certainly posed little problem.

In seventeenth-century France, a device known as the "flying chair" occasionally brought passengers to the upper floors of higher buildings. Similar to hoists used by stablemen to lift bales of hay to a loft, the flying chair was operated by a rope running around a wheel at the top of the building exterior. One end of the rope was attached to the chair, the other end to a counterweight. To rise, a passenger threw off a sandbag attached to the chair—the counterweight would then descend and the much lighter chair and passenger would rise. Not a very pleasant ride, as you might imagine. Even so, at the end of the upward journey, the passenger had to climb in through the window.

In a sense the flying chair was similar in operation to the dumb-

The first successful nonhydraulic elevator was built by Henry Waterman in New York City in 1850.

waiter, a pulley-and-counterweight device used chiefly to lift food from kitchen to dining room. An apocryphal story credits Thomas Jefferson with the invention of the dumbwaiter; we do know that Jefferson used one of the world's first dumbwaiters in his Virginia home to deliver food from a basement kitchen to the dining room. The dumbwaiter was later used in this country to deliver garbage to the basement of many apartment buildings.

In the early nineteenth century, the hydraulic elevator became popular for moving goods in factories and warehouses. The platform of a hydraulic elevator was mounted atop a plunger that rose or fell in a hollow cylinder according to the amount of water in the cylinder. A steam engine pumped water into the cylinder to lift the plunger; valves released the water to lower the plunger and car. But the hydraulic elevator had one serious disadvantage: since the length of the plunger had to be equivalent to the height of the shaft, the cylinder in which the plunger sank had to be buried to a depth equal to the height of the shaft. Thus the heights to which an elevator could go were severely limited.

The problem was partially solved by an American, Cyrus Baldwin, who designed a new kind of hydraulic elevator, in which a much shorter plunger turned wheels at the top of the shaft. Ropes wrapped around the wheels actually raised and lowered the platform. These later models did away with the need for extensive excavation for the cylinder, and allowed some platforms to attain the blinding speed of 600 feet per minute—about seven miles an hour. The hydraulic elevator is still used in some warehouses and parking garages where speed is less important than strength.

The first successful non-hydraulic elevator was built by Henry Waterman in New York City in 1850, and was installed in a Manhattan warehouse to hoist barrels to the upper floor. Waterman's elevator was a crude platform lifted by a cable that wound around a cylindrical drum known as the windlass. The windlass was turned by steam power in one direction to lift the platform; then turned in the other direction to lower it. But these devices also limited the height of an elevator shaft, since the drum afforded only so much room to safely accept the winding rope.

Like the hydraulic elevator, windlass elevators were used only for hauling freight. Why not passengers as well? Well, for one thing, few people at the time were ready to trust their lives to the hemp ropes then used as cables.

Then, along came Elisha Graves Otis. Though Otis is often called the inventor of the elevator, he initially contributed only one major innovation to elevator design. But that innovation was significant enough to make him, in effect, the father of the passenger elevator.

Vermont-born Otis was working in a furniture factory when he was asked to design a machine for lifting lumber and other materials from floor to floor. Otis's invention made its debut at the 1853 Crystal Palace Exposition in New York, where it was billed as "An elevator, or machine for hoisting goods."

Elisha Graves Otis was the father of the modern passenger elevator.

Elisha Otis giving a public demonstration of his safety elevator at the Crystal Palace Exposition, New York City, in 1854.

Otis's elevator was a simple platform that moved between two guide rails, with a steam-powered windlass at the top of the shaft to raise or lower the cable. The innovation was a safety device that could stop the fall of the elevator in the event the cable broke. The simple device consisted of two metal hooks and a spring, attached to the cable where it met the platform. If tension in the hoist rope was relaxed—in the event of a cable break, for instance—the hooks immediately sprang to a horizonal position, where their ends would catch in teeth cut into the guide rails and stop the elevator's descent. Sounds a bit shaky? Well, it's basically the safety device modern elevators rely on today—and it's totally reliable.

According to some accounts Otis demonstrated the safety of his invention by holding regular cable-breaking exhibitions at the exposition. Spectators would watch in amazement as Otis climbed on the platform, rose to the top of the shaft, and then cut the cable! His expected fall would be checked by the safety hooks.

By 1857, Otis had installed the world's first commercial passenger elevator in the Haughwout Department Store in New York. A steam-driven lift, the elevator rose five stories at a speed of forty feet per minute—barely faster than a stairway. At first, shoppers were reluctant to risk their lives on the newfangled device, but as more and more people took the—er, plunge, it soon became clear that the passenger elevator was here to stay.

Early steam-driven elevators required a large space for the steam engine, and often spewed thick smoke into the shaft. The next step was obvious: an electric elevator. In 1880, a German named Werner Siemens built a crude electric elevator, with a motor under the platform turning cogwheels that fit into notches in the guide rails.

In 1887, William Baxter built an unsuccessful electric machine in Baltimore. The world's first *successful* electric elevator was installed two years later by the Otis Elevator Company in the Demarest Building in New York—and was in continual use until the building was demolished in 1920.

The Demarest Building elevator's thirty-year life span pales next to the endurance record of the world's oldest operating elevators, three hydraulic machines installed in a Grammercy Park, Manhattan apartment building in 1883, and still operating after more than ninety years of service.

IN A LONDON "LIFT."

FAIR AMERICAN: *I wonder why they call elevators lifts in this country.*

LIFT BOY: *Hi can tell you, marm. Hi can lift you hup, and hi can lift you down. Hi can helevate you hup, but hi can't helervate you down.*

In 1895, the Englishmen Frost and Strutt invented a device called the teagle that offered a marked improvement over the windlass. Instead of a drum at the top of the shaft, the teagle employed a pulley wheel and counterweight, with the cable pressed so tightly against the wheel that it turned with the pulley. The teagle eliminated the cable-length limitations of the earlier windlass elevators—now buildings could rise toward the sky.

The Otis Elevator Company now installs from 20,000 to 25,000 new elevators and escalators each year.

By the turn of the century, the problems of speed, safety, and height limitation had been successfully challenged. There remained only improvements in convenience and economy. The push-button elevator, introduced in 1894, was both more reliable and cheaper to operate than the hand-operated manned elevator you can still find in the moldiest of city buildings. Automatic leveling, which brings the car to rest precisely at floor level, made its debut in 1915, but the cry of "watch your step" will live on forever. By the middle of this century, automation had rendered the elevator operator nearly extinct.

Haute hotel life in Philadelphia—the elevator.

The Otis Elevator Company, the world's largest manufacturer of elevators, now installs from 20,000 to 25,000 new elevators and escalators each year, and services an estimated 400,000 Otis elevators functioning around the world. Otis was exporting elevator equipment to thirty-one countries as early as the 1890's. Nowadays, Otis operates twenty-nine plants worldwide, with over 44,000 employees.

Modern elevators are "gearless traction" machines. An electric motor turns a wheel, called the traction sheave, at the top of the shaft. The cable runs over the traction sheave, around a smaller wheel below the traction sheave, back around the traction sheave, and down the shaft. One end of the cable is attached to the car, the other to the counterweight. Another cable, called the compensating cable, stretches from the bottom of the car to the bottom of the counterweight, after first passing over an idler wheel at the bottom of the shaft. The compensating cable is needed to—yep—compensate for the unequal distribution of cable weight when the car is near the top or bottom of the shaft.

The earliest electric elevators with push-button controls simply carried a passenger from point A to point B without stops—no matter how many people on intermediate floors impatiently watched the car glide by. A modern elevator answers all calls in one direction, then responds to calls waiting in the other direction. Large office buildings with many elevators use group control systems, which keep the cars correctly spaced and send only the closest elevator to answer a call.

Thanks to Otis, elevators are now almost 100 percent—five times safer than a staircase, according to the elevator industry. Cable failure is extremely rare, for each of a modern machine's eight woven steel cables can support a load eight times the capacity of the car. Safety devices similar to Otis's assure that even if the cable does break, the car won't fall very far in the shaft. And a device at the bottom of the shaft, called the buffer, will break the fall of an errant elevator in the unlikely event the car does plummet.

An airplane once crashed into a New York office building and struck directly into the elevator shaft, destroying the cables. The car plunged seventeen floors—but the buffer saved the life of the elevator's lone passenger!

Modern elevators travel at many times the speed of the earliest machines, with express elevators in some taller buildings speeding along at 1,200 feet per minute—fast enough to require machinery to adjust changing air pressures in the car. And newer elevators, such as those in the Sears Tower and the John Hancock Building in Chicago, travel at speeds of up to 1,800 feet per minute!

One of the largest elevators in the world—a hydraulic model—raises, lowers, and revolves the stage at New York's Radio City Music Hall. But the largest commercial elevator on record was constructed to raise and lower a full swimming pool on the stage of the Hippodrome Theater in New York. The device had a capacity of 250,000 pounds—that's equal in weight to thirty-five hippopotami—and moved at a speed of twelve feet per minute, slower than the most sluggish hippopotamus!

A second means of vertical transportation, the escalator, was developed while the electric elevator was still in its infancy. A patent for an escalator was issued in 1859, but the first working escalator—a stepless conveyor belt with cleats for traction—was installed by Jesse Reno in 1896 on a pier in Coney Island, New York. About the same time, Charles Seeburger constructed a similar conveyor with horizontal steps. Seeburger coined the word "escalator" for his invention, combining the Latin *scala* ("steps") with the first letter and ending of "elevator." Seeburger's device forced riders to step on and off to one side—at their own risk. The Otis Elevator Company acquired both inventions. By 1921, Otis had developed the kind of horizontal-step escalator in use today.

Escalators eliminated both the need for an elevator operator and, more important, long waits for an elevator car. Escalators were installed extensively in deep subway stations, transporting a steady stream of riders and thereby eliminating bottlenecks at elevator doors. In fact, the longest escalator in the world can be found in the Leningrad subway, with a vertical rise of 195 feet.

The steps of an escalator are moved by an endless chain powered by electricity, usually at speeds of about 100 feet per minute. The underside of each step is triangular in shape, and mounted on four wheels running in tracks under the steps. When the step begins its ascent, the rear wheels rise to keep the top of the step horizontal.

As anyone who's had to climb to the eighth floor of a department store via seven escalators is well aware, the escalator will never re-

Photo courtesy of the British Tourist Authority and the British Travel Association.

Passengers ride the escalators at one of Britain's underground stations in London.

Among recent elevator innovations is Otis's glass-walled, double-deck affair that runs on the exterior of the building.

place the elevator for long distances. As buildings rise higher and increase in floor area, engineers have had to keep pace with constant innovation. The major problem faced by the engineers is how to minimize the space taken up by elevator shafts when many elevators are needed for a building. One answer is the dual elevator—two cars running in one shaft. The first dual elevator was placed in service in Pittsburgh in 1931, with the upper car running as an express, the lower car as a local. Another development, the double-deck car, was introduced in 1932, with two attached cars that stop one floor above the other.

The designers of the 110-story World Trade Center in New York arrived at another solution for minimizing elevator shaft space. In each of the two towers, express elevators speed passengers to "sky lobbies" on the forty-fourth and seventy-eighth floors. Local elevators run only between one lobby and another. Thus three local cars can

The latest word in elegant elevators is the outdoor glass-cab elevator, such as this one at the Hyatt Regency at O'Hare International Airport in Chicago.

run in the same shaft, each serving one-third of the tower, and the amount of floor space occupied by elevator shafts is cut by almost two-thirds!

Round elevator cars serve a Johnson Wax Company building in Racine, Wisconsin, designed by renowned architect Frank Lloyd Wright. Another Wright creation, the Price Tower in Oklahoma, is served by hexagonally shaped elevator cars.

And who says an elevator can go only straight up? The Eiffel Tower boasts elevators that move along dizzily inclined tracks, as does the George Washington Masonic Monument in Virginia. And the outdoor elevator is now coming into vogue, as demonstrated by the new Hyatt Regency Hotel in Atlanta, served by glass-cab elevators running in rails on the outside of the building.

Beats a flying chair, doesn't it?

FRANKFURTERS

There are over 200 varieties of sausage made in this country, by some 3,000 individual processors. The frankfurter is by far the most popular.

There is no truth to the notion that frankfurters are unavailable today in Germany, the land of their birth. Stop by a roadside eatery or pop into a quick-lunch restaurant in Germany and you'll have little trouble finding a frankfurter of some dimensions, complete with bread, mustard, and sauerkraut.

But there is one difference between the German frank and the hot dog you'll find at an American stand: in Germany, you'll be served your frank piecemeal, with a sausage, a pile of sauerkraut, and a piece of bread on a plate. The frank-on-a-bun, like its cousin, the hamburger-on-a-bun, is a product of American ingenuity.

The frankfurter and hamburger are both medieval inventions, but the sausage itself predates recorded history. The word comes to us from the Latin *salsus*, *salted* or *preserved*. The word *salami* was mentioned often in the pre-Christian period, perhaps associated with the Greek city of Salamis on Cyprus.

Since meat preservation was a problem before the invention of refrigeration, preserved meat was always popular. In the Middle Ages, sausage makers developed individual formulas for seasoning their products, which frequently took the name of the city where they originated. From Frankfurt, of course, came the frankfurter; from Bologna—well, need we say more?

The southern European preferred dry, heavily salted sausage, such as *genoa salami* from Genoa; in northern Europe, cooks preferred fresh and cooked sausage such as *head cheese*, *blood sausage*, and *bratwurst*.

The frankfurter was brought to the United States by German immigrants. Like the hamburger, it first became popular in the Cincinnati area. As to why the frank became more popular than any other sausage—well, who's to account for tastes?

Today, frankfurter meat is cured with various combinations of

Photo courtesy of Oscar Mayer and Co.

chemicals, such as sodium chloride and sodium nitrite or nitrate, along with sugar. The pork or beef is chopped, seasoned, stuffed into its collagen or intestine skin, and then smoked and cooked. In some frankfurter manufacturing plants, computers select raw materials daily and feed them into a continuous hot-dog processing machine, untouched by human hands. Frankfurter production that formerly required nine hours now takes as little as forty-five minutes.

There are over 200 varieties of sausage made in this country, by some 3,000 individual processors. The *frankfurter* is by far the most popular. Americans gobble up close to sixteen billion weiners each year—about eighty per person!

Wieners roll off the "hot dog highway" at Oscar Mayer at a rate of 36,000 links per hour.

The original Nathan's Famous hot dog stand on Coney Island was founded in 1916. This photograph shows the stand in 1920. The little boy in his father's arms is Murray Handwerker, current chairman of the board and president of Nathan's Famous, Inc.

Franks with beans were popular on the American frontier, since both would remain fresh for long periods of time. Though refreshment stands at early baseball parks sold such items as tripe, planked onions, and cherry pie, the hot dog eventually became the overwhelming favorite of the bleachers. In fact, the term *hot dog* was coined in 1919 at the Polo Grounds, a major-league ballpark in New York City. Today, a baseball park without hot dogs would be an affront to the sport.

Americans gobble up close to sixteen billion weiners each year—about eighty per person.

In 1967, a gala celebration was held at Nathan's to honor the 50-year jubilee of the Coney Island hot dog.

Once, Babe Ruth devoured so many hot dogs at a depot stand that he had to be rushed to a hospital emergency room.

Though the frankfurter remains popular, it certainly is no longer fashionable—except perhaps for the tiny frank-and-bun concoction known as *pigs in a blanket that are de rigeur* at so many cocktail parties. And some frankfurter makers now adulterate their product with—your grandparents would shudder—chicken!

We have no idea of the contents of the 20 two-ounce franks that Jimmy Davenport of Kentucky wolfed down in just three and a half minutes in 1976, setting the world's record for hot-dog consumption. But we know that a mammoth weiner exhibited by a California hotel to celebrate the American Bicentennial in 1976 consisted of forty pounds of pork and beef, and measured 148 inches in length. To our knowledge, no patriot volunteered to single-handedly devour the dog.

GELATIN

There's always room for
JELL-O.
—*Advertising slogan*

To the modern American, the sweet gelatin dessert known as Jell-O is an institution. Just tear open the wrapper, pour boiling water over the powder, and refrigerate in a bowl or mold. Jell-O's a lot easier to make than pie.

Sure, we take Jell-O for granted, until we realize what our forefathers—or foremothers—had to go through to serve a bowlful of the shimmering dessert.

Before the turn of the century, gelatin was a functional food item rather than a treat. Jellies and aspics had been used since the days of ancient Greece to bind, glaze, and preserve other foods. Just think of the canned hams packed in aspic you buy today.

We think of gelatin basically as a dessert; but in former times, cooks flavored their gelatins with vinegar, wine, almond extract, and other items that produced a tart rather than sweet product. Those cooks hardly had need of a sweet jelly, since the items they glazed were more often meats than sweets.

As long ago as the Renaissance, chefs took pride in constructing elaborate gelatin molds, and no dinner party was complete without at least one jelly construction worthy of the best modern-day wedding cake baker. In the nineteenth century, the most popular mold designs were castles and fortresses complete with doors, windows, and crenellated turrets.

Before this century, the glue needed for gelatin—called *collagen*—had to be laboriously extracted from meat bones. In the Middle Ages, deer antlers were a popular source of the glue; and later, calves' feet and knuckles. Housewives in the nineteenth century used isinglass, made from the membranes of fish bladders.

Gelatin-making was a daylong affair, requiring the tedious scraping of hair from the feet, hours of boiling and simmering with egg whites to degrease and clarify the broth, and careful filtering through jelly bags or "filtering stools." The transparent finished product was then dried into sheets, leaves, or rounds.

Not the easiest process in the world, you'll agree. Charles B. Knox thought so, too. In 1890, the Jamestown, New York man was watching his wife make calves'-foot jelly when he decided that a prepackaged, easy-to-use gelatin mix was just what the housewife needed. Knox set out to develop, manufacture, and distribute the granulated

gelatin, while his wife invented recipes for the new kitchen staple.

A few years later, a Le Roy, New York woman named May Wait *didn't* wait for Knox to flavor his gelatin, and concocted a mix of sugar, powdered gelatin, and artificial fruit flavors that she christened Jell-O. Actually, a powdered gelatin dessert had been invented fifty years earlier by the same Peter Cooper credited with the invention of the "Tom Thumb" locomotive. But it wasn't until the development of the icebox at the end of the century that America was ready for gelatin desserts.

Wait's product found its way to few American tables before it was bought by the food tycoon Frank Woodward, who was already marketing a coffee and tea substitute named Grain-O. A genius in packag-

In the early 1900's, JELL-O salemen toured the country in special JELL-O company automobiles, demonstrating the simple preparation of "America's Most Famous Dessert" at fairs, church socials, banquets, and picnics.

Photo courtesy of General Foods Corporation

Pictures of Elizabeth King, "the JELL-O girl," appeared in JELL-O advertisements, recipe booklet covers, dessert dishes, and souvenir spoon handles, between 1904 and 1908.

Photo courtesy of General Foods Corp.

By the 1930's, JELL-O had become a way of life.

ing, mass marketing, and advertising, within a few years Woodward turned Jell-O into a household word. The ten-cent carton advertised a "delicious dessert" that was "delicate, delightful, and dainty," and the Jell-O trademark of a young girl with carton and kettle in hand soon appeared on store displays, dishes, spoons, and other promotional articles.

To show the housewife how versatile the product was, Woodward's company distributed free booklets with Jell-O recipes. One booklet alone ran to a printing of 15 million copies!

By 1925, Jell-O was a big-money industry. In that year Jell-O joined Postum to form General Foods, today one of the largest corporations in America. Talk about humble beginnings!

By the 1930's, Jell-O had become a way of life. In the Midwest, no Sunday dinner was complete without a concoction known as Golden Glow salad—Jell-O laced with grated carrot and canned pineapple and served with gobs of mayonnaise.

Knox Gelatine tried to discourage the rush toward Jell-O with ads warning shoppers to spurn "sissy-sweet salads" that were "85 percent sugar." While Knox stressed the purity of their odorless, tasteless, sugarless gelatin, Jell-O highlighted their product's versatility.

As for the belief that gelatin is good for the hair and nails, the only claim made by either Jell-O or Knox is that their product "may" do some good for "some people's" hair and nails.

Today, you'd be hard put to find a beanery that didn't offer at least one flavor of the fruity dessert. Gelatin is very popular among dieters, especially the sugarless D-Zerta variety, and many restaurants serve elaborate specials of Jell-O, fruit, and cottage cheese. In modern health-conscious America, Jell-O has become the highly touted alternative to "junk food" desserts.

Strawberry Bavarian Soufflé is one of the spectacular desserts that can be made with gelatin.

Photo courtesy of Knox Gelatine

GOLF

The early 1970's marked a major milestone in golf history: the opening of the 10,000th golf course in the United States. Figuring conservatively at 6,000 yards per course, we can estimate that some 60 million yards—or 34,100 miles—of this country are regularly traversed by some 10 million golfers.

Assuming a figure of eighty yards as the average fairway width, we can conclude that a total area of about 1,550 square miles is now devoted solely to the practice of swatting a small ball into a four-and-a-quarter-inch hole—a total area larger than the state of Rhode Island!

The world's most land-consuming game is most often traced to humble beginnings in Scotland, but there is no firm evidence that golf originated in that country. Similar games were played in other nations centuries before golf appeared in the British Isles. In the early days of the Empire, the Romans enjoyed a game they called *paganica*, played with a bent wooden stick and a leather ball stuffed with feathers. Roman legionnaires may well have brought the game to Britain.

Cambuca, a game similar to *paganica* that was played in fourteenth-century England, may have been an early ancestor of golf. The Dutch played a game called *kolven* on frozen rivers and canals. In kolven, the players used a wooden club to putt a ball toward a stake pressed into the ice. Sixteenth-century illustrations from Bruges, in Belgium, show players putting a ball at a hole in the ground. The Soviets recently claimed that golf originated in Denmark in the fifteenth century, and the Chinese have long claimed that the game was born in the Orient two or three centuries before Christ.

In any case, we first find a reference to golf in Scotland in a 1457 decree ordering that the game "be utterly cryit doun and nocht usit," since it interfered with the practice of archery, a more useful sport to the defense of the realm. Another ordinance of 1471 decried the playing of "golfe and futeball;" and in 1491, yet another decree stipulated punishments for law-breaking linksmen.

This last edict was the work of King James IV, who for a time forbade golf in Scotland, declaring: "It looketh like a silly game." But within a few years of his decree, the king himself became a keen golfer, and entries showing the purchase of balls and other golf equipment appear in accounts of James's lord high treasurer.

In 1592, the laws against golf were modified to forbid the sport only on the Sabbath. That law was later softened to outlaw golf only "in tyme of sermons."

Since the time of James IV, golf has remained a popular royal sport in Britain. Golf has long been officially known as the "royal and ancient game." James's son, James V, was a regular on the links. His daughter, Mary Stuart, was seen with clubs in hand just a few days after the murder of her husband—an indelicacy that should not surprise many of today's more avid linksmen. Perhaps you've heard the one about the duffer whose partner dropped dead on the golf course? The bereaved player was mournfully sipping his cocktail at the clubhouse bar when a friend rushed up to offer his condolences.

"I heard you carried poor old Willie all the way back to the clubhouse," the friend said. "That was quite a job. He must've weighed a good 250 pounds."

"Oh, carrying him wasn't difficult," the duffer replied, shrugging. "What bothered me was having to put him down at every stroke, and then lift him up again."

Golf was regularly played in England at least as early as 1603, when King James I—a Scot—appointed an official clubmaker, and budgeted funds for the purchase of golf balls.

Before assuming the English crown in 1685, James II played a challenge match against two Scottish noblemen, choosing for his partner a shoemaker named Johne Patersone. Evidently Patersone was a ringer, for the king won the match, and Patersone bought a house in London with the money he earned from the royal victory.

During the eighteenth century, golf clubs and associations became popular throughout England and Scotland. The reasons are obvious: anyone can set up a tennis court in his yard, or play soccer in an open

Golf was once a rich man's sport, but now it has millions of poor players.

Playing golf in 1810.

The most famous Scottish course, the Royal and Ancient Golf Club of St. Andrews, was founded in 1754, and remains the supreme authority on the sport.

field, but even a four- or five-hole golf course requires a vast expanse of well-tended land. Only by pooling their resources, and sometimes their land, could golfers provide themselves with an adequate course.

The first golf club in England, *The Royal Blackheath*, was founded around 1787, when there were already six clubs in Scotland. The most famous Scottish course, the Royal and Ancient Golf Club of St. Andrews, was founded in 1754, and remains the supreme authority in the sport, framing and revising rules for clubs throughout the world—except for clubs in the United States, which has its own governing body. There are now some 1,800 golf courses dotting the island of Great Britain.

Golf was being played in the United States at least as early as 1779.

Professional golf began in earnest in the early nineteenth century. The earliest pros not only played for cash, but lent their talents to the manufacture and design of golf clubs and balls, and instructed beginners as well. The most famous of the early pros was Old Tom Morris, the proprietor of the golf shop at Prestwick, Scotland. Old Tom won the British Open four times between 1861 and 1867 before relinquishing his title in 1868—to his son, Young Tom Morris. Young Tom had entered his first professional tourney at the tender age of thirteen. He was only seventeen when he won the British championship. He won four successive championships and was undoubtedly the premier player of his time.

Golf was being played in the United States at least as early as 1779, when an advertisement for golfing equipment appeared in a New York paper. The game may actually have been enjoyed much earlier here, for upon the death of William Burnet, governor of New York and Massachusetts, in 1729, the Burnet estate listed "nine golf clubs, one iron ditto, and seven dozen balls." There is also evidence of golf in South Carolina and Georgia in the late eighteenth century. But the game apparently did not catch on here at the time, for almost a century passed before golf was mentioned again in official records.

> I regard golf as an expensive way of playing marbles.
> —Chesterton

The father of American golf is Robert Lockhart, who returned from Scotland in 1887 with a supply of balls and clubs and laid out a course in a pasture in Yonkers, New York. A year later, Lockhart and his friends founded the first modern American golf club, named St. Andrews after the landmark Scottish course.

Within the next five years, more than two hundred clubs were organized here, among them the Chicago Golf Club, the first American course with eighteen holes.

By 1895, there were over 50 clubs, and by the turn of the century,

The secret of good golf is to hit the ball hard, straight, and not too often.

In thē 1700's, the "royal game of golf" was played in the Borghese Gardens in Rome.

There are three ways to improve your golf game: take lessons, practice constantly—or start cheating.

more than 900, with at least one club in each state. A 1901 golfing guide listed 982 clubs, including 66 six-hole courses, 715 nine-hole links, and 92 eighteen-holers. One hundred nine courses were listed without mention of size. The 1920's saw a rapid increase in the number of golf courses and players. By 1930, there were over 5,000 courses in operation, with an estimated $830 million in property value and some 2¼ million players—along with 800,000 caddies.

Many Americans considered golf an effete sport until 1913, when a former caddy named Francis Ouimet defeated two British stars to win the U.S. Open. After Ouimet's victory, golf was increasingly accepted by the general public.

Today, there are three types of golf course in the United States: the private course open only to club members; the private course open to the general public (for a price); and the municipal course owned and operated by the city and available to all for a small fee. In addition to the 10,000 regular courses, there are hundreds of small pitch-and-putt courses, and untold numbers of miniature links.

Today, the four major tournaments are the U.S. Open, the

Victorian ladies played golf at the "Westward Ho!" Ladies Golf Club in Bideford, Devon.

Masters, the PGA (Professional Golfers Association) Championship, and the British Open. A victory in all four contests in one year constitutes the "grand slam" of golf. Bobby Jones, perhaps the greatest amateur golfer of all time, is the only man to win "the whole ball of wax."

Jones's four victories in 1930 came in the four major tournaments of *his* time—not the four major tourneys of today.

Today, a modern pro can earn well into six figures in a single year, without winning even one major tourney. Jack Nicklaus, 1975's biggest money-earner, brought home a nifty $298,149 in purses during that season.

Among women golfers, Sandy Palmer was the leading money-winner that year, with over $76,000 in purses. Kathy Whitworth, eight times the leading money-winner among women golfers, has

Amy Pascoe, English Ladies' Champion of 1896, demonstrates the finishing stance for the approach shot.

The confident golfer teed up his ball, looked toward the next green, and declared to his caddy, "That's good for one long drive and a putt." He swung violently, topped the ball, and watched it roll a few feet off the tee.

The caddy stepped forward and handed him the putter, smugly muttering, "And now for one hell of a putt!"

---

grossed over a half-million dollars in purses during the last fifteen years. But to most minds, Mildred "Babe" Didrikson Zaharias remains the Babe Ruth of women golfers. A star in track and field, tennis, baseball, and basketball before she turned to golf, Babe won more than fifty major golf tournaments in her career, including a streak of seventeen straight triumphs. In 1950, the Associated Press voted Babe the greatest female athlete of the half-century.

Golfers, of course, have their own magazines. *Golf Digest,* the leading publication in this field, has a circulation of close to one million copies.

In addition to a hall of fame of great players, golf has certainly produced some marvelous additions to our vocabulary. The word *golf* itself is probably derived from the Dutch *kolf* or *kolven,* or the German *Kolbe.* Some authorities claim that the source is the Scotch

An amateur golfer is one who addresses the ball twice—once before swinging, and once again, after swinging.

gowf, "blow of the hand." The game was long known as *goff*, *gouff*, or *gowff* in Scotland.

The word *caddie* (the youth who carries the golfer's bag and often chooses the club for each shot), comes from the French *cadet*, "young lad." The term *putt*, like the verb "put," is rooted in the Middle English *putten*, "push" or "thrust."

The rules of golf, unlike the rules of many other sports, have changed little over the centuries, but the equipment used in the game has undergone a number of major alterations. The earliest golf sticks were made with thick wooden shafts and long heads. Modern clubs are manufactured with steel shafts and either persimmon wood or chromium-plated steel heads.

Today, we use numbers to designate each club; but until the 1920's each club had its own name. The woods were numbered from one to five, and were known as follows:

No. 1 . . . THE DRIVER
No. 2 . . . THE BRASSIE
No. 3 . . . THE SPOON
No. 4 . . . THE BAFFY
No. 5 . . . THE CLERK

The irons were numbered one through nine:

No. 1 . . . THE DRIVING IRON
No. 2 . . . THE MIDIRON
No. 3 . . . THE MID MASHIE
No. 4 . . . THE MASHIE IRON
No. 5 . . . THE MASHIE
No. 6 . . . THE SPADE MASHIE
No. 7 . . . THE MASHIE NIBLICK
No. 8 . . . THE PITCHING NIBLICK
No. 9 . . . THE NIBLICK

Many a golfer prefers a golf cart to a caddy because it cannot count, criticize—or laugh.

Golf is a game in which the slowest people in the world are those in front of you, and the fastest are those behind.

Other clubs include the putter, the jigger or chipper, and various wedges, however, no golfer in tournament play is permitted to carry more than fourteen clubs.

Before 1848, golf balls were made of leather, stuffed with "as many feathers as a hat will hold." The leather balls were expensive and virtually useless when wet, so the guttie, a ball of solid gutta percha (a rubberlike substance) caught on quickly in the 1850's. Golfers using the guttie quickly noticed that a new ball tended to hook and slice erratically when hit: but old, pockmarked gutties traveled straight. So the practice began of manufacturing golf balls with small depressions, or dimples, on the outer surface.

Rubber-cored balls appeared in 1898; and at first, were known as "bounding billies." Since then, golf's governing bodies have legislated the size and weight of the balls to be used in all official play. At present, official U.S. balls are equal in weight but slightly larger in diameter than the balls used in Britain and the rest of the world.

By the way, the golf tee was the brilliant invention of one George F. Grant of Boston, who patented a tapered wooden tee in 1899.

Golfing records are difficult to compare, since golf courses vary in difficulty. But the lowest golf score ever recorded for an eighteen-hole course of at least 5,000 yards was a fifty-five, achieved by E.F. Staugaard in California in 1935, and matched in 1962 by Homero Blancas in Texas.

The longest golf drive on record is 515 yards, by Michael Hoke Austin in Las Vegas, Nevada, in 1974. Prior to that, the record belonged to Englishman E.C. Bliss, who walloped a ball 445 yards during a 1913 match. Unofficially, it's been claimed that a golfer known only as "Ohio Fats" has hit drives considerably longer.

Many talented golfers go through life without once tasting that dream of all linksmen, the hole-in-one. But at least fifteen players have achieved the remarkable achievement of holes-in-one on successive holes. The greatest of these feats was accomplished in 1964, when Norman Manley recorded back-to-back aces on two *par-four* holes in Saugus, California.

You can be certain that no one will ever score a hole-in-one on the seventeenth hole of the Black Mountain Golf Club in North Carolina.

Golf: A five-mile walk punctuated by disappointments.

For the complete golfer: This sturdy, transparent tube clips onto the golf bag and dispenses tees.

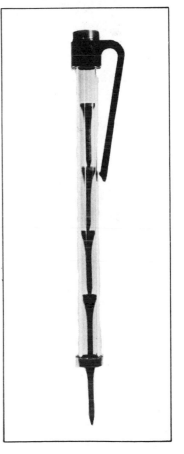

The par-six hole, the longest in the world, measures 745 yards from tee to cup.

The world's largest club in the world is undoubtedly the Eldorado Golf Club in California, which includes fifteen individual courses!

Among the remarkable lore of golf are the following stories:

Let us here set down the enviable record for the most strokes taken on a single hole—an outlandish 166! In the 1912 Shawnee Invitational for Ladies in Pennsylvania, an experienced woman golfer, who shall mercifully remain nameless, had the misfortune of duffing a drive into the Binniekill River. With the ball floating insolently in the water, she set out in a rowboat to "play the ball where it lies," with her husband at the oars. After flailing away for what must have seemed an eternity, she finally succeeded in driving the ball to dry land one-and-a-half miles downstream. By the time she hacked her way back through the woods and holed out on the sixteenth green, the distraught duffer had taken 166 strokes— all meticulously recorded by her loving husband.

*   *   *

Bobby Jones, one of golf's great immortals, played in his first tournament at the age of 14. The year of the tournament was 1916.

Justice McKenna of the United States Supreme Court was a dedicated golfer, but a rather unsuccessful performer. Hoping that his game might be improved if he took instruction, he engaged a professional for a course of lessons.

One day, while practicing on a course just outside the Capitol, he placed his ball on the tee, swung mightily, and missed. The same thing happened on three successive strokes: each time his club hit several inches behind the ball. The golf pro watched in silence.

The Justice was chafing. Finally, in white heat, he glared at his ball, which hadn't moved a fraction of an inch, and muttered, "Tut! Tut!"

The instructor gravely walked towards the jurist, and said, "Sir, you'll never learn to play golf with *them* words."

*   *   *

Lew Worsham leaned over his putter on the 18th green of the Jacksonville Country Club. He needed to sink the ball in 2 to win the 1948 Jacksonville Open Championship, a $10,000 feature. He moved his putter carefully behind the ball. Suddenly, he straightened, dropped his club, and went to the side of the green.

"I touched the ball," he told the tournament official. "Call a penalty stroke."

Worsham then returned to take the 2 putts that would have won, the 2 putts that now gave him only a tie.

The next day, Lew lost the playoff to Clayton Haefner on the 21st green.

But even in defeat Worsham was marked as a great champion—a champion in sportsmanship. Not even his victory in the 1947 National Open earned him the respect he won by calling against himself a penalty nobody else had seen.

This picture of Britain's early masters was taken in 1902. Left to right are J.H. Taylor, Harry Vardon, B. Sayers, William Auchterlonie, Alexander Kirkaldy, Willie Fernie, and James Braid.

GOLF'S MOST COLORFUL TERMS

BIRDIE   Score of one stroke less than the par for that hole.

BISQUE   Handicap stroke that a player may use on any one hole of his choosing, provided he announces his decision to use the stroke before teeing off on the following hole.

BOGIE   Score of one stroke more than the par for that hole.

BULGER   A driver whose face bulges into a convex shape.

BUNKER   Sand trap.

DIVOT   Piece of turf cut out of the ground by a player's stroke.

DUB   To hit the ball poorly, or a shot poorly executed.

FORE   A cry of warning to people within range of a shot.

GOBBLE   Hard-hit putt that drops into the cup, but would have traveled far beyond the cup had it not dropped in.

HOSEL   The socket on an iron club into which the shaft fits.

MULLIGAN   A poor shot which a player, by agreement, is allowed to cancel and replay.

SCLAFF   To strike the ground behind a ball before making contact with the ball.

There's no game like golf: you go out with three strangers, play eighteen holes, and return with three enemies.

Dave White's round at the Winchester Country Club started fine, but he blew up on the fifth hole and took a horrifying 13! Then the Massachusetts pro settled down with a vengeance. He shot 10 straight birdies to salvage a par round of 72.

*　　*　　*

The day was August 19, 1962. Longview, Texas, was agog. Homero Blancas, a 24-year-old graduate of the University of Houston had just completed the first round of the Premier Invitational Tournament in 55 strokes! His card of 27 for the front nine, and 28 for the back, was the lowest round of golf ever played on a course measuring more than 5,000 yards.

All seven brothers of the Turnesa family, who were born and reared in Elmsford, N.Y., became outstanding golfers. Mike Turnesa was a greenskeeper at Fairview Country Club in Elmsford, and he started his kids in the game. They learned fast.

Six of the boys—Mike, Jr., Frank, Joe, Phil, Doug, and Jim—became professionals. The only Turnesa who didn't turn pro was Willie, the youngest. But he, too, was a superb golfer. Willie won the U.S. Amateur in 1938, and again in 1948; and he won the British Amateur in 1947.

Among them, the seven Turnesa brothers won a host of tournaments, and in 1952, Jim won the Professional Golfers Association championship.

The Turnesa Brothers of Elmhurst, New York were a golfing phenomenon.

HAMBURGERS

The English called the burger "Salisbury steak" after Dr. James J. Salisbury, who in the 1880's recommended to his patients that they eat well-done beef patties three times daily, with hot water before and after, to relieve colitis, anemia, asthma, and other ailments.

Sure, everyone knows that the hamburger comes from Hamburg and the frankfurter from Frankfurt. What could be plainer? But it may interest you to know that while the meats themselves are German in origin, the idea of placing a hamburger or a frankfurter on a bun is an American innovation—and institution. The fact is, those countries that do regularly consume the frank and the burger are more likely to import them from the United States than Germany!

The hamburger is a more recent invention than the frankfurter. During the Middle Ages, traveling merchants from Hamburg learned from the Tartars of the Baltic lands how to scrape raw meat and season it with salt, pepper, and onion juice for what came to be known as "Tartar steak." Many restaurants still serve a similar dish known as *steak tartare.*

No one knows the name of the first cook to shape scraped or chopped beef into a patty and broil it, but we do know that the first hamburgers were browned on the outside and almost raw inside. When the hamburger arrived in America, it was eaten quite raw—the way the French, for instance, still prefer their meat.

The English and Irish were the first to cook their beef patties well-done throughout. The English called the burger *Salisbury Steak* after Dr. James H. Salisbury, who in the 1880's recommended to his patients that they eat well-done beef patties three times daily, with hot water before and after, to relieve colitis, anemia, asthma, and other ailments.

Modern doctors might scoff at Salisbury's ideas. But you'll still find Salisbury Steak on many dinner menus side by side with the burger.

The difference? Well, many diners buy their chopped meat frozen in large plastic bags. To prepare hamburger patties, an implement such as an ice cream scoop is used to extract thawed meat from the bag and set it on pieces of wax paper. The chef then forms the patties by swatting the lumps of chopped meat with a heavy can of vegetables—round, of course. For the Salisbury Steak, however, an *oval* can (usually a sardine can) is used to shape the meat.

Burgers were first popularized in the United States by German immigrants settling around Cincinnati. But the first burger wasn't laid between the halves of a bun until early in this century. The sandwich—meat of any kind between pieces of bread—has been with us since at least the eighteenth century. The sandwich was reputedly the brainstorm of inveterate gambler John Montagu, fourth earl of Sandwich, who stuffed his meat between bread slices so that he could dine at the gambling table. Officially, the first *hamburger sandwich* appeared at the 1904 Louisiana Purchase Exposition in St. Louis, Missouri—also the birthplace of the ice cream cone.

As for the modern hamburger, the last decade has seen a huge increase in burger corruption, with soy protein a common culprit. But consider yourself lucky. A Welsh zoologist has been working on a high-protein burger made from rat meat. And other scientists with tainted tastebuds have proposed a burger made from cotton—talk about flannelmouth!

If the popularity of the frankfurter has tapered off somewhat in recent years, the hamburger is certainly on the rise. Chopped meat now accounts for about 30 percent of all consumer meat sales. As late as the 1920's, many American dictionaries still did not contain the word *hamburger* though most did mention the *Hamburg steak*. Today, it would be hard indeed to find a restaurant, diner, coffee shop, or roadside stand that did not serve the burger in some shape or form. Burger joints have been mushrooming all over Europe, too, led by a British chain known as Wimpy's. And you'll have no trouble in Paris finding a McDonald's for *Le Cheeseburger*.

McDonald's is a story in itself. A chain known as the White Castle was the first to serve cheap, mass-produced hamburgers. Since then, hamburger joints have proliferated. Today, McDonald's is definitely the leader of the pack. Beginning with a stand in Des Plaines, Illinois,

Nutrition is an inexact science: it cannot explain how teen-agers manage to thrive on hamburgers and Coke.

McDonald's famous "Big Mac" hamburger.

which raised its now-famous yellow beams on April 15, 1955, McDonald's has grown into a huge corporation with well over several billion dollars in annual sales. McDonald's sales average a billion hamburgers every three months!

To date, McDonald's has sold 25 billion hamburgers—stack them up and you'd have twenty piles the size of the tallest building in the world, the Sears Tower in Chicago.

The McDonald's Corporation is run from a complex near Chicago called "Hamburger Central." Since 1968, new franchisers have been taught the ABC's of hamburgerology at a school in Elk Grove Village, Illinois, known as *Hamburger University*.

The McDonald's philosophy: in three out of four families, it's the children who decide where to eat. Please the child and you've captured the entire family.

That idea has certainly worked. The McDonald burger has now spread from coast to coast, and through much of Europe and Japan. As of January 9, 1978, there were 4,612 McDonald's stands throughout the world. And, yes, there's a McDonald's in Hamburg!

In 1975, a group of Australians exhibited a 2,859-pound hamburger which was over 17 feet in circumference.

If the McDonald's burger has lost little in translation, some of the firm's terminology has not fared so well. When McDonald's was laying plans for its first Paris franchise, *Gros Mec* seemed the appropriate translation for the "Big Mac"—until red-faced McDonald's officials learned that *Gros Mec* also meant "big pimp" to the Frenchman.

McDonald's may hold the record for the number of hamburgers sold, but certainly not for the largest burger. That honor belongs to a group of Australians who in 1975 exhibited a 2,859-pound burger which was over seventeen feet in circumference. Hopefully, they had a few tons of catsup on hand.

And McDonald's would be delighted to serve Ronald Sloan, who in 1976 established a hamburger-eating record by devouring seventeen burgers, with buns, in a mere thirty minutes—appropriately enough, in Cincinnati.

ICE CREAM

I scream, you scream, we all scream for ice cream.
—Street rhyme

True or false: (1) Ice cream will cool you off on a hot summer day; (2) Americans invented the dessert; (3) Since mechanical refrigeration techniques were not developed until late in the nineteenth century, ice cream is obviously a recent arrival to man's dessert table.

If you answered "false" to all three of the above statements, you've proved you really have the scoop on man's favorite frosty confection. In fact, three answers of TRUE would place you among the majority of Americans, who are ice-cold when it comes to the finer points of ice cream lore.

First, ice cream is not a cooler. Oh, it may cool your taste buds momentarily, and its psychological effect may convince you that you're cooling off. But ice cream is chock-full of calories, the unit of measurement of heat. So, the ultimate effect of a bowlful of ice cream is to make you warmer, not cooler!

Modern American refrigeration techniques and ice cream infatuation notwithstanding, the frozen dessert is neither a recent concoction nor a product of Yankee ingenuity. Most historians would trace the first bowl of ice cream to fifteenth- or sixteenth-century Italy, or perhaps England, but the story of ice cream's rise to gustatory prominence is a good deal more interesting than a simple date.

In ancient Rome, the Emperor Nero had snow transported from nearby mountains to cool his wine celler, and reportedly concocted some of the first water-ice desserts by mixing the snow with honey, juices, and fruit. But the first frozen dessert made from milk didn't reach Europe until the thirteenth century, when Marco Polo returned from the Orient with a recipe for a milk-ice, presumably similar to sherbet.

Improvements in ice- and sherbet-making probably led to the invention of ice cream some time in the sixteenth century. We know that early in that century Italian noblemen were enjoying a frozen milk product called "flower of milk." Yet Anglophiles may proudly point to a fifteenth-century manuscript reporting on the coronation of Henry V that mentions a dessert called *creme frez.* If creme frez was indeed ice cream, then the manuscript proves that the reputedly Italian invention was actually being made in England before the sixteenth century.

Italian ice cream arrived in France in 1533, along with Catherine de Medici and her retinue of chefs, when the fourteen-year-old Florentine moved to Paris to marry King Henry II. (Modern French cooking, by the way, is actually Italian in origin, descended from the Florentine cuisine of Catherine's chefs.) For many years, the chefs of various French noblemen tried to keep their recipes for ice cream a secret from other chefs—and from their masters, who were frequently astounded by their cooks' talent for serving a cold dessert even in the warmest weather.

"Peaches and Cream" is the title of this drawing by illustrator James Montgomery Flagg.

Ice cream remained a treat for the rich and regal until 1670, when Paris's first cafe, the Procope, opened its doors and made the frigid dessert available to the masses for the first time. Other cafes quickly followed—including the Café Napolitain, whose proprietor, a Monsieur Tortoni, concocted the creamy delight that still bears his name.

The first mention of ice cream in America occurs in 1700, but the dessert was not made here in any quantity until much later in the century. Both George Washington and Thomas Jefferson were known to be ice cream fanciers. Jefferson, who had learned how to make French ice cream during a visit to France, was one of the first rulers to serve the confection at a state dinner. Jefferson once served a dessert of crisp, hot pastry with ice cream in the middle, perhaps the first ice cream sandwich in America.

Ice cream remained an expensive dish until the early nineteenth century, which saw the invention of the insulated icehouse and the hand-crank ice cream freezer. By the 1820's, the dessert was being sold by street vendors in New York City, who beckoned passersby with shouts of "I scream ice cream."

Many vendors peddled a concoction they called *hokey pokey*,

In 1898, the first Schrafft's Ice Cream and Candy Shop was opened on Broadway in New York City.

Photo courtesy of Schrafft's Ice Cream Co., Ltd.

made from milk and eggs boiled to form a custard, then frozen in pewter vessels surrounded by salt and ice. Hokey pokey could thus be considered the ancestor of today's frozen custard. The term, by the way, is thought to be related to "hocus pocus," since one could never be quite sure what went into cheap ice cream. By the middle of the century, ice cream was so popular that a magazine editor was moved to write: "A party without ice cream would be like a breakfast without bread or a dinner without a roast."

The father of the American ice cream industry was Jacob Fussell. Beginning in 1851 with a small ice cream store in Baltimore, Fussell was soon selling his wares in shops from Boston to Washington, and during the Civil War the ice cream entrepreneur sold huge quantities of ice cream to Union supply officers. By the end of the century, ice cream could be bought almost anywhere in the nation. New inventions such as steam power, mechanical refrigeration, electricity, and the homogenizer made the ice cream plant virtually as modern as it is today.

In the early decades of this century, the popularity of the soda fountain made ice cream an American institution. Temperance preachers urged listeners to give up the grape in favor of the cool confection. Baseball star Walter Johnson—no relation to Howard—boasted that all he ever ate on the day he was to pitch was a quart of ice cream.

Beginning in 1921, officials at the Ellis Island immigration station in New York, intent on serving the newcomers a "truly American dish," included ice cream in all meals served at the station.

By that time, the three mainstays of the ice cream parlor—the soda, the sundae, and the cone—were already popular from coast to coast. The first to appear was the ice cream soda. In 1874, a soda-fountain manufacturer by the name of Robert M. Green was busily vending a cool drink made of sweet cream, syrup, and carbonated water (now known as the egg cream) at the semicentennial celebration of Philadelphia's Franklin Institute. One day, Green ran out of cream and substituted vanilla ice cream, and the new treat quickly became a sensation. Green went on to make a fortune selling ice cream sodas. His will dictated that "Originator of the Ice Cream Soda" be engraved on his tombstone.

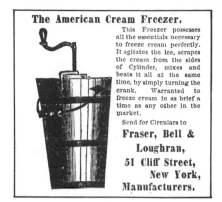

The American Cream Freezer.

This Freezer possesses all the essentials necessary to freeze cream perfectly. It agitates the ice, scrapes the cream from the sides of Cylinder, mixes and beats it all at the same time, by simply turning the crank. Warranted to freeze cream in as brief a time as any other in the market.

Send for Circulars to

Fraser, Bell & Loughran,
51 Cliff Street,
New York,
Manufacturers.

Ice cream freezer, circa 1870.

There are many claims for the invention of the ice cream sundae, which emerged during the 1890's. But then contemporary laws that forbade the sale of soda on Sunday undoubtedly had a hand in popularizing the dessert. The first sundaes were sold in ice cream parlors only on Sunday, and thus were called "Sundays" or "soda-less sodas." The spelling change to "sundae" was made later by ice cream parlor proprietors eager to see the dish shed its Sunday-only connotation.

The best-known explanation for the invention of the ice cream cone traces its origin to the 1904 Louisiana Purchase Exposition in St. Louis. According to the tale, an ice cream salesman by the name of Charles E. Menches gave an ice cream sandwich and a bouquet of flowers to the young lady he was escorting. She rolled one of the sandwich wafers into a cone to hold the flowers, then rolled the other wafer into a cone for the ice cream. But some researchers claim that nineteenth-century Frenchmen occasionally ate ice cream from paper or metal cones.

Ice cream parlors were an integral part of American life early in this century, in many ways the social forums of their time. In these emporia, busy soda jerks developed a lingo all their own. *Adam's ale*, for instance, was water, while *belch water* meant seltzer. *A pair of drawers* could mean only one thing: two cups of coffee. The expression *fix the pumps* was used to call attention to a female customer with large breasts.

Fortunes were made in the ice cream trade during the heyday of the soda fountain. Louis Sherry, a Frenchman from Vermont, began his career as a famed restauranteur when he was granted the ice cream concession at the Metropolitan Opera House in New York. In 1925, Howard Johnson—the father of American franchisers—opened his first ice cream store in Wollaston, Massachusetts. Johnson, incidentally, once sold 14,000 ice cream cones in a single day at his Wollaston Beach stand.

Americans presently consume over a billion gallons of ice cream, ices, and sherbet each year—enough to completely fill the Grand Canyon.

"The Soda Fountain" by William Glackens.

Courtesy of the Pennsylvania Academy of Fine Arts.

And while we're looking at ice cream statistics: During the 1930's one soda fountain chain reported that each of its fountains, on the average, sold 3,145 gallons of ice cream, 455 gallons of chocolate syrup, 45 gallons of vanilla syrup, 300 pounds of malt powder, and 26 quarts of cherries each year.

In 1921, the *Eskimo pie* was introduced in Des Moines, Iowa by the same Russell Stover who was to go on to fame and fortune in the candy trade. The *Good Humor*, meanwhile, was the handiwork of one Harry Burt, an ice cream parlor owner from Youngstown, Ohio. Before starting out in the ice cream business, Burt had sold a lollypop he called the *Good Humor Sucker.* The bright idea to mount a chocolate-covered Eskimo pie on a lollypop stick led to ice-cream-on-a-stick, and the familiar white wagons that still ply our streets with their tinkling bells. Good Humor bars are now sold in most supermarkets as well.

Today, the manufacture of ice cream is, of course, mechanized. Factories first produce a liquid product made of 80 percent cream or butterfat, milk, and nonfat milk solids, and about 15 percent sweeteners. Next they pasteurize, homogenize, whip, and partially freeze the mixture, then add flavoring, package, and fully freeze the product in its containers at temperatures of about 240 degrees below zero. The finished product is frequently as rich in vitamins as an equivalent amount of milk.

Frozen mousse is a cold dessert made from sweetened whipped cream, flavoring, and gelatin. *Sherbet* consists of milk, sweeteners, and fruit flavoring, while *Italian Ices* is made from fruit juices, water, and sweeteners. *French ice cream* is definitely different from other varieties: in this country, only ice cream made with eggs can legally be sold as "French."

The quality of ice cream products differs greatly from brand to brand, due to such factors as the amount of fresh milk, cream, or eggs used, the naturalness of the flavoring ingredients, and the presence of preservatives and synthetic flavor and texture enhancers. If the ice cream you've been enjoying recently leaves something to be desired in the taste bud department, consider yourself lucky. A U.S. Department of Agriculture scientist has suggested that ice cream may someday be made from powdered soybean milk!

PARTIAL MENU OF "THE FLICK"

These are just a few of the ice cream concoctions offered by The Flick Ice Cream Parlor *in New York City.*

Dish of Ice Cream or Sherbet or Yogurt 1.75

SUNDAES

Large Sundae 2.25
Your choice of 2 flavors ice cream, topping, nuts, whipped cream and cherry

Extra-Large Sundae 3.95
4 Scoops ice cream, topping, nuts, whipped cream and cherry

Gibson Girl 3.95
4 scoops mixed ice cream, butterscotch sauce, wet walnuts, whipped cream and burgundy cherry

A Sherbet Delight 3.95
Fresh fruit topped with Flick orange and lemon sherbet

Fresh Fruit Flick Delight 3.95
Giant bowl of fresh fruit, your choice of 2 flavors of ice cream, whipped cream and cherry

Flaming Desire 3.95
4 Scoops of ice cream of your choice, topping, whipped cream and burgundy cherry. Set aflame and served to delight you

Mission Impossible 4.25
Egg nog, rum raisin and burgundy cherry ice cream topped with hot fudge, marshmallow, butterscotch, crushed pineapple, whipped cream and cherry

Virgin's Delight 3.95
Vanilla, cherry-vanilla and cocoanut ice cream with a blanket of marshmallow sauce, whipped cream and red cherry

> **The ultimate effect of a bowlful of ice cream is to make you warmer, not cooler!**

Americans presently consume over a billion gallons of ice cream, ices, and sherbet each year—enough to completely fill the Grand Canyon. Americans are by far the world's largest consumers of ice cream. The average person in the United States puts away about twenty-three quarts each year—that's roughly equivalent to a cone per person every other day. Only Australians, Canadians, and New Zealanders eat even half that much. Compare that figure with the average yearly consumption of 100 years ago—about one teaspoon per person!

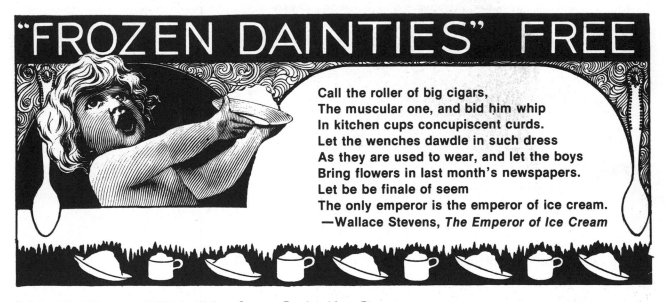

"FROZEN DAINTIES" FREE

Call the roller of big cigars,
The muscular one, and bid him whip
In kitchen cups concupiscent curds.
Let the wenches dawdle in such dress
As they are used to wear, and let the boys
Bring flowers in last month's newspapers.
Let be be finale of seem
The only emperor is the emperor of ice cream.
—Wallace Stevens, *The Emperor of Ice Cream*

Only in America, then, could you expect to find the largest ice cream sundae of all time. The 3,956-pound monster, concocted in Mc-Lean, Virginia in 1975, contained 777 gallons of ice cream, six gallons of chocolate syrup, over a gallon of whipped cream, and a case of chocolate sprinkles.

The world's largest popsicle, meanwhile, was a paltry 2,800 pounds. The largest banana split ever thrown together—measured one mile in length and contained 33,000 scoops of ice cream and over 10,000 bananas! This whopper was the pride and joy of a St. Paul, Minnesota ice cream parlor.

Most ice cream stores today point with pride, not to the size of their wares, but to the sheer length of their flavor list. The Baskins Robbins company lists over 300 flavors in its repertoire, and the number is still climbing—though you'll have a tough time finding half that many in any one store. The winner of the Baskin Robbins America's Favorite Flavor Contest, by the way, was Chocolate Mint ice cream. The modern ice cream maker will go to any length to outdo the competition with bizarre new taste treats, and novelty flavors such as *iced tea*, *bubblegum*, *root beer*, and *mango* ice cream, the newcomers occasionally outsell the old standbys *vanilla* and *chocolate*.

The largest banana split ever thrown together measured one mile in length and contained 33,000 scoops of ice cream and over 10,000 bananas.

But don't think that exotic flavors belong solely to the modern ice cream maker. A recipe book dating from 1700 shows that even at that date, French confectioners were turning out such tempting ice cream flavors as *apricot*, *violet*, and *rose!*

MONEY

Wine maketh merry, but money answereth all things.
—Ecclesiastes

An old fable tells of a miser who buried his gold in the forest. Each day, he crept into the woods, dug up the trove, counted his coins, and buried them again. But one day, another man spied him counting his gold, and returned that night to steal it. The next morning, the miser discovered that he had lost everything.

A friend tried to comfort him. "Take a pile of stones and bury them in the hole," he suggested, "and make believe the gold is still there, for when it was, you did not make the slightest use of it."

The fable cleverly points up the real nature of money—coins and bills—at least as we use them today—are almost worthless in themselves. The long history of money has actually been a steady movement away from the immediately useful toward the symbolically valuable. That movement is continuing.

One writer has termed money "the poor man's credit card," for the well-to-do have the luxury of receiving their income by check, depositing it, purchasing items and services with credit cards, and then paying their credit card bills by check, perhaps without ever laying eyes on a dime of cold cash! The movement of wealth, which once dealt solely in the transfer of land, animals, or metal, has become largely a simple movement of paper.

Until the seventh or eighth century B.C., money per se did not exist. Early man's commerce was built on the barter system, involving a simple exchange of goods. A craftsman, for instance, might trade a tanned hide or a carved icon for a supply of grain or milk. But the barter system presented a number of problems. First of all, a successful barter deal depended upon a double coincidence: the man who needed the hide had to have a supply of grain to spare, and the man who tanned the hide had to need and want the grain. Many bartered goods were not partitionable; for example, a man making a coat in the hope of receiving two bushels of wheat could not trade half a coat for one bushel.

In a limited way, the barter system has continued right into the present day. A servant or laborer will often accept food and lodging in partial payment for his services, and sharecropping farmers trade a portion of their crop for the use of the land they till. But standards and mediums of exchange began to appear well before recorded history.

Among early hunters, tanned hides were useful as a medium of exchange, for everyone could put the hides to use for clothing—and hides, unlike grain or meat, would keep almost indefinitely. Leather money was used in Russia right up until the seventeenth century, as was tea money in China. Hundreds of other items have served for a time as legal tender, including slaves, tobacco, gunpowder, pig jawbones, and glass beads. Manhattan Island, you recall, was bartered for twenty-four dollars worth of glass trinkets. Salt once passed for dough in Ethiopia, and skulls were hard cash in Borneo.

In Western cultures, cattle became a favored standard of exchange at a very early date, since cattle to a great extent already formed the basis of wealth. Cattle were generally owned by rich and poor alike; land, only by the aristocracy. Our words *capital* and *chattel* come from "cattle," or rather from "head of cattle," based on the Latin *caput*, "head."

Cloth money served as legal tender in ancient times in the Orient.

Right up until the seventeenth century, leather was used for money in Russia, and tea was used for money in China.

You might conjure up the image of a shopper walking to the store with four head of cattle shuffling behind him as his "pocketbook." But cattle were used more as a *standard* of exchange than as a *medium* of exchange. The value of bartered goods was determined by relating

The Onondaga Indians used wampum belts for money.

their worth to cattle; most often the cattle themselves did not serve as money. In our modern monetary system, coins and bills are the mediums of exchange, and gold, at least until recently, the standard of exchange.

But even as a standard of exchange, cattle presented problems, for one steer might be well fed and another scrawny. As actual items of exchange, cattle required upkeep—although they had the happy advantage of occasionally multiplying. The use of metals, then, certainly offered a number of obvious advantages. First of all, metal required neither upkeep nor extensive storage space, and precious metals were valuable in themselves for decorative use.

Iron money was used for a time in ancient Sparta. According to some accounts, Spartan monarchs cleverly minted coins so large they could barely be carried—to prevent its citizens from leaving the country.

At first, metals had to be weighed and assayed at each transaction, but later, pieces of uniform size were stamped to indicate their weight and purity. And that is exactly what a coin is: a piece of metal whose worth has been guaranteed. The first metal coins were minted in the kingdom of Lydia, in Asia Minor, around the year 650 B.C., although there is evidence of silver money in Iran as early as 760 B.C.

By the time of the Roman Empire, land and cattle speculation were already common—thus, these items were valued not for their immediate usefulness, but for their value in metal currency. The Romans adopted a form of gold standard, and stored their reserves in the Temple of Juno Moneta. Moneta became the mint, and Juno was regarded as the goddess of money. Such was the origin of this almighty word. Copper coins, melted into the floor during a fire, could be seen for a time among the temple ruins.

During the early Middle Ages, the coinage of the Eastern Empire at Byzantium, and later, the coinage of the Arabs, became the most important species in the eastern Mediterranean. In Western Europe, in the late eighth century, Charlemagne sanctioned the abandonment of the gold standard and established a monetary system based on silver. A silver penny, or *denarius*, was the basic unit, with 240 pennies to a pound of silver. The words *livre*, *lira*, and *pound* as used in British currency, date from this era. The Pound Sterling was original-

The Aboo Bekr *was an ancient Egyptian coin.*

ly 240 sterlings, or silver pennies, and literally weighed one pound.

Gold came back into use during the thirteenth and fourteenth centuries, with the florin, from Florence, among the more important coins. But the older silver system remained in use, so that through the Renaissance two basic monetary systems were current in most of Europe. Financial calculation was indeed a laborious job.

In the fifteenth century, the Venetian gold ducat—a word which

An 18th-century Chinese money-changer examines his wares.

*A 19th-century Chinese
coin from the reign of
Emperor Hien-Fung
(1851-1861).*

comes from "duchy"—became the most valued coin in much of
Europe. Although bills of exchange had been in use since thirteenth-
century Italy, the first bank notes were not placed in service until
1661, in Sweden. Paper money is a Chinese invention, dating from the
seventh century although some Chinese historians claim that paper
money was actually first printed there in 119 B.C.

Why are gold and silver so appropriate as mediums of exchange?
First of all, the metals were always highly prized for their sheen and
utility in personal adornment and religious statuary. Gold and silver
will neither deteriorate nor rust. And the supply of these metals, while
large enough to fill the bill as a medium of exchange, is not *so* large
that the metals become worthless.

But through the ages metal money has presented its own problems. European monarchs frequently debased their currency—reduced the gold or silver content of the coins—to pay for expensive
wars, and many avaricious individuals were wont to clip their coins to
steal a few grains of precious metal. The wide variety of money standards in use in medieval and Renaissance Europe often made business
transactions difficult—and made the moneychanger an absolute necessity. Gradually, the moneychanger came to fulfill many of the
functions now performed by banks. And with the rise of moneylend-
ing and capital accumulation, paper money, otherwise worthless, became reliable as a medium of exchange.

Paper money is, of course, the hardest cash throughout the world
today. But many of the terms we still use when discussing matters
monetary reflect earlier standards and mediums of exchange. As we
mentioned, *pound, livre, lira*, and also *ruble*, refer to weight. The
Greek *drachma* originally meant "handful."

"Pecuniary" comes from the Latin *pecus*, which means "cattle".
"Coin," comes from the Latin *cuneus*, which indicates "stamp" or
"die"; and "fee," derives from the Anglo-Saxon *feoh*, or "cattle." "Fi-
nance" is related to *final*, since a money transaction was regarded as
the "final act" of a deal.

The English *guinea* comes from the African area where gold for
the coin was originally mined. *Franc* is an abbreviated *Francorum
Rex*, "King of the Franks." And the word *money* itself is the legacy of
the Roman goddess Juno Moneta.

During the sixteenth century, when heavy silver coins were widely used throughout Europe, Bohemian coins minted in St. Joachimsthal were considered the purest. They therefore formed the standard of excellence. From Joachimsthaler comes the older words *thaler* and *daler*, and, of course, the almighty *dollar*.

In the early days of our nation, English, French, and Spanish monies all circulated through the American colonies, with a concomitant confusion of trade. In 1785, the dollar was adopted by Congress

A heavy purse makes a light heart.

—Ben Jonson

This document passed for a $20 bill in Colonial America.

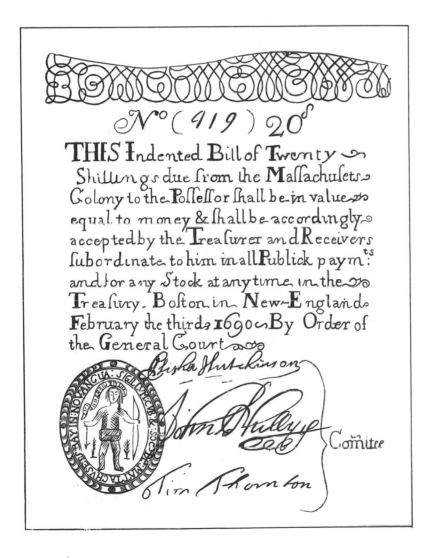

as the unit of exchange, and the decimal system as the method of reckoning. The U.S. monetary system was established in 1792: the first mint began operation in Philadelphia the following year.

Many coin and bill denominations have come and gone since then. Among the coins no longer in use are the *half-cent*, the *two-cent*,

CURRENCY VALUES

Nation	Currency Standard	Value per U.S. $1*
Argentina	peso	74.50
Australia	dollar	.80
Austria	schilling	18.20
Belgium	franc	39.00
Brazil	cruzeiro	9.42
China	yuan	1.96
Czechoslovakia	koruna	11.66
Denmark	krone	6.07
Egypt	pound	.56
Finland	markka	3.84
France	franc	4.69
Germany, East	mark	2.55
Germany, West	mark	2.55
Greece	drachma	35.40
Haiti	gourde	5.00
Hungary	forint	20.44
Iceland	krona	184.30
India	rupee	8.90
Indonesia	rupiah	415.00
Iran	rial	70.00
Iraq	dinar	.30
Ireland	pound	.52

*As of mid-1977.

Washington half-dollar.

the *three-cent*, the *twenty-cent*, and the *silver half-dime*. The nickel was not introduced until 1886. Today, gold coins are no longer minted, and you may be surprised to learn, no bills larger than $100 are now placed in circulation.

The money we use in America was originally based on the gold

CURRENCY VALUES

Nation	Currency Standard	Value Per U.S. $1*
Israel	pound	8.25
Italy	lira	880.00
Japan	yen	299.70
Mexico	peso	20.50
Morocco	dirham	4.38
Netherlands	guilder	2.69
Nigeria	naira	.62
Norway	krone	5.51
Philippines	peso	7.80
Poland	zloty	33.20
Portugal	escudo	29.34
Romania	leu	12.00
Saudi Arabia	riyal	3.53
South Africa	rand	.87
Soviet Union	ruple	.75
Spain	peseta	66.90
Sweden	krona	4.40
Switzerland	franc	2.54
Turkey	lira	15.15
United Kingdom	pound sterling	.58
Yugoslavia	dinar	18.00

*As of mid-1977.

Broad *of James I.*

He was subject to a kind of disease which at that time they called lack of money.
　　　　—François Rabelais

**Never ask of money spent
Where the spender thinks
    it went.
Nobody was ever meant
To remember or invent
What he did with every cent.**

— **Robert Frost**

standard. A bill was, in effect, a promise to pay the bearer on demand the dollar amount of gold stated on the note. But our money no longer has a gold or other commodity backing, and you cannot turn in your bills for gold. A person is willing to accept otherwise valueless paper money because he knows that others will accept these bills from him. Coins, too, are symbolic in value: a dime, for example, does not contain ten-cents' worth of metal.

As long as monetary systems were tied to a gold or silver standard, there were self-imposed restraints on the system: the amount of gold or metal in a nation's reserves limited the amount of money that could be minted. But without a commodity backing to its currency, a government can overprint paper money, and problems such as runaway inflation often arise.

The worst inflation in history occurred in Hungary in 1946, when

At the Federal Reserve Bank of New York, gold is stored in 121 vault compartments. Foreign gold deposits are earmarked and segregated by account.

Photo courtesy of the Federal Reserve Bank of New York.

American mines produce some $47 million in gold each year.

a single gold pengo was valued at 130 trillion paper pengos! A simple purchase might require so many bills that a wheelbarrow was needed for a trip to the store, and notes were issued in denominations as high as 100 trillion pengos!

The inflation rate in Chile, between 1950 and 1973, was an outlandish 423,100 percent— meaning, in American currency, that what could once be bought for one dollar eventually cost $4,232!

Speaking of high denominations, the highest valued paper currency ever printed were U.S. gold certificates issued in 1934, worth $100,000. In case you've never seen one, the bill bore the head of President Woodrow Wilson. The highest denomination notes still in circulation are U.S. Federal Reserve Bank notes worth $100,000, but none has been printed since 1944; and according to present plans, no further bills over $100 will ever be issued.

The least valuable bill in existence today is the *one-cent* Hong Kong note, worth just one-fifth of a U.S. penny.

In terms of sheer size—which matters not a whit in legal tender—the largest and smallest bills in history are, respectively, the *one-kwan* note of fourteenth-century China, which measured nine by thirteen inches, and the 1917 *ten-bani* note of Rumania, barely more than an inch-and-a-half square.

As for coins, the smallest in size was the Nepalese silver *quarter-dam* of 1740—you'd need some 14,000 to equal an ounce.

At the other end of the scale, the Swedish copper *ten-daler* coin of 1644 weighed up to 43.4 pounds. And natives of the Yap Islands in the South Pacific at one time used stone coins some twelve feet wide, weighing up to 185 pounds!

The lowest denomination coin in existence today is the *five-aurar* piece of Iceland, which when issued in 1971, had a face value of only .1311 of a U.S. penny—you'd need 762 aurars to equal a dollar.

And the highest denomination coin was the 1654 gold *200-mohur* coin of India, worth the equivalent of $1,400.

Money may be a curse, but you can always find someone to take the curse off you.

Abe said to his friend Willie, "Willie, lend me twenty dollars."

Willie took out his wallet and handed Abe a ten dollar bill.

"Willie," said Abe, "I asked you for twenty."

"Yes, I know," said Willie. "This way you lose ten and I lose ten."

In the late 19th century, California gold miners used hydraulic methods.

At recent gold prices, this baby is worth a cool $2,660, the greatest intrinsic value of any coin ever struck. But the 200-*mohur* is not the most valuable coin in history—that honor goes to an Athenian silver *drachma*, sold to a coin collector in 1974 for $314,000!

How much money is there in the world today? It's almost impossible to estimate, since the value of various currencies changes from day to day. But there's an estimated $49.7 billion in gold bullion in the central banks of the world, with the largest single chunk in the Federal Reserve Bank in New York City: $17 billion.

Rich or poor, it's nice to have money.

The Pound Sterling was originally 240 sterlings, or silver pennies, and literally weighed one pound.

The United States is the nation with the largest gold reserves, but we're not the world's largest gold-producing country. American mines produce some $47 million in gold each year (based on a selling price of thirty-eight dollars per ounce), an amount equal to the entire production of Asia or Latin America and three times the total European figure. Yet the United States ranks third in gold production, behind Canada—about $60 million per year. South Africa is far and away the leader with over a billion dollars worth of gold.

With all of this money floating around, you may wonder why more of it hasn't found its way into *your* pocket. Don't be ashamed if you feel an uncontrollable hankering for more of the green stuff. After all, *money* is not the root of all evil. The Bible actually says that "the *love* of money is the root of all evil." And that's quite a difference.

Money isn't everything, but it's way ahead of whatever is in second place.

The first money coined in the United States looked like this.

NEWSPAPERS

As you may have heard, the famous Battle of New Orleans, won by Andrew Jackson and his troops over the British during the War of 1812, was fought on January 8, 1815—15 days *after* the war had ended. A treaty ending the conflict had been signed in Europe, but the news failed to reach either Jackson or the British troops before the battle. Moreover, Jackson's superiors in Washington were unaware of both the battle *and* the treaty!

It's no surprise that news traveled slowly before the introduction of electronic media and the up-to-date newspaper. But before you laugh too hard, you might consider the results of a 1969 poll taken in Morocco, revealing that only 56 percent of those asked knew that a man had set foot on the moon. And of these, more than half thought the story was a hoax!

The modern newspaper could only be the product of the best printing processes and news-gathering networks, both developments of the twentieth century. But written news reports, undependable as they were, date back to classical times. Romans of the fifth century B.C. distributed newsletters with reports from the capital for those residing nearby on the Italian peninsula.

Upon assuming the consulship in 60 B.C., one of Julius Caesar's first acts was to establish a daily bulletin of government announcements, the *Acta Diurna*, to post in the forum. Posted proclamations and the announcements of town criers—and the grapevine—provided the news to many city residents for centuries, but it wasn't until the seventeenth century that newspapers proper began to spring up around Europe on a regular basis.

Though the Chinese claim the world's first newspaper, a court gazette first published in the seventh century B.C., Chinese newsletters were actually printed by hand or from blocks until movable wood type was introduced in China in the seventeenth century. Thus, the printed newspaper can properly be termed a European development.

One of Europe's first printed news reports was the work of Englishman Thomas Raynalde who, in 1549, translated German news pamphlets documenting recent political events, murders, and marvels—a style of journalism not unknown today. Early English news reports, translated from German or Dutch, came to be known as *corantos*, a term related to "current."

In 1776, there were 53 newspapers in London.

The early corantos reported news only from the Continent, and were for the most part prohibited, or at least hindered, from relating domestic events. But, in 1641, with the abolition of the tyrannical court, the Star Chamber, freedom of the press in England took a major step forward. That year saw the publication of *Diurnal Occurrences* (a title identical to Caesar's), the first news pamphlet to contain domestic news, written in London by Samuel Pecke.

Most seventeenth-century news publications were partisan, printed with the approval, or direct sponsorship, of either the monarchy or parliament. Despite their titles, these journals of "diurnal" occurrences were published weekly. The first bona fide daily newspapers in England were not published until 1702.

Daniel Defoe, best known for his novels, published a weekly entitled The *Review* between 1704 and 1713. At various times a paid political pamphleteer, a secret agent, and a hack, Defoe was wont to take his political point of view from the highest bidder, and often switched sides when it suited him. The author of *Robinson Crusoe* once edited a Tory newspaper actually sponsored by the Whigs, and a Whig publication sponsored by the Tories—both at the same time! Nevertheless, Defoe is considered the first important journalist in England, and the originator of the serial story.

Most early English newspapers were political in nature, devoted mainly to domestic and foreign news and commerce reports. The famed journalists Sir Richard Steele and Joseph Addison were among the first to introduce social commentary to the newspaper. The pair began with the *Tatler* in 1709, then, beginning in 1711, brought out the *Spectator*, a daily. Between them, they wrote about 90 percent of the papers themselves. The *Spectator* eventually ran to some 555 issues, and reached a circulation of over 3,000. It was read by many times that number.

Addison and Steele's papers were to have many imitators in England, including the *Idler* and *Rambler* of Samuel Johnson, brought

Novelist Daniel Defoe was also a crackerjack newspaper editor and major figure in the evolution of modern journalism.

out in the 1750's. By 1753, English newspapers had passed the 7 million mark in annual circulation; by 1760, 9 million; and by 1767, 11 million. In 1776, there were fifty-three newspapers in London alone—presumably, most of them made reference to a burgeoning conflict in England's far-off American colonies.

Most eighteenth-century English newspapers were designed for the well-educated. Many of the essays from the *Spectator* or *Rambler* are considered among the finest English writing in this form. Taxes kept the newspaper out of the hands of many people until late in the

In 1850, the arrival of the daily newspaper was a major event in English life.

century, when William Cobbett first tried to reach the masses with a cheap weekly paper.

The *London Times* was begun in 1785 by John Walter, who promised his readers the paper would have no part in political partisanship or scandal-mongering. Walter spent a few sojourns in Newgate prison for his journalistic independence. But by the middle of the nineteenth century, the *Times* was the pre-eminent British newspaper, with a daily circulation of about 50,000. Even at that late date, each issue contained but twelve pages.

The first American publication that could justifiably be termed a newspaper was brought out in 1690 by Benjamin Harris, a bookseller who had been forced to flee England after publishing a seditious news pamphlet. Harris called his Boston paper *Publick Occurences Both Foreign and Domestick,* and promised it would be issued "once a moneth (or if any Glut of Occurrences happen, oftener)." Harris's four-page paper was suppressed after only one issue for certain comments found distasteful by Massachusetts governor Simon Bradstreet.

In 1704, a postmaster named John Campbell brought out the *Boston News-Letter*, the first continuously published newspaper in America. Printed by one Bartholomew Green in a back room of his house, the paper was published in some form right up until the Revolution, and was without competition for fifteen years—reaching the astronomical circulation figure of 300! By the way, one of the first printers of the *Gazette* was James Franklin, and his apprentice was a certain thirteen-year-old brother named Benjamin—perhaps you've heard of him?

Benjamin Franklin later moved to Philadelphia to work as a printer and occasional writer; and in 1728, bought a paper begun the previous year by Samuel Keimar. Franklin shortened the paper's eleven-word title to the *Pennsylvania Gazette*, and published the sheet successfully for nineteen years—by which time Franklin probably had a number of more pressing matters to attend to.

You might have heard that Benjamin Franklin founded the recently defunct *Saturday Evening Post* in 1728, for the claim appeared directly on the cover of each issue. The fact is, Franklin had nothing whatsoever to do with this magazine, which first appeared in 1821—not 1728. The magazine's publishers fabricated the claim in 1899, and

Were it left to me to decide whether we should have a government without newspapers, or newspapers without a government, I should not hesitate a moment to prefer the latter.
—*Thomas Jefferson*

In 19th-century Paris, a newspaper market was held on Rue du Croissant.

never abandoned it even when the claim was proved patently false.

The first New York newspaper was the *New York Gazette*, brought out by William Bradford in 1725. The Gazette was basically an organ of the Colonial government, and gave impetus to patriot Peter Zenger's opposing paper, the *New York Weekly Journal*, which he began publishing in 1733. Zenger was eventually jailed for his work. The court case that followed, exonerating Zenger, did much to establish the principles of freedom of the press in America.

Many claims have been heard for the first daily newspaper to be published in the United States, but it's generally accepted that the honor goes to the *Pennsylvania Packet and Daily Advertiser*, which first appeared as a daily in 1784. Newspapers were not widely read here until the 1830's, when the penny press began to appear. These papers—costing, as you might imagine, one cent, when the going rate was six cents—were the first to be available to people at all economic levels.

The first successful daily in this genre was the *New York Sun*, launched in 1833. In 1841, Horace Greeley founded a rival paper, the *New York Tribune*. Ten years later, three publishing entrepreneurs is-

---

As the founder of New York's highly successful newspaper, the Tribune, *Horace Greeley expanded the concepts of news coverage and developed a high-caliber staff. A dedicated journalist, he had one peculiarity: he was convinced that the word "news" was plural. His staff disagreed, but Greeley was adamant.*

Once, while traveling, Greeley sent a telegram to the home office, asking: "ARE THERE ANY NEWS?"

A reporter responded: "NOT A NEW."

---

sued the first copy of the *New York Times*, today generally regarded as the premier American newspaper. The paper was failing in 1896 when it was taken over by Adolphe Ochs, previously the publisher of a Tennessee paper. Och's early years saw the adoption of the slogan "All the news that's fit to print," along with a slogan that promised: "It does not soil the breakfast cloth"—a reference to the so-called yellow journalism of the day.

The term *yellow journalism* originated in the 1890's when San Francisco publisher William Randolph Hearst invaded the New York market and instituted an all-out rivalry between competing papers. When the *New York World* published the first color comic strip in 1893—"The Yellow Kid" by Richard Outcault—Hearst lured the artist away and published the strip in his own New York paper, the *Jour-*

English journalists of the Victorian era would rush from the estate of the Prince of Wales in Sandringham, England, to get stories of the future Edward VII's activities to press.

nal. The continuing rivalry between the various New York papers pandering to lurid tastes soon took on the name "yellow journalism." Many papers of this era were much like the modern tabloid or scandal sheet, featuring large banner headlines, plenty of pictures, and sensationalist features.

The twentieth century has seen the gradual consolidation of American newspapers and the founding of the newspaper chain. Hearst himself bought or established some forty daily papers. The peak year for American papers—in terms of sheer numbers—was 1916, when 2,461 dailies were published across the nation. By 1944, consolidation and bankruptcy had brought that figure down to 1,744.

New York City once had dozens of papers; but by the 1950's, most remaining papers were combinations of earlier publications—the *New York Herald Tribune* and the *New York World Telegram and Sun*, for instance. Today, there are but three daily publications that can be called "New York" newspapers: the *Times*, the *Post*, and the *Daily News*. The latter was founded in 1919 by three Chicago publishers. Within six years, the *Daily News* had become the largest newspaper in the United States, a title it still holds by virtue of selling some two million copies daily.

The single newspaper with the largest daily circulation is the Russian Pravda, **with a reputed circulation of 10 million copies.**

Much of the news coverage now provided by the daily newspaper is the work of the wire agencies, which maintain a news correspondent in almost every large or capital city in the world. The Associated Press was founded in 1848 by six New York papers to divide the cost of transmitting news by telegraph. By 1950, the agency had some 300,000 miles of wire in operation in the United States alone. The other major American news agency, United Press International, was founded in 1907 by E.W. Scripps, uniting three older news agencies.

Close to one-fourth of the newspapers published in the world today are brought out in America—1,768 in 1975—with a total paid circulation of close to 62 million copies daily. But the single newspaper with the largest daily circulation is the Russian *Pravda*, with a reputed circulation of 10 million copies. *Pravda* (which means "truth" in Russian) was begun in 1912. After the 1917 revolution, it became the leading organ of the Russian Communist party. *Izvestia*, the official daily newspaper of the Soviet government, is the second newspaper in the world in terms of circulation, with eight million copies sold per day. Those who believe that the high figures attributed to the Soviet papers are due to the fact that there are no other papers published in that country might be surprised to learn that there are some 7,200 papers published altogether in the Soviet Union, though there are only about 650 dailies.

The Japanese daily *Asahi Shimbun* ranks third in circulation, at just over seven million copies per day, and two other Japanese papers claim a circulation in excess of five million. The largest paper in England is now the *London Daily Mirror*, with some four million copies sold per day, and both the *Daily Sun* and the *Daily Express* own circulations close to the three million mark. And the *Evening News*, with an average circulation of over a half-million copies, is the world's best-selling evening newspaper.

I sing of News, and all those vapid sheets
The rattling hawker vends through gaping streets;
Whate'er their name, whate'er the time they fly,
Damp from the press, to charm the reader's eye:
For, soon as morning dawns with roseate hue,
The Herald of the morn arises too:
Post after Post succeeds, and all day long,
Gazettes and Ledgers swarm, a noisy throng.
When evening comes, she comes with all her train
Of Ledgers, Chronicles, and Posts again,
Like bats, appearing when the sun goes down,
From holes obscure and corners of the town.
—George Crabbe, The Newspaper

Newsboys loudly hawked their wares on the streets of New York in the early 1900's.

After the New York Daily News, *the* Los Angeles Times *is the nation's best-selling newspaper, with about one million copies sold per day. The* New York Times *follows in the number-three position.*

After the *New York Daily News*, the *Los Angeles Times* is the nation's best-selling newspaper, with about one million copies sold per day. The *New York Times* follows in the number-three position. Rounding out the top ten are, in order, the *Chicago Tribune, Detroit News, Detroit Free Press, Chicago Sun-Times, Philadelphia Bulletin, New York Post*, and *Washington Post*. But the *Wall Street Journal*, published around the nation rather than in one particular city, officially ranks as the number-two American daily, with a circulation of some one-and-a-half million copies. In all, American advertisers will spend about eight-and-a-half billion dollars this year on newspaper advertising!

Americans are far from the world's greatest newspaper readers, however. That honor goes to the Swedes, who pore through about 564 papers for every 1,000 persons. (In the United States, the figure is 300 papers per 1,000 persons.) And the newspaper that comes closest to total national saturation is the *Sunday Post*, published in Glasgow, Scotland and read by about four-and-a-half million people each Sunday—more than 77 percent of all Scots of presumed newspaper-reading age.

No one who has carried home a copy of the *New York Sunday Times* could entertain any doubt as to the world's largest newspaper in sheer bulk. The largest Sunday *Times* ever published, on October 17, 1965, consisted of 946 pages in fifteen sections, and weighed a whopping seven-and-a-half pounds! Let's see—if the Sunday *Times* has a circulation of about one-and-a-half million copies, we can calculate that the average issue of that paper comprises a total of some 10 million pounds of paper. Now, that's a small forest!

PEANUTS

About half of the United States' annual peanut harvest of some 4 billion pounds is used for peanut butter.

"Peanut" may sound like a plant that can't quite make up its mind where it belongs in the world of botanical classification. What's your guess? A nut, you say? Nope—the goober is actually more a pea than a nut. The versatile, tasty morsel we call the peanut is the pod or legume, and not the nut, of the *arachis hypogea* plant, a member of the same botanical family as the ordinary green pea.

But the peanut is an unusual member of the pea family, since its pods have the peculiar habit of ripening underground. After the plant's flower is pollinated, a stalklike structure called a *peg* begins growing from the base of the flower toward the soil. Only when the tip of the peg is below the soil surface do the fertilized ovules begin to develop their characteristic pod.

These pods also appear to serve as roots to some extent, absorbing minerals from the surrounding soil. The one to three "nuts" found inside the shell are the seeds of the plant, although the tiny morsel found inside the nut when it's split open is the only part of the seed with reproductive powers.

Most Americans would probably guess that the peanut is a native of Africa, perhaps because of its popular association with African slaves in the Southern United States. True, the goober did cross the ocean with the slaves, but that's only half the story.

The peanut is in fact a native of tropical South America. Spanish conquistadores exploring the New World found South American Indians eating what many called *cacohuate*, or "earth cocoa."

The goober was gradually transplanted in West Africa as a food and fodder crop. Subsequently, slave traders found that the peanut could provide cheap, nutritious food for Africans being carried across the ocean on slave ships. Eventually, some African peanuts were brought to Virginia and planted for livestock fodder. Thus the peanut made two transatlantic journeys before becoming a North American crop.

These peanuts are grown in Red Level, Alabama.

Photo courtesy of USDA and photographer Steve Wade.

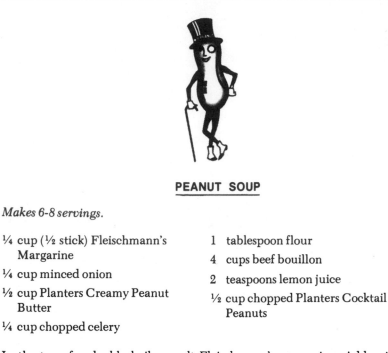

PEANUT SOUP

Makes 6-8 servings.

¼ cup (½ stick) Fleischmann's Margarine

¼ cup minced onion

½ cup Planters Creamy Peanut Butter

¼ cup chopped celery

1 tablespoon flour

4 cups beef bouillon

2 teaspoons lemon juice

½ cup chopped Planters Cocktail Peanuts

In the top of a double boiler, melt Fleischmann's margarine. Add onion and celery; saute until tender. Place over boiling water. Add Planters Creamy Peanut Butter and flour; blend well. Stir in beef bouillon and lemon juice. Cook for 20 minutes, stirring occasionally. When serving, garnish with chopped Planters Cocktail Peanuts.

SOUTHERN PEANUT PIE

Makes one 9-inch pie

1 cup sugar

¼ cup light corn syrup

½ cup (1 stick) Blue Bonnet Margarine, melted

3 eggs

½ teaspoon vanilla extract

1½ cups Planters Dry Roasted Peanuts

1 9-inch unbaked pastry shell

Combine sugar, corn syrup, melted Blue Bonnet Margarine, eggs and vanilla in large mixing bowl. Beat with rotary beater until thoroughly blended. Stir in Planters Dry Roasted Peanuts. Turn into unbaked pastry shell. Bake in moderate oven (375 degrees Fahrenheit) for 45 minutes. Serve warm or cold. Garnish with whipped cream, if desired.

Recipes courtesy of Planters Peanuts.

Initially, peanuts were most used in Virginia as fodder for pigs, and the soft, juicy ham made from peanut-fattened hogs has ever since been known as *Virginia Ham*.

The peanut has also been called *groundnut* and *earthnut*, both aptly suggestive of the plant's peculiar subterranean habits, if not its true botanical classification. The word *goober* is reputedly of African origin, from the Bantu *naguba*—although some etymologists have drawn a connection between *goober* and the ancient English word *gouber*, meaning "an afternoon's repast" or "snack." Indeed, the peanut was once billed by advertisers as the "nickel lunch."

George Washington Carver is the man most responsible for widespread cultivation of peanuts in the United States. Carver's work in the early part of this century showed that the peanut could help free the South from its dependence upon cotton, and restore needed nitrogen to soil depleted by cotton cultivation. When Carver began his research in the 1890's, the goober was not even recognized as a crop; by 1940, the peanut ranked as one of the six leading crops in America, and the largest crop in the southern United States after cotton.

Carver, the son of a slave, not only demonstrated the ecological advantages of peanut cultivation, but later found new uses for the crop after it had become over-abundant here as a foodstuff. Carver discovered some 300 derivatives of the goober, including cheese, milk, flour, coffee, ink, dye, plastics, soap, wood stains, linoleum, cosmetics, and medicinal oils. And in his spare time, Carver managed to find over 100 derivatives of the sweet potato!

Peanut butter is one peanut derivative we can't thank Carver for. That great favorite of the schoolboy was introduced by a St. Louis doctor in 1890 for patients who needed an easily digestible form of protein. Thereafter the peanut batter became a fad. Today, about half of the United States' annual peanut harvest of some 4 billion pounds is used for peanut butter, with the remainder going to salted nuts, candies, oil, and livestock fodder. Only about 10 percent of our crop is used to manufacture peanut oil; but throughout the rest of the peanut-growing world, the goober is grown almost exclusively for its oil.

Planters Peanuts, the world's largest dealer in peanut products, was founded in 1906 by Amedeo Obici, an Italian immigrant who had

The extra calories needed for one hour of intense mental effort would be completely met by the eating of . . . one half of a salted peanut.
—Francis G. Benedict, The Energy Requirements of Intense Mental Effort

journeyed alone to America as a twelve-year-old boy. Starting as a peanut vendor in Wilkes-Barre, Pennsylvania, Obici built Planters into a ten million dollar a year business within a quarter-century.

"Mr. Peanut," the company's trademark, began his association with Planters in 1916, when the firm offered a prize for the best trademark suggestion. A fourteen-year-old Virginia boy submitted a drawing for an animated peanut, another artist added the familiar cane, hat, and monocle, and "Mr. Peanut" was soon appearing plumping Planters peanuts everywhere.

The peanut requires at least five months of strong sunshine and twenty-four inches of rain annually, and thus is restricted to the warmer regions of earth. India is the largest peanut-producing nation, followed by China and West Africa, with the United States fourth in total production.

As a food, the goober is one of the most concentrated sources of nourishment known to man. Pound for pound, the peanut provides more protein, minerals, and vitamins than beef liver, more fat than heavy cream, and—dieters beware—more calories than sugar. Recent

---

Recent experiments in Africa have shown that the discarded shells of the peanut can also be used as animal fodder!

---

experiments in Africa have shown that the discarded shells of the peanut can also be used as animal fodder!

Peanuts may be basically a snack food in the United States, but in many parts of Africa and Asia the goober is an indispensable part of the diet. To demonstrate the importance of the peanut in other nations, we might note that the first American to be honored with a monument in India was none other than George Washington Carver. In 1947, the peanut growers of India unveiled a monument in Bombay to commemorate the American's outstanding work.

Remember the days of the "nickel lunch?" Today, this small bag of peanuts costs a quarter.

PLAYING CARDS

Ask even a hard core cardsharp about the origin of playing cards and pointing to the king and queen in their Renaissance raiment, he may well answer smugly that, of course, the cards originated in Europe during the fifteenth and sixteenth centuries. Well, the reply would be half correct; yes, the design of modern playing cards can be traced back to fifteenth- and sixteenth-century Europe. But the cards themselves are a good deal older than the paper money often used to wager on them.

The exact origin of playing cards remains uncertain, but most historians agree that China is their most probable birthplace. But no matter where they originated, cards—like their gaming counterparts, dice—were probably used, at first, exclusively for fortune telling.

In early times, cards were connected with various religious rites. Some ancient Hindu cards, for instance, were divided into ten suits representing the ten incantations of the god Vishnu. The four-suit deck may be symbolic of the four hands of the god, as represented in Hindu statuary.

No one seems quite certain how cards found their way to Europe. Marco Polo may have brought them back from China in the thirteenth century. Other theories credit—or blame—the gypsies with bringing cards from Arabia to Europe, or claim that the Arabs themselves introduced cards in Europe during their occupation of Sicily and Spain. Probably, all of these sources were in some part responsible.

The first reference to playing cards in Europe appears in an Italian manuscript of 1299, although cards did not become well known on the continent until the fourteenth century. A receipt, dating from 1392, shows that Charles VI of France purchased three decks of cards in "gold and diverse colors." By 1495, playing cards were so well established in Europe that card manufacturers in various nations petitioned their kings for protection against imports.

Many believe that Tarot cards are the forerunners of the modern deck. The fact is the two decks developed independently—Tarot cards were unknown in China, and playing cards were virtually unheard of in Europe before the thirteenth century.

The Tarot deck consists of twenty-one pictorial representations of material forces, elements, virtues, and vices, plus the Fool—the precursor of the joker that found its way into the playing card deck. For centuries gypsies have claimed the ability to foretell the future based on their interpretations of the Tarot cards, which show characters and dress strikingly similar to those of the Romany tribe.

Renaissance Venetians were probably the first to combine the twenty-two-card Tarot deck with the then current fifty-six-card playing deck. The playing deck of the time consisted of a king, a queen, a knight, a page, plus number cards from one through ten in each of four suits—*cups*, *coins*, *swords*, and *wands*. Several games derived from the combined seventy-eight-card deck—twenty-two Tarot plus fifty-six playing cards—are still played in some countries.

Further combinations of number and picture cards resulted in decks of thirty-two or thirty-six cards in Germany, forty cards in Spain, and fifty-two cards in France. The English adopted the French deck, with its designs which originated in fifteenth-century Norman-

This engraving shows a French card factory in the era of Louis XIV.

dy. The picture cards were in royal dress from the period of Henry VII.

The English retained the French symbols for the four suits, but changed their names. If you want to call a spade a spade in France, you would say *pique*, literally "pike." The French *carreau* ("tile" or "square") became in England the diamond; the *trefle* ("cloverleaf") became the club; and the *coeur* ("heart") remained the heart.

In Germany, the spade, diamond, club, and heart are known respectively as the *Grun* ("leaf"), *Schelle* ("bell"), *Eichel* ("acorn"), and *Herz* ("heart"). In Italy, it's *spada* ("sword"), *denaro* ("coin"), *bastone* ("rod"), and *coppa* ("cup").

In Soviet Russia, government officials once tried to replace the corrupt monarchy with proletarian revolutionary figures, but the tradition of Russian card design was so well entrenched that the attempt had to be abandoned. The famous nineteenth-century poet Pushkin wrote a novel, *Queen of Spades*, in which card playing leads to the death of the three main characters, and then Tchaikovsky based a celebrated opera on Pushkin's novel.

The earliest European playing cards were laboriously hand paint-

Morrisey's Gambling House at Saratoga, New York was a popular 19th-century casino.

Odds at Poker

Hand	Number Possible	Odds Against
Royal Flush	4	649,739 to 1
Other Straight Flushes	36	72,192 to 1
Four of a Kind	624	4,164 to 1
Full House	3,744	693 to 1
Flush	5,108	508 to 1
Straight	10,200	254 to 1
Three of a Kind	54,912	46 to 1
Two Pairs	123,552	20 to 1
One Pair	1,098,240	4 to 3 (1.37 to 1)
Nothing	1,302,540	1 to 1
	2,598,960	

ed. Later, they were printed with wood-block techniques. German card makers were perhaps the first wood-block engravers in Europe.

In 1832, Thomas de la Rue invented a typographic process for card manufacture, and institutionalized the design of "double-headed" cards, readable from either end.

Early mass-produced playing cards were printed on pasteboard, with two sheets gummed together and lacquered.

At various times, card makers have tried to introduce different types of deck. One such effort was a deck with five suits. Metal cards intended for play on magnetized boards, have been manufactured, and these come into view, occasionally, on a windy day at the beach. But basically, card design has remained unchanged for centuries.

European governments have always found playing cards an ideal subject for heavy taxation. England began taxing card imports in 1615. By 1628, the tax on each deck had risen to a then exorbitant half-crown. Taxes on playing cards once became so high in Austria that card makers began selling oversized decks that could be gradually trimmed as their edges became worn, thus lasting two or three times as long as a regular deck.

Did you ever wonder why the ace of spades in every pack is so dis-

Card parties are no novelty—this scene depicts a card party of the 15th century.

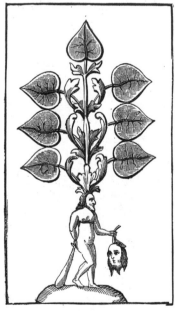

These old German tarot cards were used to tell fortunes. The top card is the seven of clubs; the bottom card is the seven of diamonds.

tinctive, with the central spade by far the largest symbol in the deck? Well, the ace of spades was the card designated to bear the tax stamp. Even today, card makers use the ace of spades to carry their trademark or brand name.

More than 70 million editions of what the Puritans termed "The Devil's Picture Book" are now sold in this country each year—one deck for every three persons. The figure is misleading, though, since Las Vegas casino operators probably account for a large chunk of the total—owing to their practice of throwing away a deck after just a few rounds of blackjack.

The number of games that can be played with cards is virtually limitless. New games are invented continually. Yet almost all games can be divided into one of two categories: rank games and combination games.

The earliest Chinese games were rank games, in which the player turning over the highest card won the round. Many modern games are based on that simple idea, with variations such as the trump suit—a designated suit from which any card beats any card of the other three suits. Among the popular games in this category would be *loo*, *euchre*, *whist*, and *bridge*.

Combination games are those in which the winner of a round is determined by the entire hand he holds and the combinations formed by his cards—*poker* and *gin rummy*. Games which are a combination of the two are: *pinochle* and *klobriash*.

Poker became popular in the United States in the nineteenth century, especially among gold-digging forty-niners. The game was actually based on an older Spanish game called *primero* that included elements of betting and bluffing just like the modern game. According to Shakespeare, Henry VIII played *primero* the night Queen Elizabeth was born. The term *poker* comes to us from the German *pochen*, "to brag" or "to knock," or from a similar German game called *pochspiel*.

Reportedly, there are over 350 different versions of that great boon for a rainy day—*solitaire*.

The popularity of a card game varies greatly from country to country, and from one era to the next. In the United States today, most people have at least heard of *canasta*—a Latin American invention—and also have heard of *poker*, *rummy*, *bridge*, *gin*, *blackjack*, *war, go, cassino, keno, pinochle,* and *old maid.* In the past, such games as *faro, whist,* and *euchre* were more popular.

Blackjack is easily the most popular casino game in the United States today. Actually, all popular casino games—*baccarat, banque, chemin-de-fer,* and *blackjack*—date from the fifteenth and sixteenth centuries. All were extremely simple to play. In each of these games, the object is to reach a number of close to—but not above—a predetermined limit. In blackjack, it's 21; in baccarat, it's nine.

The record for the greatest number of stories in a house of cards is 39—using 1,240 cards.

You may have been confused in the casino, or in your reading, by the games of baccarat and chemin-de-fer. The rules of play are actually the same in both games, but the betting procedure is different in each. Baccarat is *the* big-money game in most American casinos, while chemin-de-fer remains more popular in Europe. In both games, six fifty-two-card decks are used, shuffled together and placed in a wooden box known as the *sabot.*

Speaking of rules, Edmond Hoyle has been credited with formulating the rules to many popular card games. Actually, Hoyle wrote only two books on cards, and never heard of most of the games for which he is supposed to have formulated the rules. Among them is poker, which was not invented until almost 100 years after Hoyle's death.

If you're a real card freak, you may want to take a gander at some of the world's great playing card collections. The most notable are in the British Museum in London, the Morgan Library in New York, and the Cincinnati Art Museum, which includes a display donated by the U.S. Playing Card Corporation.

And talking about card freaks: a Canadian by the name of John Wilson holds the record for the greatest number of stories in a house of cards—39 stories in a tower of 1,240 cards. Joe E. Whitlam of England bettered that feat by building a house of seventy-three stories—a stupendous 13 feet, 10¼ inches—but Joe cheated a bit by bending some cards into angle supports.

The well-rounded card player might like these round cards, which can be read no matter how you hold them.

We might also mention what must be the single largest loss in a game determined by the turn of one card. William Northmore of Okehampton, England, an inveterate gambler of the early eighteenth century, lost his entire fortune of $850,000 on the turn of an ace of diamonds!

William Northmore gambled $850,000 on the ace of diamonds—and lost!

Northmore's tale does have a happy ending, though. After the game, Northmore vowed never to gamble another penny. The townspeople of Okehampton, in sympathy for his plight, elected Northmore to Parliament, where he served for nineteen years until his death.

Suit Distribution at Bridge

The odds against finding the following distributions are:

4-4-3-2	4 to 1
5-4-3-1	9 to 1
6-4-2-1	about 20 to 1
7-4-1-1	about 249 to 1
8-4-1-0	about 2,499 to 1
13-0-0-0	158,755,357,992 to 1

Without doubt, the card game most widely played over the world today is *Contract Bridge,* a partnership game played by four persons.

Bridge is derived from *Whist,* which can be traced back to 1529. The earliest treatise on Whist written by Edmund Hoyle in 1742, was a bestseller.

Duplicate Whist was played in London as early as 1857. The idea of Duplicate Whist was to eliminate luck and transfer the game into a contest of skill.

In 1891, the American Whist League was established. My, how the game has grown! Today, bridge is played by over 30 million people in the United States, of whom 200,000 are dues-paying members of the American Contract Bridge League.

It is estimated that over 60 million people play bridge throughout the world. In Sweden, Holland, and Belgium, the game is even more of a rage than it is in the United States. Today, champions compete on television, and there are bridge columns in newspapers throughout the world.

During the 1930's the big name in bridge was Ely Culbertson, who developed a system of bidding which took the bridge world by storm. With a host of bridge teachers under his tutelage, Culbertson turned the game into a multi-million dollar business. He wrote a number of books on the Culbertson System, which sold in the hundreds of thousands. Included in his hoopla were matches played by himself and his wife as partners against such topnotch bridge stars as Sidney Lenz and P. Hal Sims. These Culbertson matches became parlor chitchat throughout the country and turned the name of Culbertson into a household word.

During the 1940's, the ascendant star was Charles H. Goren, who ruled the world of bridge for some twenty years.

Apart from being played in tournaments, bridge is, of course, also played for money; sometimes, it is rumored, for fairly high stakes. In the early days of the game, Charles F. Schwab, the steel magnate, is reputed to have run a game where the stakes were a dollar a point. In today's clubs, the stakes run as high as 10 cents a point, which on a bad evening when Lady Luck frowns, might cost a player around $500.

Ely Culbertson was a critical figure in the history of bridge playing. Culbertson turned bridge into a multi-million dollar industry.

POCKETKNIVES

The pocketknife is obviously a recent invention, right? After all, the technological skill required to craft a workable fold-up knife must be a product of the industrial age. Besides, what need would men have had for a pocketknife in the days before pockets? Well, don't be surprised if you come across a rusty, time-worn pocketknife among the display cases of a museum—a tool, say, 2,000 years old!

Knives themselves, of course, have been with us since the Stone Age. Primitive man used cutting tools and weapons made from stone and flint, and later, from bronze and iron. The ancient Romans were skilled metalworkers, spreading their craft throughout their Empire—and the Romans left us the world's first known fold-up pocketknives.

The Roman implements were about three inches long when shut, fashioned without a spring or "nail nick"—the groove used to open the blade. The handles were often elaborately carved. One pocketknife surviving from the first century features an ivory handle skillfully carved into the shape of an armored gladiator. Another Roman knife, now in the British Museum, had the carver's name scratched into the handle.

Table knives did not exist in the Middle Ages—each diner was expected to bring his own knife which between meals, doubled as a dagger. Nor did innkeepers provide table cutlery. Affluent travelers often carried sets of elegant tableware among their baggage. Obviously, the pocketknife would have been an ideal all-purpose tool for the medieval European, but few pocketknives were in existence at the time. Most men preferred an unfolding knife in a scabbard to a pocketknife—owing either to the lack of good spring knives or to the shortage of pockets.

Until the eighteenth century, the only kind of pocketknife generally available was the jackknife, a heavy tool with one blade that closed into a groove in the handle. Then cutlerers began using springs to secure the blade in both the open and closed positions, providing a safer, firmer tool. From that time on, pocketknife manufacture became known as spring knife cutlery.

As the craft improved, multibladed tools began to appear—the penknife by far the most important. No, *penknife,* is not, strictly speaking, interchangeable with *pocketknife.* A penknife was a specialized pocketknife with one-blade opening at each end of the handle.

The smyler with the knyf under the cloke.
—Chaucer,
Canterbury Tales

The smaller of the two blades was used to trim and sharpen quill pens.

Throughout the eighteenth and nineteenth centuries, anyone who wrote had to own a penknife, and spring knife cutlery became a major industry in Europe and the United States. The penknife was the premiere product of the cutlerer's craft, for the fitting of a spring knife demands highly skilled work. The blades were made from high-grade steel, tempered slightly harder than table knives. The more expensive models were finished by jewelers, with handles fashioned from silver, ivory, pearl, horn, ebony, and tortoise shell. An American cutlery catalogue from 1893 lists some 1,500 pocketknife models, which might suggest both the size of the industry and the variety of product available at the time.

Since at least the fourteenth century, the English cutlery industry had been centered around the city of Sheffield, while German knife

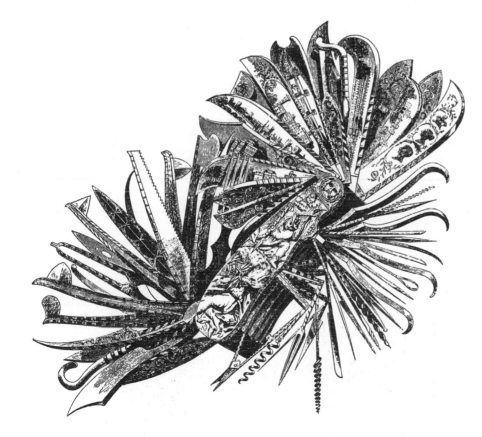

This 80-blade English pocketknife, inlaid with gold and mother of pearl, was exhibited at the Great Exhibition of 1851 in the Crystal Palace, in Hyde Park, London.

The Norfolk Sportman's Knife, manufactured in 1851, was fitted with 75 blades, and took two full years to manufacture.

makers from Solingen have long excelled at their craft. It was nineteenth-century Sheffield cutlerers who began fitting pocketknives with various other tools, among them buttonhooks, files, leather borers, tweezers, gimlets, saws, and implements curiously known as "castrating blades." One interesting Sheffield creation sported both a pistol and a dagger.

The jack-of-all-trades knife—often known as the sporting knife—is today the most popular kind of pocketknife, fitted with nail files, clippers, scissors, corkscrews, forks, spoons—you name it. Special sporting models have been designed for fishermen, engineers, and campers, some combining a tool chest of implements into one handy pocketknife.

The Norfolk Sportman's Knife, manufactured in 1851, was fitted

Four models of pocketknife in vogue during the late nineteenth century were The Dainty Knife, The Congress Knife, The Gentleman's Knife, *and* The Indian Trapper.

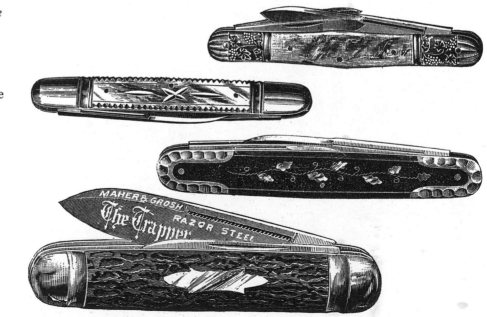

with seventy-five blades, and took two full years to manufacture. But the award for pocketknife-blade proliferation surely goes to the Year Knife, made—like the Norfolk—by the world's oldest cutlery firm, Joseph Rodgers and Sons Ltd. of Sheffield. This knife was introduced in 1822 contained 1,822 blades, and the firm has added one blade to the knife each year since. By now, of course, it's far from a "pocket" knife. In 1977, this one-of-a-kind tool was fitted with its 1,977th blade, and the number will continue to match the year until 2000 A.D., when there will be no further room for blades in this gargantuan tool.

Though we have little need for the penknife today, pocketknives are still widely manufactured. In the recent past, young boys often carried pocketknives for whittling, or for games like mumblypeg; but after the teenagers of the 50's took to carrying switchblade and push-button knives for less savory purposes, we no longer look kindly upon knife-wielding youths. Laws have been passed in some states stipulating the maximum length for a pocketknife blade—a longer blade is considered a deadly weapon.

If you number yourself among the ranks of pocketknife owners, take note: pocketknife manufacturers warn that their products demand constant attention. The spring joints of each blade should always be kept well oiled. And most important, a pocketknife blade should never be used as a screwdriver or lever. The blades are made from special steels tempered to maintain an edge, but not to withstand the strains of bending. If you need a screwdriver, you'll have no trouble finding a pocketknife fitted with one.

POTATOES

"Meat and potatoes" are the foundation of most American cooking, and of many European cuisines as well. The spud is so rooted in Western cooking that it's sometimes hard to believe the vegetable was totally unknown in Europe just a few hundred years ago.

In the mid-sixteenth century, Spanish conquistadores in South America discovered that the Incas ate a white tuber they called "papa." (Perhaps it was the "father" of their diet.) The Incas used the plum-sized vegetables in hundreds of ways, baking them in hot ash, eating them raw or dried, and even pounding them into a flour.

The Spaniards thought the tuber was a form of truffle, since the Incas found them underground. Pedro Cieca, an officer of Juan Pizarro, shipped a load of the spuds back to Spain. From there, they were sent to the Pope for inspection, and eventually to a Belgian botanist for classification.

The botanist called the vegetable *taratoufli*, "little truffle," a word

The Idaho, *prized for its thick, tasty skin, is the ideal baking potato.*

recognizable in the present German word for potato, *kartoffel*. But the Spaniards found the spud similar to the sweet potato, called *patata* after the African *batata*, and christened the new vegetable by the same name. The English for a time also called both vegetables by the same name: *potato*.

Within twenty years of their arrival in Europe, potatoes were being grown, sold, and eaten in Spain, though far less than the sweet potato. After Sir Walter Raleigh planted potatoes on his Irish estate, spud farms began to sprout up all around the Emerald Isle. But in England and Scotland, the potato remained unpopular for two hundred years—defamed as "Ireland's lazy root."

In the late seventeenth century, the German monarch Frederick William decided that the potato could solve his nation's food shortage, and he decreed that all peasants should plant spuds. Those who refused to would have their noses and ears cut off. It's unknown how

Nineteenth-century Breton peasants are depicted harvesting potatoes in the field.

This woodcut shows German farmers gathering the potato crop.

many farmers lost their features because of the bog apple, but Frederick's decree may help explain why potatoes have become so popular in Germany.

The English, with considerably less encouragement to plant the spud, did not become large-scale potato eaters until the latter half of the eighteenth century. The Scots, meanwhile, continued to resist the spud, with some Presbyterian clergymen declaring that since the vegetable was not mentioned in the Bible it could not be fit for human consumption.

France was the last European nation to accept the potato. A soldier who had spent considerable time in Germany returned to his homeland to convince fellow Frenchmen that the potato was both edible and delicious, despite medical advice that the vegetable was "toxic and the cause of many illnesses."

The first potato to reach the shores of North America arrived around 1622, imported by Virginia colonists as a food. The first potato cultivation didn't begin in America until 1719, when Irish immigrants planted spud fields in New Hampshire. Thomas Jefferson, by the way, was the first American to serve french fries with beefsteak, a combination now as institutionalized in America as the Declaration of Independence. And it was the German immigrants you can either thank or blame for potato salad.

Of all the foodstuffs indigenous to the Americas, none is as useful as the potato. Potatoes are easy to cultivate and can be stored for long periods of time. To give you an idea of the fecundity of the potato, in 1968, an English farmer reported that just six seed potatoes had yielded a whopping 1,190 pounds of spuds.

The potato is also one of the most versatile vegetables. You can do almost anything to the spud and still it insists on remaining edible. Potatoes can be *home-fried, french-fried, deep-fried, mashed, hash-browned, baked, boiled, oven-roasted,* or made into *chips, sticks, salad, pancakes.* They can be coal-roasted as *mickies,* or powdered into *instant potatoes*—well, you get the idea.

Spuds can also team up deliciously with many other foods, and the list of dishes featuring the potato is virtually endless. *Potatoes O'Brien* joins diced, fried spuds with onions, green peppers, and pimientos. For *potatoes Lyonnaise,* boil potato slices, then brown and add

This wire potato scoop is available from Sears Roebuck.

onions. *Dumplings* are made from grated spuds and baking soda, while *potato knishes* wrap mashed potatoes and onions in a pastry dough. Popular potato soups include *vichyssoise*, made from onions, leeks, potatoes, cream, and consomme, and usually served cold. For *scalloped potatoes*, spread alternate layers of thin-sliced potatoes and onions in a casserole dish, add milk, and bake.

Photo courtesy of USDA.

New potatoes, boiled and served with a green onion sauce made from evaporated milk, flour, butter, and scallions.

Speaking of thin-sliced spuds, the well-known *Saratoga chips* were invented, not surprisingly, in Saratoga, New York, when a guest-house chef appropriately named George Crumb lost his patience with a guest who insisted on thin french fries. Crumb cut a potato into paper-thin slices, dropped them in oil, and—presto!—another American institution was founded.

In 1969, Australian Paul Tully set a record for potato chip devouring by consuming thirty two-ounce bags in twenty-four-and-a-half minutes—without a drink. And while we're on the subject, the record for potato gobbling is three pounds in four minutes and forty-five seconds, set in Worcestershire, England in 1976. We have no idea if the spuds were peeled or unpeeled—or served with or without Worcestershire sauce.

To settle an oft-heard dispute: no, the sweet potato and the yam are *not* the same vegetable. The yam is in fact almost never seen in this country—no matter what food packagers claim to the contrary!

More than one American tourist has been known to ask his confused French waiter for *french fries*. The French actually call them *pommes frites*—and the French word for potato is *pomme de terre*, literally "earth apple."

The French have also contributed *pommes soufflées*, or souffled potatoes, to our gastronomic repertoire. The delicacy was reportedly created by the personal chef of Louis XIV. In this case, necessity was definitely the mother of invention. One afternoon, the king left the palace to inspect his army, then engaged in warfare with the Dutch. On the return voyage to the palace, the Sun King's coach was delayed by a downpour that made the roads impassable. When his master did not appear at the expected hour, the Royal Chef began to panic. The Great Monarch was a most fastidious diner, who insisted that his repasts be served the instant he arrived at the royal dinner table. The cook had prepared a huge batch of the king's beloved *pommes frites*, but as the hours passed and still Louis failed to appear, the fries began to frazzle and turn cold and soggy.

Suddenly, a herald announced the entrance of the king. The agitated chef, in dismay, grabbed the deep-fat fryer and submerged the wilted french fries in sizzling oil, shaking the fryer madly from side to side. Et voilà!—a dish fit for a king was born. The potatoes emerged from this second bath in deep hot oil all puffed up—golden brown and heavenly delicious.

To make *pommes soufflées* is a culinary feat. It is said that the heat of the oils must be perfect. Consult a good cookbook and try it. You, too, might achieve gastronomic immortality.

According to another tale, however, the origin of souffled potatoes is considerably less regal. A nineteenth-century French chef was charged with preparing a banquet to celebrate the opening of a new railroad line. While preparing the repast at one of the new stations, the chef was notified that the train carrying a coachload of dignitaries to the banquet would be delayed. So he took his half-cooked french fries out of the oil and began preparing a fresh batch. Then he was notified that the train was pulling into the station, on time after all. Frantic, the chef plunged the half-cooked potatoes back into the fat, and the soggy fries puffed into crisp ovals—*pommes soufflées!*

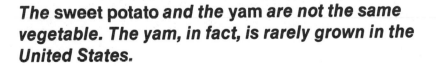

The sweet potato *and the* yam *are not the same vegetable. The yam, in fact, is rarely grown in the United States.*

Today, Americans consume literally billions of spuds each year—production usually hovers around 34 billion pounds—with the most well-known varieties hailing from Idaho, Maine, and Long Island.

Potatoes remain, pound for pound, one of the cheapest foodstuffs available, perhaps because they can be grown so easily. If you believe some mothers, they'll even grow behind the dirty ears of little boys.

This potato digger is a handy contraption for unearthing spuds from the soil.

REFRIGERATION

A prominent encyclopedia has suggested that the invention with the greatest impact on worldwide economic life since the railroad is—no, you'd never guess—the refrigerator! Isn't the refrigerator more of a convenience item? Hardly. Refrigeration technology has completely revolutionized farming and led to the rapid development of a worldwide food trade. It would be difficult indeed to find a person in the world today who has not benefitted in some way from the introduction of refrigerated food preservation.

The growth of cities and suburbs in the last century has steadily moved most of us further and further away from our food source, the farm. Without food-preservation techniques, especially refrigeration, it's doubtful that this urban growth could have moved ahead so rapidly. And since the advent of refrigeration, a nation no longer has to feed itself—the abundant supply of one nation can balance the scarcity in another, allowing many nations to industrialize more quickly. Improved food preservation has also helped increase the world's food supply by eliminating much waste. Foods that would otherwise perish can remain in storage until needed.

Refrigeration may be a recent advance, but food preservation itself has engaged man's attention since the beginning of time. Cheese and butter may, in a sense, be regarded as preserved milk; wine, as

Without bacteria, edibles would last almost indefinitely.

preserved grapes. For thousands of years, meat and fish have been preserved by salting or drying, or more recently, by curing with sugar or nitrate compounds. Most of these early stratagems were discovered by chance—they worked, but no one knew why. Only when the existence of bacteria and their influence on foodstuffs became known, could man begin to deal adequately with food preservation.

Without bacteria, edibles would last almost indefinitely. All food-preservation techniques, then, are designed to kill or limit the growth of bacterial life. For instance, the process of drying works because bacteria cannot grow in the absence of moisture. Sterilization by heat—cooking—will completely destroy bacterial life, but the effects are temporary. Cooked food will spoil as rapidly as uncooked food if left untreated or uneaten.

Cooling does not kill bacteria, but it does stop their growth. Once scientists learned that most bacteria cannot grow at temperatures below the freezing point of water, and also that long-term freezing or cooling of foods does not influence their nutritional content, they knew what was needed for the perfect food-preservation system—a refrigerator. It remained only to invent one.

It had long been known that low temperatures would, for some then unknown reason, preserve food. People in Arctic lands often stored their meat in snow and ice. But to preserve food, people in warmer climes needed man-made ice.

Ancient Indians made ice the simplest and least dependable way possible—leaving water in special outdoor receptacles overnight. The ancient Romans cooled their wine cellars with snow brought from nearby mountains. They also discovered, as did the Indians, that water could be cooled with the addition of saltpeter. The Romans sometimes chilled liquids by immersing bottles in vessels filled with

This ice-house was used by George Washington at Mount Vernon to preserve food.

The first refrigerator in the United States was invented in 1803 by Thomas Moore of Baltimore.

water and saltpeter, and rotating the bottles rapidly. The records of a Roman doctor, Blasius Villafranca, show that cooling water with saltpeter was still common in the sixteenth century.

Primitive cooling techniques could chill food and drink, but not freeze them; the beneficial effects were temporary. During the eighteenth century, many scientists developed an interest in mechanical refrigeration, but with neither electricity not the means to manufacture large quantities of ice, the scientist's road to the new "ice age" was a long and difficult one.

This Victorian precursor of the refrigerator had detachable parts that were easy to assemble and disassemble.

The first "refrigerator" in the United States was invented in 1803 by Thomas Moore of Baltimore, but Moore's machine was really a "thermos" device—two boxes, one inside the other, with insulating material in between. Food stored with ice in the inner box would remain cool for a time, but not cool enough to inhibit bacterial growth for very long.

The next giant step toward successful refrigeration came in 1834, when Jacob Perkins, an American living in England, developed an ice-making machine functioning on the compression principle. Gases subjected to high pressures will remain in the liquid state at temperatures beyond their normal boiling point. Perkins showed that when these compressed liquids were used as refrigerants, they would absorb a great deal of heat before changing to the gaseous state.

In 1851, an American engineer named John Gorric took Perkins' techniques one step further, filing a patent for "an improvement in the process for the artificial production of ice." Gorrie stunned a dinner crowd by exhibiting blocks of man-made ice the size of bricks. Gorrie's compression-principle machine failed as a dependable refrigerator for a number of reasons, but his primitive machine formed the basis of much later work.

The 1870's saw vast improvements in refrigeration techniques. A refrigerator car—really a rolling icebox—had made its earliest appearance in 1851, when several tons of butter made the journey by rail from Ogdensburg, New York to Boston. But the first application of refrigeration technology to marine food transportation came in 1880, when the steamer *Strathleven* carried a meat cargo from Australia to England. Oddly enough, the meat was meant to be cooled, not frozen—but freezing did take place, and the excellent results led to the subsequent freezing of all meat cargoes.

The domestic refrigerator was not to be used on any scale until this century. In the past, urban Europeans had often hung dairy products out the window to keep them cool for a time. The larder was also used throughout the West for temporary preservation. Earlier in this century, most American homes relied on the icebox for their victuals. The icebox, however, left much to be desired, especially when the iceman did not cometh.

The modern domestic refrigerator is based to a great extent on the

A primitive icebox used in India in the 1870's.

This refrigerator train car of the 1880's was patented by Henry Tallichet, of Austin, Texas.

This advertisement appeared in Century Magazine *in 1888.*

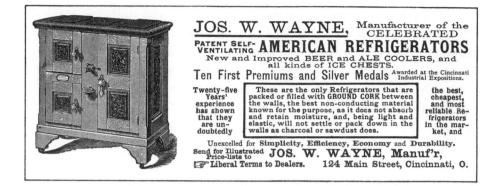

work of the Frenchman Edmond Carré. In the 1830's, Carré perfected the first refrigerating machine to be widely adopted for individual use. Carré's machines were used in many Paris restaurants for the production of ice and ice cream products. The first household refrigerator patent in the United States was granted in 1899 to one Albert T. Marshall of Brockton, Massachusetts.

Modern refrigerators and freezers use a circulating refrigerant that

By 1906, refrigerators had begun to resemble the modern 'fridge.

continually changes from the gaseous to the liquid state. Most machines use dichlordifluoromethane and other refrigerants mercifully known under the trade name of Freon. The liquid refrigerant changes to a gas in the evaporator, then absorbs heat from the food chamber and carries it to the condensing coils, where the refrigerant is cooled by air passing over the coils, and is reconverted into liquid. The cycle is then repeated, spurred on periodically by a small electric motor. Incidentally, your refrigerator is probably your greatest electricity consumer—after your air conditioner.

Wartime restrictions limited the growth of the domestic refrigerator in this country, but after World War II the 'fridge found its way into almost every American home—and so did frozen foods. The American, Clarence Birdseye, is responsible for the development of methods for freezing foods in small packages for the retail trade. The General Foods Corporation introduced the now familiar Birds Eye commercial pack in 1929. Since then, the use of frozen foods has grown with the refrigerator. As early as 1944, Americans were consuming some three billion pounds of frozen meats, vegetables, fruits, fish, and dairy products each year.

During and after World War II, military and industrial research led to the development of the science of cryogenics, the study of matter at extremely low temperatures. Basically, cryogenics—from the Greek word *kryos,* "icy cold"—deals with the production of temperatures below that of liquid oxygen (-297 degrees F.). You hardly need such frigid temperatures to keep your eggs fresh, but cryogenic engineering has had an impact on many elements of modern life, from medicine to space travel.

Scientists are now freely discussing the ultimate cryogenic marvel, suspended animation. Living organisms, including man, can theoretically be kept in a deep freeze almost indefinitely, and resume normal life functions upon thawing. Persons with presently incurable diseases could be frozen before death in the hope of reviving them when cures are found. Intergalactic space travelers could be frozen and revived upon reaching their destination thousands of years later. And think of the possibility of a living time capsule, a human being frozen for thousands of years, to be resurrected by some future civilization to see how we lived in the twentieth century!

A refrigerator is a place where you store leftovers until they are ready to be thrown out.

RESTAURANTS

The restaurant is such a seemingly natural and necessary institution that you'd suspect it's been with us for as long as man has lived in cities. But the restaurant, as we know it today, is a surprisingly recent development. That's not to say there weren't any commercial eating places before our time. But the menu, with its choice of dishes, is only about 200 years old. The fact is that the diner or the coffee shop in which you may have lunch today offers more of a menu selection than the best of restaurants of the world did just a few centuries back.

The earliest forerunners of the restaurant were the medieval tavern and cookshop. The tavern customarily provided a daily meal, or "ordinary," at a fixed hour and price, usually serving just one dish, much like a household cook providing dinner for a large family. Cookshops primarily sold cooked meat for carry-out, but some did, on occasion, serve food on the premises.

By the sixteenth century, Englishmen of all classes were in the habit of dining out often. Local taverns offered fixed price meals, wine, ale, and tobacco, and served as a meeting place and informal clubhouse to boot. Entry was generally restricted to men. Among the more famous Elizabethan taverns in London were *The Falcon*, a popular haunt of actors, and *The Mermaid*, oft frequented by William Shakespeare.

Beginning in England around 1650, the coffee house began taking over many of the tavern's social functions. At first, the coffee house served only coffee, tea, and chocolate—all new arrivals to Europe. Then, the coffee house began providing wine, ale, and occasional hot meals. Another attraction was its supply of gazettes and newsletters regularly kept on hand for coffee swillers on their way to and from

---

For the first real restaurant, we must naturally turn to France. In 1765, a soup vendor named Boulanger opened a shop offering diners a choice of dishes rather than the then standard "ordinary" or table d'hote dinner.

The Old White Hart Tavern on Bishopsgate Street, London, a popular Renaissance establishment, was one of the precursors of the modern restaurant.

work. The clientele evidently was quite varied. An early eighteenth-century writer noted: "Some shops are a resort for learned scholars and wits; others are the resort of dandies, or of politicians, or again of professional newsmongers, and many are temples of Venus."

For the first real restaurant, we must naturally turn to France. In 1765, a soup vendor named Boulanger opened a shop offering diners a choice of dishes rather than the then standard "ordinary" or "table d'hôte" dinner. The sign above Boulanger's door read *"Restaurants,"* meaning "restoratives," referring to the hot soups and broths available inside. The term restaurant or a derivative, was eventually adopted by many other nations and languages, although the word was not generally used in England until the late nineteenth century.

Hungry Parisians so enjoyed the new eating place that hundreds of similar establishments began springing up around the city, one offering close to 200 different meat dishes daily.

The first "luxury" restaurant to open its doors in Paris was *La Grande Taverne de Londres*, founded in 1782 by Antoine Beauvilliers. He was later to write a cookbook that became a standard work on French culinary art. According to the rotund gastronomist Brillat-

Savarin, Beauvilliers' establishment was the first to offer the four essentials of a fine restaurant: "an elegant room, smart waiters, a choice cellar, and superb cooking."

Prior to the French Revolution, aristocrats maintained elaborate culinary staffs. When the aristocracy was driven from power, their cooks were likewise driven from the kitchen. Many sought work in restaurants or opened their own eating places. By 1804, there were well over 500 restaurants in Paris.

The great culinary establishments of nineteenth-century Paris included the *Véry*, whose menu listed twelve soups, twenty-four fish dishes, fifteen beef dishes, twenty mutton specialties, and scores of side dishes. In 1869, the *Véry* was merged with a neighboring restaurant to form the *Le Grand Véfour*, which still ranks near the top among French restaurants. Another great restaurant of the era, the *Café Anglais*, had a chef, Adolphe Duglère, who created the famed "Three Emperors Dinner" in 1867 for three well-heeled diners: Tsar Alexander II of Russia, his son, the future Alexander III, and William I, the future emperor of Germany.

Across the English Channel, by the end of the nineteenth century, the tavern had given way to the restaurant and the tea shop. The first teahouse opened in 1884, initially serving only teas. Later, it offered full meals. Teahouses became immediately popular among women, who for the first time had a place where they could eat in public without a male escort. Meanwhile, the lower classes turned to cheap eateries nicknamed "dives" due to their customary underground location.

In the United States, the earliest restaurants on record appeared in Philadelphia around 1680. The *Blue Anchor Tavern* was among the first. New York's *Fraunces Tavern*—the site of George Washington's farewell to his troops—was a popular watering hole in Revolutionary times, and still operates today.

The major American innovations in the field of eateries were the self-service restaurant and the automatic restaurant. The first self-service eatery in New York opened in 1885, but self-service establishments called *cafeterias* first became popular in San Francisco of the gold rush era.

The first automatic restaurant was opened by the Horn & Hardart Baking Company in Philadelphia in 1902, using mechanisms imported from Germany. Other American innovations were the specialty restaurant—the steak house and seafood restaurant, for example—the Pullman diner car, and the riverboat dining room.

By 1955, there were close to 200,000 eating places in the United States—one for every 800 persons—serving over 60 million meals a day with a staff of 1.3 million workers. Annual sales totaled about 9 billion dollars, making the restaurant the third largest retail business in this country. About 20 percent of all restaurant sales are now rung up on the cash registers of large American chains. These include *Howard Johnson's, McDonald's,* and other various hamburger drive-ins.

Today, the last word in gastronomic excellence is the guide published by the Michelin Corporation, a French tire firm. Michelin annually rates restaurants in thousands of towns and cities, awarding

Hope springs eternal in the human breast—that's why a new restaurant is crowded.

Rector's Specialties

Onion Soup
Chicken casserole, Catalane
Boneless Squab en cocotte, Nerac

Lobster, Thermidor
Sweetbread, Prince of Wales
Venice Peaches, Mephisto

Luncheon

1894

OYSTERS 25   CLAMS 25

Soups

Julienne, Pea or Tomato 25 40   Chicken Gumbo 35 60
Mongole 25 40   Consommé Brunoise 25 40 .   Oyster Stew 50

Fish

Filets of Sole, Marguery 40 75 *9 minutes*
Aiguillette of Kinglish, Rector 50 90 *9 minutes*
Oysters and Oyster Crabs, Opera 75 *6 minutes*
Brook Trout, maître d'hôtel 45 80, *10 min.*   Bluefish au gratin 40 70, *12 min.*
Frogs' Legs, Poulette 60 1 10, *5 minutes*   Filet of Bass, Mornay 40 70, *7 minutes*

Hot

Roast Beef 40 60   Spring Lamb
Braised Beef with noodles 35 60, *ready*   **Irish Lamb Stew 35 60**, *ready*
Shirred Eggs, chicken livers 50, *5 minutes*   Omelette à l'Espagnole 50, *5 minutes*
Emincé of Lamb, green peppers 40 70, *4 min.*   Lamb Fries, Béarnaise 40 70, *8 min.*
Pig's Feet, sauce moutarde 35 60, *6 min.*   Calf's Brains, brown butter 35 60, *4 min.*
Corned Beef Hash browned, poached eggs 40 70, *7 minutes*
Brochette of Chicken Livers, Madeira sauce 40 70, *9 minutes*
Tripe en casserole, nouvelle mode 40 70, *4 minutes*
Deerfoot Sausage, purée of peas 35 60, *6 minutes*
Ham and Spinach, demi-glace 40 70, *5 minutes*
Fresh Mushrooms on toast 60 1 00 *9 minutes.*

Vegetables

New Peas or Beans 50   New Asparagus 1 00
Potatoes Sarah 20 30 Oyster Plant 30 Egg Plant 40 Spinach with egg 25 40
Bouldin Island Asparagus 35 60   Asparagus Tips au gratin 35 60
Céleri braisé au jus 30 50   Macaroni, Spaghetti or Noodles 25 40

Game, Etc.

Ruddy Duck 2 00   Squab Chicken 1 25   Teal Duck 1 00
Squab, Plover, Snipe or Railbird 80   Spring Chicken 1 50 75
Broiled Half Capon 1 25   Half Spring Turkey 1 50

Salads

Hot House Tomato or Cucumber 35 60   Chiffonade 40 70   Rector 45 75
Lettuce, Chicory, Celery or Escarole 30 50   Romaine 35 60
Fetticus with beets or dandelion 30 50   Mayonnaise 10

Dessert

Fresh Strawberries with cream 75   French Pastry [assorted] 25
Brandied : Figs, Peaches, Cherries or Plums 25 40

Ices

Fancy Ice : Plombière au kirsch 40 Souveniers : Pin Cushion 50
All Plain Cream or Ices 25 mixed 30
Cheese   Fruits
COFFEE : French 15 Turkish 20 Special 25

HALF PORTIONS FOR ONE PERSON ONLY

Rector's

Courtesy of The New York Historical Society, New York City

THE FOUR SEASONS

Sea and Fresh Water Fish

❦ The Four Seasons LOBSTER Soufflé (30 minutes) 18.50

STRIPED BASS FOR TWO: Flamed on Fennel with Pernod 26.50

. . . or Poached in White Wine and Herbs 24.50

The Classic TRUITE AU BLEU 11.50

❦ SHRIMPS and SCALLOPS Sautéed in Tarragon Cream 15.50

This Evening's Entrées

Filet of PLUME DE VEAU with CRAB MEAT and ASPARAGUS 16.50

Sautéed CALF'S LIVER with Avocado 12.75

Escalope of VEAL Sautéed in Lemon Butter 14.50

Steaks, Chops and Birds

BROILED OVER CHARCOAL

CALF'S LIVER — Thick, Sage Butter 12.50

SIRLOIN STEAK or FILET MIGNON 15.00

Twin Double LAMB Chops 15.50

Skillet STEAK with Smothered Onions 16.50

Spring Salads

AS A MAIN COURSE

Planked STEAK Tartare 13.50

A NIÇOISE Salad 12.50

AVOCADO and SHRIMP, Louis 12.50

The Four Seasons SHELLFISH PLATTER 18.50

Partial menu of The Four Seasons, one of New York's most prestigious restaurants.

The dollar lunch was still a possibility at the posh restaurant Rector's in 1894.

When it comes to the cost of dining out, times have really changed. At New York's elegant Four Seasons restaurant, the entrees are now close to 30 times as expensive as similar dishes were in the Gay Nineties.

each from zero to three stars according to culinary quality. One star indicates good quality in its class; two stars suggests the restaurant is well worth a detour; and three ranks the establishment among the best in the world.

In a recent typical year, Michelin rated a total of 3,036 restaurants in France: 2,382 were rated but unstarred; 581 received one star; 62 received two stars; and only 11 restaurants earned the highest Michelin compliment of three stars. Five of these gastronomic palaces were in Paris, among them *Le Grand Véfour* and *La Tour D'Argent*, the oldest surviving restaurant in Paris.

Many culinary connoisseurs, however, maintain that for the best in *haute cuisine* you'll have to travel to Vienne, near Lyons, where you'll find the renowned *Pyramide*. Other gourmets would name Paul Bocuse's *Auberge Pont de Collonges*, near Lyons, as the world's premier restaurant, or perhaps the *Auberge de l'Ill* in Illhausen, Alsace, or the *Hotel Cote D'Or* in Saulieu, near Dijon.

France, of course, has no monopoly on fine food. (Modern French cuisine, by the way, is Italian in origin.) Many gourmets avow that

---

A man walked into a restaurant in a strange town. The waitress came over and asked him what he wanted.

Feeling lonely he replied, "Two fried eggs, and a kind word."

The waitress said nothing but went inside to give the order. When she came back with his food, the out-of-towner said, "Thanks for the eggs, but where's the kind word?"

The waitress leaned over and whispered, "Don't eat 'em!"

Chinese cuisine is actually the world's finest, and excellent Oriental restaurants can be found in most cities of the world.

It's been estimated that a New Yorker can dine out every night of his life until age sixty-five without visiting any establishment twice!

Among New York's restaurants, *Lutece* and *La Grenouille* have been given high marks by Michelin, and certainly rank among the finest restaurants on this side of the Atlantic. *Windows on the World,*

The way of a man with a maid usually leads to an expensive restaurant.

Two men sat down in a restaurant and ordered their main dishes. Then they closed their menus. The waiter said, "Thank you, gentlemen, and would any of you wish a beverage with your meal?"

One man said, "Well, I usually have coffee, but today, I think I'll have a glass of milk."

The other man said, "That sounds good. I'll have milk, too. But make sure the glass is clean!"

"Very good," said the waiter, and he left.

Soon he came back with a tray and two glasses of milk, and said, "Here you are, gentlemen. Now which one of you asked for the clean glass?"

---

located atop one of the 110-story World Trade Center towers, has been lauded for its view more than its food. Reservations for dinner at the sky-high restaurant must sometimes be made weeks in advance. And any list of Gotham's posh restaurants must include *The Palace* where dinner prices are, at this writing, $75 per person—without drinks!

ROSES

There are about 35 species of rose thought to be native hybrids of North America.

Quick, name a flower. Well, you may not have said *rose*, but if you were to experiment with the question you'd probably find that, of the estimated 300,000 species of plants on earth, the rose is the first flower to pop into most minds.

Why? It's difficult to say. Many other flowers are larger, more colorful, more fragrant, or more valued. But no single flower is so universally known, so closely connected with the culture of many civilizations, so rich in poetic and mythologic significance as the rose. Symbol of beauty, romance, love, secrecy, perfection, elegance, and life itself, the rose has figured in legend, heraldry, and religion, and has served as the favorite of poets and artists from time immemorial.

Immortalized in songs, such as *The Last Rose of Summer, Sweet Rosie O'Grady,* and *My Wild Irish Rose,"* the rose has been, and will likely forever remain, the king or queen of flowers.

A rose by any other name would smell as sweet.
—Shakespeare,
Romeo and Juliet

The botanical family Rosaceae, which includes close to 200 species and thousands of hybrids, has flourished for millions of years. Indeed, roses have been cultivated for so long that it's impossible to determine where or when the flower was first domesticated. The Egyptians were familiar with cultivated roses by 3000 B.C., building rose gardens in their palaces and often burying roses in their tombs. By the time of Cleopatra's reign, the rose had replaced the lotus as Egypt's ceremonial flower.

The mythologies of various ancient cultures touched on the rose. Most agreed that the flower was created when the gods were still on earth. The Greeks called the rose "the king of flowers" until the poet Sappho, in her *Ode to the Rose*, dubbed it the "queen of flowers" forevermore. According to the Greeks, the rose first appeared with the birth of Aphrodite, the goddess of love and beauty. When Aphrodite (in Roman mythology, Venus) first emerged from the sea, the earth produced the rose to show that it could match the gods in the creation of perfect beauty. The well-known painting by Botticelli, *Birth of Ve-*

nus, depicts dozens of roses in a scene of the goddess emerging from the sea.

Another myth tells of a beautiful maiden named Rhodanthe (*rhodon* in Greek means "rose") who was tirelessly pursued by three suitors. To escape her pursuers, Rhodanthe fled to the temple of Artemis, where her attendants, convinced that Rhodanthe was even more beautiful than Artemis, flung a statue of the goddess from its pedestal and demanded that Rhodanthe be represented there instead. The god Apollo, angered by the insult to his twin sister, Artemis, turned Rhodanthe into a rose and her attendants into thorns. The three suitors were changed into the three courtiers of the rose: the bee, the worm, and the butterfly.

Yet another myth blames the god Eros, or Cupid, for the rose's thorny stem. According to the tale, the god of love was enjoying the aroma of the thornless rose when he was stung by a bee lurking in the petals. To punish the flower, Cupid shot the stem full of his arrows, and the rose forever after was cursed with arrowhead-shaped thorns.

The Madame de Watteville Rose (left).

The Papa Gontier Rose (right).

A root in the right soil,
Sun, rain, and a man's toil;
That, as a wise man knows,
Is all there is to a rose.
—Orgill Mackenzie,
Whitegates

Yet according to a Chinese proverb, "The rose has thorns only for those who gather it."

According to some Biblical scholars, the Rose of Sharon was not a rose at all, but a tulip, a narcissus, or perhaps a meadow saffron.

Christian lore relates that the rose became thorny only when man had been driven from the Garden of Eden. In *Paradise Lost*, the poet Milton tells of "flowers of all hue, and without thorn the rose." Legend also tells us that after betraying Christ, Judas hanged himself on a thorn tree, which then burst into bloom with roses, as a sign that Christ died for the sinner as well as for the saint.

The word *rosary* comes to us from the Latin *rosarium*, meaning a "rose garden," and later the word came to mean "a garland of roses." Christian legend tells of a monk who made a garland of 150 roses each day as an offering to the Virgin Mary. Later, the monk substituted 150 prayers for the flowers. For his piety, he was presented with a rosary of 150 beads by a "beautiful glowing woman."

Though various mythologies have explained the origin of the rose differently, almost all ancient cultures valued the rose for its beauty and fragrance. Roman aristocrats strewed roses around their banquet halls and served a wine made from roses. Moslem monarchs in India bathed in pools with rose petals floating on top of the water. According to the *Thousand and One Arabian Nights*, the Caliph of Baghdad served a jam made from roses that held captive anyone who ate it.

The use of the rose as a symbol of beauty, fraility, and love is quite understandable, but the flower has also symbolized creation, secrecy, the Church, and the risen Christ. The rose windows featured in most Gothic cathedrals are thought by some to represent life and creation, or hope radiating from faith and the Church.

As a symbol of love and romance, the rose needs little introduction. As some are fond of noting, *rose* is an anagram of "Eros." The French poem *Romance of the Rose*, one of the most popular works of the Middle Ages, uses the pursuit of the rose by a lover as an allegory for the love philosophy of the troubadors.

Robert Burns compared his "luve" to a "red, red rose, that's newly sprung in June." And a German custom dictated that a groom send a silver rose to his bride before the marriage ceremony—a custom that forms the basis of the plot of Richard Strauss's opera *Der Rosenkavalier*.

Roses are distilled to make perfume.

Since classical times, the rose has been a symbol of secrecy. In sixteenth-century England, a rose was sometimes worn behind the ear by servants, tavern workers, and others to indicate that the wearer heard all and told nothing. In Germany, roses in a dining room suggested that diners could speak freely without fear that their secrets would travel beyond the room. The expression *sub rosa*, "under the rose," is thought to originate in the custom of carving a rose over the door of the confessional in a Catholic church.

Exactly why the rose came to be a symbol of secrecy is open to speculation. Perhaps the unopened rosebud suggests beauty or truth hidden by the closed petals. In any case, medieval alchemists used the rose as a symbol of the need for secrecy in their art, and as a representation of certain highly guarded scientific principles important in their work. The secret society of the Rosicrucians—from "red cross"—used a cross with a red rose as their symbol.

In medieval England, many families employed a representation of the rose in their coat of arms: the red rose of Lancaster and the white rose of York are two well-known examples. During the fifteenth century, these two houses fought for control of the English crown in a struggle that came to be known as the War of the Roses.

Some historians have claimed that the name of the conflict originated not in the emblems of the two houses, but in the names of two London taverns, the White Rose and the Red Rose, where partisans of each side met in secret. In his dramatic chronicles of the war, Shakespeare offers another explanation. At one point in *Henry VI* (Part I), the Duke of York challenges his future foes in a rose garden with these words:

> *Let him that is a true-born gentleman,*
> *And stands upon the honor of his birth,*
> *If he suppose that I have pleaded truth,*
> *From off this briar pluck a white rose with me.*

Whereupon Somerset, a future ally of Lancaster, replies:

> *Let him that is no coward nor flatterer,*
> *But dare maintain the party of the truth,*
> *Pluck a red rose from off this thorn with me.*

Curiously, during a key battle of the War of Roses, the Lancastrian forces mistook the star symbol of an ally for the "rose-and-sun" of their enemy, and set upon them in error, costing their side the victory. The house of Tudor, which took over the English crown after the war, shrewdly combined both red and white roses in its emblem.

The rose has, of course, proved useful in more ways than the symbolic. Rose water was first distilled around the time of the Crusades. When the Moslem leader Saladin retook Jerusalem from the Crusaders, he refused to enter a mosque until all the walls and the objects had been purified with rose water. Over fifty camels were required to transport the aromatic cargo from Baghdad to Jerusalem.

Rose oil, used in perfumes and lotions, likewise originated in the Near East, and did not appear in Europe until 1612.

A seventeenth-century German book lists thirty-three diseases that supposedly can be cured by rose water or oil.

During the eighteenth century, rose petals occasionally were in-

This woodcut adorns the title page of French humanist Symphorien Champier's Rosa Gallica, *a treatise on medicine, history, and cooking, published in 1514.*

cluded in English salads, and essence of roses was used to flavor ice cream.

Today, roses are grown extensively in many parts of the world, especially in France, India, and the Balkans, and attar of roses is used in perfumes, cosmetics, and flavoring syrups. Rose hips, the fruits of the rose plant, are used to make tea, or as a source of Vitamin C.

The Empress Josephine of France, the wife of Napoleon, put the rose to a more singular use. Josephine built a huge rose garden at her estate at Malmaison, with over 250 varieties of the flower flourishing—every variety known at the time. The Empress often carried in hand a Malmaison rose that she could raise to her lips when smiling, since she was particularly sensitive about her imperfect teeth.

The rose has been cultivated and hybridized for so long that there are, strictly speaking, no species of purely wild rose left on earth. The flowers extant today range in size from just half an inch in diameter to varieeties that spread to more than seven inches. Colors range from white through yellow, pink, red, and maroon.

Some roses smell like—well, roses, while others suggest green tea,

These white climbing roses were promoted in an ad in Harper's Magazine *around the turn of the century.*

PURE WHITE PERPETUAL BLOOMING HARDY CLIMBER "MARY WASHINGTON ROSE"

"NAMED AND RAISED BY" GEO. WASHINGTON

hay, or various spices. Biologically, the rose's fragrance is quite important, since roses normally do not secrete nectar and depend mostly on aroma and color to attract pollinating insects.

There are about thirty-five species of rose thought to be native hybrids of North America. Various roses are the state flowers of Iowa, North Dakota, and New York. While the Greeks and Romans named

---

Various roses are the state flowers of Iowa, North Dakota, and New York.

---

their roses after gods, and the English after court figures, in America the preference is for descriptive or geographical names, such as the *pasture*, the *prairie*, the *smooth*, the *prickly*, or the *California rose*. The Chinese, meanwhile, have long used metaphoric names for the flower. The names of some Chinese rose varieties translate as *After Rain*, *Clear Shining*, *Tiny Jade Shoulders*, and *Three Rays of Dawn*.

Speaking of poetic descriptions, the prominent metaphoric use of the rose through the ages has left us with a considerable body of "rosy" verse. Robert Herrick wrote *Gather ye rosebuds while ye may*, William Blake gave us *The Sick Rose*, and W.B. Yates, *The Rose of the World*. But surely the simplest observation concerning the queen of flowers came from the pen of Gertrude Stein, whose poem, *Sacred Emily* includes the line "*Rose is a rose is a rose is a rose.*"

> *The red rose whispers of passion*
> *And the white rose breathes of love;*
> *O, the red rose is a falcon,*
> *And the white rose is a dove.*
> —*John Boyle O'Reilly,*
> A White Rose

RULERS

No ruler or measuring device is completely accurate.

Here's something to think about: a dry goods dealer has a five-yard piece of thirty-six-inch wide material, and wishes to sell a customer one-and-a-half yards. But neither a yardstick, nor a tape measure, nor any other measuring device is available. Can the dealer complete the sale?

Yes, it can be done, as you'll discover later; but for now, take our word for it. Using a ruler or a tape measure would be a lot easier than figuring out this problem in your head. In fact, much of our commercial life would be next to impossible without implements for estimating length and distance. Why "estimate"? Well, if the American mission that landed a man on the moon had depended upon measuring devices only as accurate as the ruler in a schoolboy's briefcase, our astronauts would most likely have missed the moon altogether!

No ruler or measuring device is completely accurate; in fact, no measurement of any kind is ever *absolutely* correct. A measuring device is, in effect, only a reproduction of an arbitrary standard. While the standard itself is perfectly accurate, the reproduction *never* is. For instance, the standard of length measure in the United States is the yard. Theoretically, a yard is a yard is a yard, but no yardstick ever measures *exactly* thirty-six inches.

The first common unit of length was the *cubit*, used by the Egyptians and Babylonians thousands of years ago. Originally, the cubit was defined as the length of a man's arm from the elbow to the end of the middle finger (the word comes from the Latin word for "elbow"), but the actual length of the cubit varied from place to place and from time to time. Through most of Egyptian history, the cubit was equivalent to about 20.6 inches. One advantage of the cubit was that in the absence of a measuring device the unit could be easily—handily, you might say—approximated. Presumably, long-armed merchants were quite popular in Egypt.

In Egyptian, the cubit was called the *meh*, and divided into units called *sheps*, or "palms." There were seven *sheps* in a cubit, and the *shep* in turn was divided into four parts, called *zebos*, or "digits." "Let's see—I'll have two *mehs*, six *sheps*, three *zebos* of that linen . . .

The ancient Greek cubit was about 20.7 inches, but another unit of measurement, the *foot*, was more widely used. The Greek foot was about 12.5 inches, divided into twenty-five digits. The Romans adopted a *pes*, or foot, of about 11.6 inches, divided into sixteen digits.

Prior to the nineteenth century, each country in Europe had its own system of weights and measures. In medieval England, for instance, the foot was equivalent to 13.2 inches, with six feet to a *fathom*, ten fathoms to a *chain*, ten chains to a *furlong*, and ten furlongs to an *old mile*, equivalent to about 6,600 feet. The English units of measure evolved from many origins, some as old as the Roman conquest.

By 1800, length measure standards were fixed in England at their present values. The unit of length measurement was the *yard* (from the Anglo-Saxon *gyrd*, "measure"), divided into feet and inches. English kings kept a bar known as *the standard yard* in London as the ultimate arbiter of the yard's exact length.

The idea of a physical standard is an old one. Physical standards are kept, not to settle every measuring dispute by direct reference to the standard, but to have a permanent—or so it was thought—record of each measuring standard. But even a physical standard can be inaccurate. It's been estimated that the new British standard yard has decreased by .0002 inches since it was cast a little over a hundred years ago.

The original standard yard was lost when the Houses of Parliament burned in 1834. Scientific studies followed to determine a new

Only the United States, Liberia, Southern Yemen, and a handful of other small nations still employ the so-called British system, and the metric system will soon be introduced in most of these countries.

With this map-measure, you can calculate inches, miles, and centimeters.

standard and to produce a unified system of weights and measures. In 1878, the British imperial yard was defined as the distance at a specified temperature between two lines engraved on gold studs sunk in a certain bronze bar.

Measurement systems from England, France, Spain, and Portugal were all brought to America by colonists, and all were used here briefly in various places. By the time of the American Revolution, standards of measurement here were identical to those current in England. In 1832, an American physical standard was adopted, defining the yard as the distance between the twenty-seventh and sixty-third inch of a certain eighty-two-inch brass bar kept in Washington, D.C. Since 1893, the U.S. standard yard has been defined in terms of the meter.

The yard is still the standard of length measurement in this country, of course; but most other nations, including England, have gone over to the metric system. Although a decimal system for measurement was first proposed as long ago as 1670, the essentials of today's metric system were embodied in a report made by the Paris Academy of Science in 1791.

The original plan for a metric system defined the meter as one ten-millionth part of a meridional quadrant of the earth. Larger units were formed by the addition of Greek prefixes (deca-, hecto-, kilo-), and smaller units with Latin prefixes (deci-, centi-, milli-). A platinum bar was cast according to this definition for use as the physical standard, although few scientists at the time were satisfied with its accuracy.

The new measuring system did not catch on immediately. Many years passed before it was widely adopted in France and other countries. In 1875, a treaty was signed assuring international unification and improvement of the system. Four years later, the standard meter was newly defined with reference to a bar of platinum-iridium alloy. In 1927, a supplementary definition described the meter in terms of light waves, for while a platinum bar can be destroyed or altered, light wave measurement will always be available. With such a standard, a unit of measurement can be verified anywhere in the world without risking damage in transit to the physical standard.

Along with the United States, only Liberia, Southern Yemen, and a handful of other small nations still employ the so-called British system, and the metric system will soon be introduced in most of these countries as well. The exact date for total metric conversion here has not yet been fixed, but Canada began the switchover in 1977.

A number of other terms are sometimes used for length measurement. For instance, have you ever wondered what a *furlong* was? The term originated with the word "furrow," and at one time was thought to be the length most suitable for a plow furrow. The furlong is now defined as 220 yards.

The smallest unit of length measurement in the world is the atto-meter . . . your pinky is probably about 7,000,000,000,000,000,000 atto-meters long.

The word *league* has varied in meaning in different times and countries. In England, the league was equivalent to about three miles. For centuries now, the word league has been used chiefly in a figurative sense.

The *knot* is not a measurement of length, so if you ever hear a sailor say "knots per hour" you'll know he's a landlubber in disguise. The knot is actually a measurement of speed, equivalent to one nautical mile per hour.

The *nautical mile* is defined three different ways, since navigators once regarded the nautical mile as the length of one minute of the meridian at the place where they were taking the reading. The U.S. nautical mile has been identical to the international unit since 1959, measuring 6,076 feet.

The *fathom* was originally thought to be the length to which a man can extend his arms—if you can fathom that. Today, the fathom is equivalent to six feet, and is used most often in reference to water depth and cable length.

The smallest unit of length measurement in the world is the *atto-meter*, equivalent to a mere quintillionth of a centimeter. Your pinky is probably about 7,000,000,000,000,000,000 atto-meters long!

For a measuring device, early man probably first used his arms or his foot—but even during the Egyptian era, when the cubit was the unit of length measurement, a ruler of some kind was more often used. There are two basic kinds of length-measuring devices: the end standard, and the line standard. With an end standard, the unit is defined as the length from one end of the device to the other; with a line standard, from one calibration on the device to another. Most modern rulers are end standards; that is, a foot ruler is one foot long from end to end, and a yardstick is one yard long.

The handy fold-up pocket rule is an indispensible item in most households today.

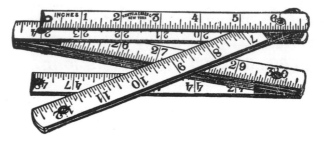

How accurate is a modern ruler? Suppose you want to draw a two-inch line on a piece of paper. First of all, the calibrations on the ruler are a fraction of an inch thick. Thus, a dot that looks correctly placed to you may appear off-center to another eye. The calibrations themselves are never absolutely precise, and the edges of most rulers are slightly warped. The chances of your line measuring precisely two inches, then, is slim, indeed.

Rulers come in many shapes and sizes, among them the three-edged or triangular ruler so often used by students—both for measuring and for launching rubber bands across the classroom.

A tape measure is used for very long measurement, or for the measurement of a bent surface. Calipers consist of two prongs joined by a pin; they are best for measuring thickness or the distance between two surfaces.

As any draftsman can tell you, there's a world of difference between a ruler and a straight edge. No draftsman worth his T-square would use a ruler for drawing an accurate straight line, since rulers are designed chiefly for measuring, not line drawing. For a crisp, straight line, it's best to use a triangle or other device specifically designed for line drawing.

You remember our dry goods dealer and his measuring dilemma? Well, here's what you would have to go through to cut the material without a measuring device.

First, take the five-yard piece of material and stretch it along the edge of a piece of paper, marking off five yards on the paper. Then add the thirty-six-inch width to the five-yard measurement on the paper, making a total of six yards. Fold the paper in half for a three-yard measure, then fold the three-yard measure in half for a yard-and-a-half measure. Finally, lay the yard-and-a-half measure over the five-yard piece of material, and mark off a yard-and-a-half on the material.

And next time, use a ruler!

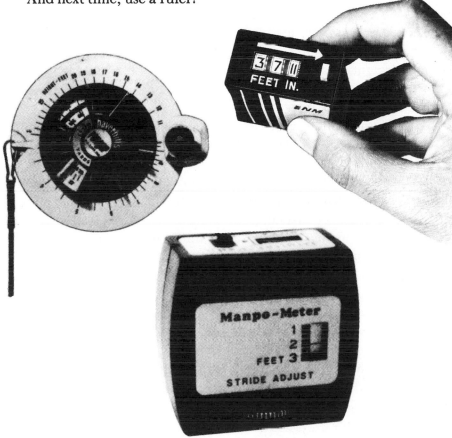

Measure for measure, these modern devices achieve maximum accuracy.

Left: The Disc Ranger measures distances from 6 feet to almost as far as the eye can see, in yards, nautical miles, and statute miles.

Right: The Tapeless Tape Measure is a skid-proof, mar-proof wheel that glides along surfaces and measures distances on a digital counter.

Bottom: The Manpo Measure Meter tells you at a glance how far you've walked.

SAFETY PINS

Relics of prehistoric man 20,000 years old include bone needles with eyes and pins decorated with heads.

On April 10, 1849, a New Yorker by the name of Walter Hunt was granted patent Number 6,281 for a device he called the safety pin. Never heard of Walter Hunt, you say? Well, Hunt was not destined to be pinned with the tag "inventor of the safety pin" for one simple reason: The safety pin, or devices virtually identical to it, had been in use for more than 2,500 years—since the days of ancient Greece!

The earliest fasteners used by man were straight pins, usually simple thorns. Relics of prehistoric man 20,000 years old include bone needles with eyes, and pins with decorated heads. The art of pin making actually predates agriculture, pottery, and metalworking.

The Egyptians didn't use the safety pin or button, but they did fashion straight pins and needles from metal. Bronze pins eight inches long have been found in Egyptian tombs, many with decorated gold heads.

Every period of classical Greece and Rome had its own forms of safety pin and clasp. In fact, the forms of each period were so distinctive that a safety pin can frequently be used to accurately date an entire archaeological find. During some periods, safety pin-heads commonly took the form of serpents, horses, and lutes; other periods produced heads with abstract designs.

Homer tells us that a dozen safety pins were presented to Penelope, the wife of Odysseus by her suitors, suggesting that the Greeks considered pins fitting gifts, even for royalty. Presumably, almost all early Greeks used safety pins to fasten their tunics, since the button wasn't to arrive from Asia Minor until considerably later.

Athenian women used long, daggerlike pins to fasten their chitons over their shoulders. According to Herodotus, when a group of angry women used the pins to stab to death an Athenian soldier, the city forbade the wearing of all but the Ionian tunic, which did not require pins. The law was later revoked; but by then, women were using buttons and safety pins.

Nothing has done so much to bring husbands and wives together as the dress that zips up the back.

This horse-shaped Etruscan safety pin dates from 700 B.C.

Courtesy, Museum of Fine Arts, Boston. Helen and Alice Colburn Fund.

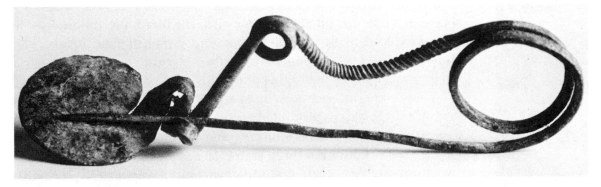

Courtesy, Museum of Fine Arts, Boston. Gift of Mrs. Edward Jackson Holmes.

The Romans called the safety pin *fibula*, a term still used for a clasp and also for a certain leg bone. A bust from the late Empire shows a consul wearing a tunic fastened by two safety pins as long as his head, suggesting that in Rome the size of a *fibula* may have indicated rank.

The Goths who overran the Roman Empire used straight pins, made most often from horn or bone, to fasten their mantles over their shoulders.

In Medieval Europe, the wealthy used elaborately fashioned safety pins of ivory, brass, silver, and gold, while the poor had to make do with simple wood skewers. By the fifteenth century, pins were being manufactured from drawn iron wire, and a pin-making industry was well established in France.

But for centuries, metal pins remained rare and costly items reserved for the rich. You've heard the expression *pin money*, meaning a small sum allotted by a husband for his wife's use, or money for incidental items. Well, when the term originated in the fourteenth century, "pin money" was just that, for at the time, pins were expensive enough to be real items in the budget. By custom, a husband would present his wife on the first or second of January with enough money to buy her pins for the year. "Pin money" went by the boards in the nineteenth century, when mass-production made pins the inexpensive purchase they are today.

The father of the American pin industry was Samuel Slocum, who in 1838, founded a pin factory in Poughkeepsie, New York, capable of

This italic fibula, or safety pin, dates from the 7th century B.C.

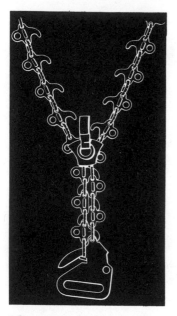

The original zipper was invented in 1891 by an engineer named Witcomb L. Judson.

turning out 100,000 pins a day. Though Slocum was not the first to design a machine for manufacturing pins, his pins were the first to be mass-produced in this country. Slocum's pins had solid heads, and came to be known as *Poughkeepsie pins.* Slocum was also the first to devise a machine for packaging pins in grooved paper boards.

There's another reason why Walter Hunt is forgotten as the "inventor" of the safety pin. The would-be pin magnate rather hastily conceived his idea, made a model, and sold his patent rights for the sum of $100—all within three hours! In any case, diaper-wearing babies have expressed their gratitude ever since, with hours of sob-free slumber.

The nineteenth century was the big era for fasteners of all kinds. Buttons are thousands of years old, but it wasn't until 1863 that Louis Hannart invented the *snap.*

And 1896 saw the first patent for a "slide fastener," a device invented five years earlier by Witcomb Judson as a "clasp locker and unlocker for shoes." The term we use today, *zipper*, originally referred only to a boot equipped with a slide fastener.

Judson, a Chicago inventor, became so tired of lacing and unlacing his high boots that he set out to devise a quicker, easier way of fastening them. At first, he peddled his invention door-to-door as the *C-Curity Placket Fastener*, using the slogan "Pull and It's Done." But Judson's zipper, a series of hooks and eyes, was crude by modern standards, and tended to open or stick.

Judson eventually sold his patent rights to Lewis Walker, who

This elaborate Etruscan safety pin dates from the 3rd century B.C.

The safety pin made a critical contribution to the wasp-waist look of the gay nineties.

with the aid of a Swede named Gideon Sundback developed the first modern zipper in 1906. Zippers began to appear on tobacco pouches, mailbags, and galoshes around 1920; but by and large, the garment industry regarded the zipper as a passing fad. At the time, the only garments fitted with zippers were theatrical costumes for quick-change artists.

The 1930's saw the development of an improved zipper, with the metal teeth die cast directly onto the zipper tape fabric. Die cast teeth with rounded edges made the zipper completely dependable for the first time. Soon, everyone was using zippers for both fastening and decoration. Zippers with multi-colored teeth were especially popular for a time. Today, zippers are used for everything from apparel and luggage to coverings for tanks and guns.

Those of you who are presently struggling with torn, toothless, or unlockable zippers might be interested to know that modern zipper manufacturers claim their products can withstand 200,000 openings and closings without showing signs of wear. Tell it to the marines!

SHOES

Step into a modern shoe store and take a look around. High-heeled and platform shoes, boots, sandals, moccasins, wooden-heeled clogs— quite a variety for today's shopper. Recent fashions? Well, not one of the footwear styles you see today is less than 400 years old!

The loftiest high-heeled and platform shoes you can find today are flat pumps compared with some of the shoes in fashion during earlier European eras. No, our ancestors didn't don stiltlike monsters to raise themselves above muddy streets, or for any other utilitarian reason. In former times, as today, shoe style was dictated by fashion—among the upper classes, at least. Class distinction via footwear? Yes—differentiation of shoe styles to indicate social rank is as old as Western civilization.

In ancient Egypt, the sandal demonstrated a person's rank in society. Slaves either went barefoot or wore crude sandals made from palm leaves. Common citizens wore sandals of woven papyrus, consisting of a flat sole tied to the foot by a thong between the toes. But sandals with pointed toes were reserved only for the higher stations of society, and the colors red and yellow were taboo for anyone below the aristocratic rank.

An Egyptian silver sandal.

Cutting sandals in ancient Egypt. Copy of a fresco in the tomb on Rekh-mi-Re, 18th dynasty (about 1450 B.C.).

The Metropolitan Museum of Art.

Shoes have been regarded as a sign of dignity since well before the Christian era. In the book of Exodus, 3:5, when God appears to Moses in the burning bush, His first command is "Put off thy shoes from off thy feet, for the ground whereon thou standest is holy ground."

Conversely, going barefoot has often demonstrated humility and piety in the presence of God. Hindu documents, thousands of years old, warn worshippers to remove their footwear before entering a shrine; and Moslem tradition demands today that shoes be removed before entering a place of worship.

In the days of ancient Greece, aristocratic women owned as many as twenty pairs of shoes, with a style to match every occasion. Slaves were employed solely to carry a supply of their lady's shoes when she left home, assuring that she would be appropriately shod throughout her travels.

The Chinese custom of binding women's feet to keep them small is many centuries old. Originally, the practice owed little to pedal aesthetics—bound feet were thought to insure faithfulness, since with such deformed feet the wife would supposedly find it difficult to travel very far on her own.

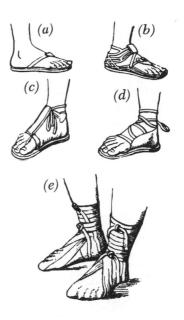

Sandals have been popular as footgear since ancient times. The sandals pictured in (a), (b), (c), and (d) above are Greek. The pair shown in picture (e) is Roman.

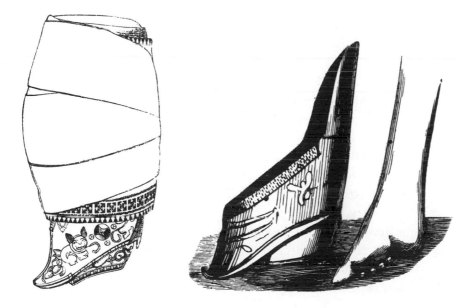

(Left) Chinese women bandaged their feet and wore dainty, embroidered shoes. (Right) A Chinese woman's shoe, and model of a foot after bandaging.

In 1851, a shoe exhibition was held by one J. Sparkes Hall of London.

(TOP LEFT AND RIGHT) *14th century English slippers.*

(BOTTOM LEFT) *Blue satin slipper decorated with honiton lace for Queen Victoria.*

(BOTTOM RIGHT) *This shoe, worn by the Duchess of York in the early 19th century, is notable for its smallness.*

A Roman divorced from his wife, being highly blamed by his friends, who demanded, "Was she not chaste? Was she not fair? Was she not fruitful?" holding out his shoe, asked them whether it was not new and well made. "Yet," added he, "none of you can tell where it pinches me."
—Plutarch, Lives

In the West, shoes have had a place in marriage ceremonies for many centuries. In some cultures, the bride's father threw his shoes at the newlyweds to signify the transfer of authority from father to husband. In Anglo-Saxon ceremonies, shoes were as indispensable as the wedding ring is today. Instead of exchanging rings with her betrothed, the bride customarily passed her shoes to her husband, who then tapped her on the head with a shoe.

During the Middle Ages, in the colder climes, the sandal gave way to more protective footwear. Often, a single piece of untanned hide was wrapped around the foot and tied with a leather thong. Beginning in the twelfth century, the sabot, a shoe cut roughly from a single piece of wood, was the predominant footwear of the European peasant. In those times, the Dutch were not unusual in their use of the wooden shoe. In England, the sabot took the form of the clog, a fabric mounted on a wooden platform. In Japan, wooden shoes mounted on thin blocks three or four inches high have been worn for centuries. The Japanese traditionally selected their wooden shoes with an ear for the sound made by the wooden blocks, for a discordant pair of clodhoppers were considered the epitome of poor taste.

The long journeys undertaken by European crusaders made stronger, longer-lasting shoes a necessity, but medieval aristocrats still took their cue from fancy. The wearing of elaborate, unwieldy footwear was an indication of lordly rank, demonstrating that the wearer did not—and could not—perform manual labor. Such shoes were genuine "loafers."

Pointed shoes originated in France, reportedly the invention of a Count of Anjou who wished to hide his deformed hooves. To assure that the peasantry did not ape the aristocrats, the twelfth-century French king Philip Augustus decreed that the points of his subjects' *souliers* should be between six and twelve inches long, depending upon one's station.

But the rush toward outlandishly long shoes went on unabated. Fashionable shoes were soon so long that their toes had to be stuffed to prevent the wearer from constantly tripping over the ends. In the fourteenth century, the points of shoes grew to such monstrous lengths that some had to be fastened to the wearer's leg just below the knee.

Poulaines, or crakows, were long, pointed-toe shoes popular in Europe in the 14th and 15th centuries. The shoes were named for Crakow, Poland, where the fashion originated.

The largest pair of shoes ever made were a colossal size 42, built for a Florida giant named Harley Davidson.

The clergy objected vehemently to the fashion, claiming that the long-pointed shoes prevented the faithful from kneeling in church. In many communities, shoe-point length was eventually limited by law to about two inches.

In the sixteenth century, aristocratic French women began wearing high-heeled shoes so steep that the—er, well-heeled wearer was literally standing on her toes when she wore them. Later, stiltlike wooden platform shoes became the rage in Venice. The heels eventually became so high that women could not walk in them, and servants were hired to help the ladies in and out of their gondolas. The fashion reportedly owed much to the Venetian husband's desire to make sure his wife didn't travel far while he was away—the same concern that motivated the Chinese to bind their women's feet.

During the 16th century "elevator shoes" were worn by Venetian prostitutes.

Among sixteenth-century Venetian prostitutes, the vogue for the stiltlike shoes was carried to absurd lengths. Eventually, high heels were proscribed by law, because of the high death-rate resulting from ladies of the night tripping and falling to their deaths.

Henry VIII initiated the vogue for wide-tied shoes in England, presumably to hide his gout-swollen feet. Shoes soon grew to such widths that Parliament passed a law limiting the width of a shoe to six inches.

That European lawmakers have historically taken such an oppressive interest in their subjects' footwear can be partly explained by the way in which fashion was dictated in earlier centuries. To a great extent, the king himself was often the trend-setter, the aristocracy was expected to follow suit, and the peasantry was forbidden to emulate their betters.

Many monarchs opted for shoes that would best veil their physical shortcomings. If the fashion didn't catch on naturally, well, laws could guarantee its implementation. For instance, the custom among men of wearing high-heeled shoes at the court of Louis XIV grew out of the Sun King's desire to mask his diminutive stature.

Compared to modern footgear, the shoes of earlier centuries were, for the most part, highly uncomfortable. It wasn't until the development of woven stockings in the seventeenth century that footwear could be made snug-fitting and shaped to the foot.

To give you an idea of the crudity of earlier shoes, it wasn't until the invention in 1818 of the left-shoe last and the right-shoe last that the left shoe was constructed differently from the right shoe. Prior to that, either shoe could be worn on either foot with equal discomfort!

Until the introduction of mass-produced footwear in the nineteenth century, shoes were usually handmade in the cobbler's shop, with nails or pegs used to bind the sole to the upper. As mechanization set in, machines were devised for sewing shoes together. By 1900, most footwear was being made, at least in part, by machine.

The first shoe manufactured in the United States was the handiwork of one Thomas Beard, a *Mayflower* pilgrim, who nailed together the first pair of American shoes in 1628. At that time, the colonists also learned how to make animal-hide moccasins from the Indians, and the moccasins became so popular in the mother country that the colonies began exporting moccasins to England as early as 1650. America's first factory for mechanized shoe production was established in Lynn, Massachusetts in 1760.

Tanned leather has been a favored material for footwear since the Arabs introduced fine leatherwork in Spain in the eighth century. The leather-making trade of the Spanish Arabs was centered around the city of Cordova—to which we owe the origin of the cordovan, a soft, fine-grained leather shoe. As leather becomes more and more expensive today, shoe manufacturers are turning increasingly to rubber and synthetic materials for their products.

By the way, the average American woman now buys about five pairs of shoes each year, and the average man, about two pairs—as a rule men's shoes last longer and remain in fashion longer than women's footwear.

Each model of a modern shoe is manufactured in some 150 sizes, with length designated by a number and width by a letter. But a size

Light she was and like a fairy,
  And her shoes were number nine;
Herring boxes without topses,
  Sandals were for Clementine.
            —*Percy Montrose*

ten shoe is not ten inches long—so where does the number come from? Believe it or not, it stands for ten barleycorns!

The English king Edward II decreed in 1324 that an inch was equal to three average-sized barleycorns laid end to end. The normal shoe was declared to measure thirty-nine barleycorns, and this size, for some reason or other, was designated with the number 13. Other sizes were graded from this standard, with one barleycorn difference between each successive size.

Today, the foot-measuring system used in England is one size different from the American system in both length and width. In metric countries, one size indicates a difference of about two-thirds of a centimeter.

Speaking of shoe size, the largest pair of shoes ever made—apart from those specially built for elephantiasis sufferers—were a colossal

---

Among sixteenth-century Venetian prostitutes, the vogue for stiltlike shoes was carried to absurd lengths. Eventually, high heels were proscribed by law, because of the high death-rate resulting from ladies of the night tripping and falling to their deaths.

---

size forty-two, built for a Florida giant named Harley Davidson. (Yes, it's the name of a British motorcycle manufacturer.) Let's see—a size forty-two equals thirty-nine barleycorns plus twenty-nine, for a total length of some twenty-two and one-half inches!

The average person has literally thousands of styles to choose from today, from the modern machine-stitched leather shoe or the rubber-soled sneaker to such ancient favorites as the sandal, the clog, the platform shoe, and the pump. The pump is thought to owe its name to the early use of the shoe for ceremonies of "pomp." Footwear ranges in price from rubber *thongs* selling for less than a dollar to mink-lined golf shoes—with eighteen-carat gold ornamentation and ruby-tipped gold spikes—sold in England for some $6,500 a pair.

The U.S. Patent Office has on file a design for boots with pockets—for use by nudists. A bit outlandish? Well, if the shoe fits, wear it!

STREETCARS

Imagine a vast network of streetcar lines connecting America's cities, with trolley cars whisking passengers between neighboring towns at speeds of seventy or eighty miles an hour. A prospect for the distant future? No, a fairly accurate description of American interurban travel around the turn of this century. Yes, that's right, we said *trolley cars!*

The first interurban streetcar line in this country connected the cities of Granville and Newark, Ohio, in 1889. The first high-speed interurban trolleys ran between Cleveland and Akron, in 1895.

Today, most people would think of the streetcar as a creature of the big city. True, most American cities have operated trolley systems

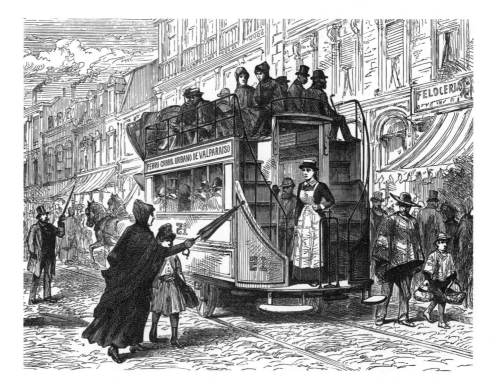

The tram was a fixture of city life in Valparaiso, Chile in 1890.

A novelty in tramway practice—putting the cart before the horses.

at one time or another. But before the country was laced with freeways and interstate highways, streetcar travel was the best means of transportation to and from the city, as well as within its boundaries. Trolley lines took salesmen to small towns to peddle their wares, and trolleys brought farmers and housewives into town to shop or deliver goods, and trolleys carried city dwellers to nearby beaches and resorts.

Interurban streetcar lines operated with heavy, individually powered cars, quite unlike the lighter, locomotive-drawn railroad cars. Trolleys ran more frequently than mainline trains, and they usually served areas inaccessible by railroad. It was common, too, for a streetcar company to construct an amusement park in an otherwise inaccessible suburban area along its trolley line in order to increase weekend and night travel on the line.

The first interurban streetcar line in this country connected the cities of Granville and Newark, Ohio, beginning in 1889, and the first

high-speed interurban trolleys ran between Cleveland and Akron in 1895. Within a few decades, many of America's cities, large and small, were linked by streetcar lines, especially in Ohio, Indiana, Illinois, and Michigan. No burgeoning town was considered major league until it was connected by streetcar line with at least one neighboring city.

Early in this century, it was possible to ride by trolley from New York all the way to Boston for less than four dollars! Of course, there were frequent changes of line.

The longest continuous streetcar route—again with frequent changes of line—ran from Freeport, Illinois to Utica, New York, a distance of over 1,000 miles!

One Colorado line climbed over a 10,000-foot peak to reach the mining boomtown of Cripple Creek.

With even the fastest modern trains rarely exceeding sixty miles per hour, it now seems hard to believe that the normal operating speed of the interurban streetcar lines was *eighty miles per hour*.

Incredible as it seems, cars of the Crandic Line between Cedar Rapids and Iowa City in Iowa once claimed tops speeds of 110 miles per hour!

Within the city, streetcars were the first motor-driven means of public transportation. Streetcars provided the first dependable intracity travel in the days before the bus, auto, and subway. Dependable,

The first New York streetcar was built in 1831.

yes; fast, often not. The first streetcar in this country, in fact, was powered by only a few horsepower—provided by, yes, a few horses!

This horse-drawn conveyance was constructed by John Stephenson in Philadelphia, and placed in service in New York City in 1832 by the New York and Harlem Railway. Called the *John Mason* after a prominent banker who had organized the railroad company, the car seated thirty passengers in three unconnected compartments. It ran between Prince Street and Fourteenth Street in Manhattan, with a later extension to uptown Manhattan. The fare was a then rather steep twelve-and-a-half cents. No, we don't know what the conductor did for change of a penny if you didn't want a round- trip ticket.

The earliest electric trolleys were powered by storage batteries,

---

The first trackless trolley began service in 1910 in Los Angeles. Despite its present automobile mania, LA once boasted one of the nation's finest streetcar systems.

---

which proved expensive and inefficient. The first electrified streetcar tracks, too, often short-circuited in the rain.

One of the world's first electric lines was constructed in London in 1860 by the American G.F. Train—that's right, Train—with two more tramlines following shortly after in that city. But it was the invention of the electric generator that led to the application of transmitted power to streetcar lines and fostered the proliferation of tramlines throughout Europe and the United States.

There are three kinds of electric streetcars. One is drawn by cable, another powered by an electrified third rail; and the third is powered by overhead transmission lines, with the car connected to the power lines by a collapsible apparatus called the *trolley*. Strictly speaking, then, only a streetcar powered by overhead lines can be called a "trolley."

There are two varieties of trolley system, one utilizing two over-

Rush-hour crowds were a problem even in 1872, in the days of horse cars.

head wires—the European preference—and the second using one wire and one electrified track to complete the electric circuit. The later type is the overwhelming favorite of American lines.

Berlin got its first electric tramway in 1881, Budapest in 1897, and Paris in 1901. A gas-powered streetcar was placed in operation in Providence, Rhode Island in 1872, while the first commercially owned electric streetcars in this country plied their course in Baltimore in 1885. The first "soundless, shockless" tracks were laid in New Orleans in 1930.

The famed San Francisco cable cars were the world's first cable-drawn cars. The Bay City's cable car was invented by Andrew Hallidie, and introduced in 1873 on Sacramento and Clay Streets.

Cable cars are drawn by an endless cable that runs in a slot between the rails. Cable cars are best suited for steeply inclined streets—thus, their early popularity in San Francisco and Seattle. But a cable car can run only at a constant speed, and a cable jam can stop every car on the line.

The Constantinople trolley was making its rounds in the 1870's.

By the turn of the century, most cable car lines had been replaced by electric trackage, although Seattle retained its system until the 1930's.

The San Francisco cable car lines still operating today are maintained chiefly as tourist attractions, with most lines long-since replaced by buses or trolleybus systems.

Streetcar lines in general began to rapidly disappear in the 1930's, in the face of competition from cars and buses. An intermediate step in the trolley-to-bus transition was the trackless trolley, a buslike vehicle that ran without tracks but was powered by electricity from overhead lines, like the trolley. The first trackless trolley began service in 1910 in Los Angeles. Despite its present automobile mania, LA once boasted one of the nation's finest streetcar systems. Brooklyn, New York maintained trackless trolleys as late as the 1950's.

London did away with its last trolley in the 50's; Paris had ripped up its streetcar tracks about twenty years earlier. Today, the streetcar is virtually extinct in America, but the trolley is still widely used in

Germany, Austria, Switzerland, and Eastern Europe.

But trolley-lovers, take heart. You can still catch a glimpse of the ancient streetcar in various museums throughout the country. The museum in East Hartford, Connecticut contains ninety-two trolleys,

In the 1870's, steam-powered trams provided public transportation in Paris.

With even the fastest modern trains rarely exceeding sixty miles per hour, it now seems hard to believe that the normal operating speed of the interurban streetcar lines was eighty miles per hour.

ranging from some 1880 relics to a New York model from the 1930's. In that museum, trolley buffs can ride an open-sided car—complete with bell—over a two-mile route.

Streetcars were inexpensive to construct and clean. Although dependable, they were not without disadvantages. Among these was the danger posed to idle strollers by a speeding trolley. The Brooklyn Dodgers of baseball fame were not so-named because of their agility on the playing field. Initially, the team was called the "Trolley Dodgers," in tribute to the maze of trolley lines crisscrossing Brooklyn at the height of the streetcar era.

Early in this century, it was possible to ride by trolley from New York to Boston for less than four dollars!

SUBWAYS

Though New York's subway is today the world's most famous—or infamous—it was not, as many people believe, the first ever constructed . . . . For the world's first underground rapid transit system we must journey to Londontown.

"Preposterous!" scoffed American tycoon Russell Sage to the first proposal for an underground transit system in New York City. "The people of New York will never go into a hole in the ground to ride."

Well, as everyone knows, Russell's counsel turned out to be less than sage. By the time of his death in 1906, subway cars were already rattling through Manhattan's first tunnel, with work proceeding on new lines in three boroughs. And every year, close to *two billion* people "go into a hole to ride" in New York City.

Though New York's subway is today the world's most famous— or infamous—it was not, as many people believe, the first ever constructed. Actually, it was the sixth to begin operation, and the second in this country. For the world's first underground rapid transit system we must journey to Londontown.

By the mid-nineteenth century, a traveler could ride by train from London's rail terminals to almost any point in England. But travel within the city itself still relied chiefly on horse-drawn streetcars and carriages. The rail lines that brought travelers to London did not reach into the city's main business and commercial center, and since the railroads and terminals were for the most part constructed by rival rail companies, there was no convenient means of transit between one depot and another.

Shortly after the opening of Marc Brunel's Thames Tunnel in 1843 had demonstrated the viability of underground rail travel, London city solicitor Charles Pearson proposed an underground railway connecting some of the city's major railroad depots. After ten years of talk, Parliament authorized the first line: a three-and-a-quarter-mile run between Paddington Station and Farringdon Road, by way of King's Cross Station.

Travel is broadening, but for the subway traveler it is flattening.

Construction was of the "cut and cover" method still used for the great majority of lines: first, a trench is dug in the street, tracks are laid at the bottom of the trench; then the trench is covered by the reconstructed street.

After three years of construction, London's first line opened on January 10, 1863. It was powered by steam locomotives fueled by coke. Despite the sulfurous smoke spewed into the tunnel by the locomotives, the "underground" was an immediate success, attracting 30,000 riders on its first day of operation, and well over 9 million during its first year.

To appreciate the English feat, remember that with a comparatively limited technology, the builders of the first subway had completed in less than three years a project that even today would require years of effort. And this despite a flood that at one point filled the ex-

Londoners stroll in the new high level Metropolitan railway station at the Crystal Palace in 1865.

The Kensington underground station was one of five new links in London's chain of Metropolitan railways. It was on the Circle Line, completed in 1884.

cavation to a depth of ten feet! Today, the London Underground is over 100 years old, but is still in excellent condition.

This line, called the "Metropolitan," was gradually lengthened over the following decades, and remained the only subway in the world for close to thirty years. But 1890 saw the opening of London's second underground line, and the first "tube tunnel" in the world. In a tube line, a tunnel is actually bored through the ground, under the building foundations.

The 1890 tube line was immediately popular, with electric power freeing the deep tunnels of noxious fumes. A trip on the three- mile line cost two pence, but the fare bought little in the way of a view. Subway cars of the time were built without windows, since in the opinion of their designers, there was simply nothing to look at in a tunnel.

On a tube line, the stations must be located far underground. The greatest depth of the London system is 221 feet, but no station is more than 100 feet underground. Thus dozens of elevators, or "lifts" as they're called in England, are needed to carry passengers between the street and the tube platform—not the most efficient way to keep people on the move, considering there might be a ten- minute wait for a rush-hour lift.

At one time, there were 240 lifts throughout the London underground system, but with the invention of a satisfactory escalator in 1911, the number of lifts began to dwindle. One escalator can do the work of five elevators, eliminating the waiting lines that plagued the earliest London tubes. Today, there are less than 100 lifts in operation in the London subway system.

On the other side of the Atlantic, the streetcar and the elevated railway were the favored forms of urban transportation until the turn of the century. The nation's first elevated line, or "El," had opened on Manhattan's Ninth Avenue in 1867, with a cable-drive system. In 1871, there was a switch to steam locomotives. The nation's first electric El did not appear until 1895, in Chicago.

The subway may not serve a humanitarian purpose, but it certainly brings people closer together.

In a rush-hour subway train, a gentleman bent over and murmured to the young lady standing beside him, "I beg your pardon, but would you like me to find a strap for you?"

"I have a strap," she retorted icily.

"Then please let go of my necktie!"

While New Yorkers were debating the pros and cons of an underground system like the one then operating in London, Boston rushed ahead with the nation's first subway. Completed in 1897, the Boston line initially ran one-and-a-half miles under Tremont Street, with trolley cars the first vehicles to ride the subway tracks.

By that time, New York had an intricate system of elevated lines. An underground line was thought to be impractical for the Big Apple, because of the hard granite rock that forms most of Manhattan Island.

The subway has put women on an equal standing with men.

After 3 years of construction, London's first line opened on January 10, 1863. . . . the "underground" was an immediate success, attracting 30,000 riders on its first day of operation, and well over 9 million during its first year.

As plans were put forward for the first underground line in the city, skeptics like Russell Sage warned that the project would prove a disaster. Property owners claimed that their buildings would collapse. The city's water board expressed fears that construction would destroy the underground water pipe system.

But the subway proponents held sway; and in 1904, the first New York subway began operation—without the collapse of any thing at all. The line ran from City Hall in Downtown Manhattan to the Grand Central Terminal in Midtown, then west to Times Square and then north to 145th Street. Another line was added almost immediate-

A rotund woman in a crowded subway stepped on the foot of a gent who was trying to read his newspaper. "Madam," he snapped coldly, "kindly get off my foot."

"Then put your foot where it belongs," the woman snapped back.

"Don't tempt me, Madam, don't tempt me," he replied.

ly, extending to 180th Street in the Bronx; but it took until 1908 for the subway to touch the shores of Brooklyn.

The London system was and still is called the *underground*, but American rapid transit pioneers had to search for an alternative term. "Underground Railroad" to most Americans suggested the network of secret way-stations that brought escaped slaves North before the Civil War; so the word *subway* was born of necessity.

The first New York subway lines, like their London counterparts, were built by competing companies, and remained privately owned until the city took over in 1940. The IRT (Interborough Rapid Transit) was the first rapid transit company in the city, operating the maiden line from City Hall and most of the Manhattan and Bronx elevated lines. The BMT (Brooklyhn and Manhattan Transit) was constructed from 1913 to 1920, and included most of the Brooklyn elevated lines. Oddly enough, the Independent Line (IND) was the only line never to be independently owned, built by the city in the 1930's.

We mentioned that the New York City system was the world's

Several French Métro station entrances are decorated with art nouveau fixtures.

Photo courtesy of the French Embassy Press and Information Division.

sixth underground railway, with London and Boston two of its predecessors. The other three? Well, the Glasgow subway was the second to be completed, opening in 1891. The Scottish line, still in operation, runs over a six-and-a-half-mile oval that never reaches the surface. Only one other subway line in the world never reaches daylight: London's Waterloo and City. On both lines, cars have to be lifted by elevator to repair shops and sidings.

In 1896, Budapest opened the first subway on the European continent, running single cars over a two-and-a-half-mile electric line. In 1900, Paris opened its first *métro*, the world's fifth, a six-and-a-quarter-mile line.

Philadelphia was the third American city to build a subway, opening its first line in 1907. Chicago, which already had a large el network, was to wait until 1943 for its first underground.

Subways were opened in Buenos Aires in 1913, in Tokyo in 1927, in Moscow in the 1930's, and in Toronto in 1954.

At present, there are sixty-seven cities operating underground rail lines of some kind. In addition to those already mentioned, there are underground transit lines in Madrid, Barcelona, Oslo, Rotterdam, Stockholm, Hamburg, Berlin, Lisbon, Milan, Rome, Kiev, and Leningrad in Europe; Osaka, Kyoto, and Nagoya in Asia; Sydney in Australia; and Mexico City and Montreal in North America.

Subway travel is the most uncomfortable distance between two points.

Construction is now proceeding on subway lines in a number of cities, including additions to the New York, London, and Paris systems. New systems are planned for Prague, Munich, Cologne, Cairo, Helsinki, Kharkov, and other cities. In America, San Francisco and Washington, D.C. have recently installed subways and Atlanta is to follow suit in the 1980's.

By the way, recent work on a new subway line in Rome has produced some unexpected benefits: excavators have discovered extensive underground ruins dating from the days of the Roman Empire. Most

Photo courtesy of the New York Board of Transit.

finds have been removed and placed on exhibit at the Termini Station.

Among all underground systems in operation today, London's is the most extensive, with 252 miles of track (77 bored tunnel, 24 cut-and-cover, and 151 outdoor) and 279 stations. A 600-train fleet with over 4,000 cars carries some 600 million passengers each year, with the one-day record standing at 2,073,134 on VE Day, 1945.

The longest continuous subway tunnel in the world stretches over seventeen miles from Morden to East Finchley in London. Compare

Construction on New York City's Sixth Avenue subway line was begun in the 1930's. The Sixth Avenue Line was completed on December 15, 1940.

An advertisement of "The Tube" by the British
Transport.

Why not use the "L?" *Egg tempera on canva*
by Reginald Marsh.
Courtesy of Whitney Museum of American Art, New Yor

New York subway riders are depicted in this
drawing by David Levine.

Riddle: **What's a place full of people**
who have no trouble making ends meet?
Answer: **A crowded subway.**

that with the longest main-line railroad tunnel in the world—the Simplon, at just over twelve miles—and the longest road tunnel, the Mt. Blanc, which is just over seven miles.

The New York system is shorter in track mileage, but far and away the busiest in the world, serving about four-and-a-half million passengers on an average weekday and over two billion a year. This massive system—one of the few to remain in operation around the clock—spans 230 miles, with 462 stations, and its 134 miles of tunnel form the largest underground network in the world.

The Paris *Métro* is 105 miles long, less than half of the London system, yet the Paris system attracts nearly twice as many passengers—over a billion each year. Some 270 closely spaced stations leave no point in the central area of the city more than 600 yards from the *Métro*!

Modern subway cars have come a long way from the early English windowless models. Those being built in America are for the most part sleek and air-conditioned, and much quieter than their forerunners. Subway stations, too, are now more imaginatively designed. In the Montreal subway, for example, an artist was commissioned to design each station, while the stations of the Moscow subway are marvels, bedecked with marble columns and elegant chandeliers.

And speaking of modern innovations, the first subway line to operate automatically without conductor or motorman began operation in New York in 1962, running between Grand Central Station and Times Square. But the city's Transit Worker's Union won a demand to place a nonfunctional motorman in each train; and today, the line is run manually, like the city's other lines. Since 1963, an automatic line has been in operation in London, running four miles between Woodford and Hainault. The San Francisco system is largely automated.

But long after the last engineers and conductors have given way to automation, the underground enthusiast will still be around to pass along subway lore. One subway buff set a record in 1968 by visiting every station in the London system in just fifteen hours! Five years later, two other determined individuals established the New York record by traveling to each of the 462 stations in just 21 hours, 8½ minutes. It takes some people almost as long just to decipher the New York system's maps!

TELEPHONES

The telephone is the greatest nuisance among conveniences, and the greatest convenience among nuisances.

"I believe," wrote Alexander Graham Bell in 1878, "that in the future wires will unite the head offices of the Telephone Company in different cities, and a man in one part of the country may communicate by word of mouth with another in a distant place. I am aware that such ideas may appear to you Utopian."

Well, if that's the case, we're now living in Utopia. Today, any American can pick up a phone and communicate not only with any other telephone in the country, but with almost any phone in the entire world—by direct dialing! The telephone has indeed brought the world to our fingertips and broadened the boundaries of our senses. Any temptation to underestimate the importance of the telephone in our lives can be quickly remedied by considering the efficiency of the modern postal system. In short, our lives would not be the same without that tool, toy, and infernal intruder, the telephone.

The man who wrote those prophetic words in 1878 is, of course, the individual most credited with the invention of the telephone. But Alexander Graham Bell was neither the first to conceptualize a voice-transmission device nor the first to design one. He was, quite simply, the first to patent one.

Before Bell began his work, other inventors in the United States and Europe had worked on systems for sound transmission to distant points. Philip Reis, laboring in Frankfurt in the 1860's, devised a crude voice-transmission apparatus employing, at the transmitting end, a diaphragm structure that controlled an electric current. At the receiving end, the electric current governed a magnetized needle that vibrated a sounding board. But twenty years later, the German patent office decided that Reis's apparatus was not a true "speaking telephone."

Alexander Graham Bell was born in Scotland in 1847. He resided in England and Canada before moving at a young age to the United States. At twenty-five, he became a teacher of the deaf at a Boston school; and the next year, a professor of vocal physiology at Boston University. At the time, Bell lived with the Sanders family in Boston, serving as a private tutor for the Sanders' deaf-mute child. He set up a workshop in the basement of the Sanders home for experiments that he hoped would lead to a "musical telegraph."

The telephone enables you to hold a long, relaxed conversation without being interrupted by the ringing of the telephone.

Bell worked mainly at night in his basement laboratory, alone and

This is the telephone into which Alexander Graham Bell uttered the historic words, "Mr. Watson, come here; I want you," on March 10, 1876. The receiver was constructed from a tuned reed.

The first commercial telephone, developed by Bell in 1876, was leased in 1877 by a Boston banker who wanted telephone service between his home and office.

In 1878, Francis Blake, Jr. invented this transmitter, which greatly improved telephone service. The instrument employed carbon to transmit sound with increased clarity.

in secrecy, for he knew that many other inventors were then engaged in similar experimentation. To guard his work, he traveled around Boston to buy his supplies in various stores. "Often in the middle of the night," Sanders later wrote, "Bell would wake me up, his black eyes blazing with excitement."

The inventor eventually lost his professorship and most of his students due to his preoccupation with telephone experimentation. Most of his friends who were familiar with his work urged him to abandon it. "If I can make a deaf-mute talk," Bell countered, "surely I can make iron talk." With money from his father-in-law and Sanders, Bell moved into a shop in Boston and hired an assistant, Thomas Watson, to pursue his dream of a "musical telegraph."

On June 2, 1875, Bell first heard over a wire the twang of a clock spring operated by Watson in another room. He then knew he was close to harnessing undulating electric currents capable of transmitting speech. Bell's rudimentary apparatus did, in fact, transmit speech the following day.

In February, 1876, Bell filed a patent for his invention. Meanwhile, Bell kept at work to perfect the device. On March 10, 1876, the first complete sentence ever transmitted by telephone reached Bell's assistant in the basement: "Mr. Watson, come here; I want you." Bell received his patent soon after—at the age of 29!

In his patent application, Bell called his invention "an improvement of the telegraph." His wife suggested the name *telephone*, which had long been in use to describe many sound-transmitting devices, such as the "string telephone" invented by Robert Hooke in 1667. When his patent was filed, Bell probably had no idea how close others were to perfecting a similar device. Elisha Gray filed a caveat (notice of intent to file a patent) a *few hours* after Bell applied for his patent. And Thomas Edison had been on the verge of success with his own telephone, when distracted by other work. The stakes? Bell's patent has been called the most valuable ever issued anywhere!

Western Union, the telegraph company, offered Bell $100,000 for his patent in 1887, but Bell rejected the offer. Western Union went on to develop its own telephone system based on the work of Gray and Edison, but an 1878 court decision ruled that Bell had sole patent rights to the telephone. Litigation involving over 600 separate cases

American phones now register about 200 billion calls per year, or about 1,400 calls per phone.

dragged on for years. Finally, the Supreme Court upheld Bell's claim for exclusive ownership.

By modern standards, the earliest telephones were crude, and conversations were barely intelligible. Many technological advances were necessary to produce the telephone we use today. In the beginning, phones were sold in pairs so that any telephone could connect with only one other.

The first commercial switchboard appeared in 1878 in New Haven, Connecticut, linking twenty-one phones.

Telephone lines were quickly strung throughout this country and Europe by Bell's company and others. By 1890, there were already 225,000 phones in use here, and there were 26,000 in Great Britain, and 22,000 in Germany. The first pay telephone reared its coin-snatching head in 1889, in Hartford, Connecticut.

The first telephone directory was in the hands of New Haven phone users in 1878—listing only fifty names.

At first, various telephone companies competed directly with one another in the United States, without provisions for link-ups. Mergers and acquisitions gradually unified the systems, so that by 1950, 82 percent of all American phones were served by the Bell System. Bell's parent corporation, American Telephone & Telegraph, today ranks as the firm with the greatest number of individual shareholders: 2,934,000 in early 1976—more than twice the number of its closest rival, General Motors. Altogether, the 582 million listed shares of AT&T stock now have a market value of almost $30 billion!

By 1900, long before the introduction of direct dialing, there were already 1.3 million phones in the United States. By 1910, the number had soared to 7.6 million; and by 1920, when "Number, please" was still the most common phrase heard through the telephone receiver, there were 13.3 million.

By the early 1950's, there were some 53 million phones in opera-

This ancestor of the upright desk set was made in 1897, and was a refinement of earlier models.

The built-in generator mechanism on this 1907 model telephone provided current for signalling the operator. Another innovation of 1907 was enclosed receiver terminals.

"Number please?" was the standard greeting of Bell operators at the main office in Kansas City, Missouri in 1904.

If there were no such thing as extrasensory perception, how would people know you're in the bathtub when they call you on the telephone?

tion here, one for every three persons. By the mid-70's, 144 million phones were in use throughout the nation. American phones now register about 200 billion calls per year, or about 1,400 calls per phone.

Today, there are some 360 million telephones in use around the world, with the United States by far the leader in phone ownership. Japan has about 35 million phones in service, Britain 19 million, West Germany 16, Italy 11, France 10, and the Soviet Union an estimated 18 million. At the other end of the scale, the Pitcairn Islands in the South Pacific can boast only twenty-nine telephones.

The nation with the highest per capita phone ownership is the tiny principality of Monaco, with 825 phones per 1,000 persons, compared with about 670 in the United States. The nation with the lowest per capita phone use is the Himalayan kingdom of Bhutan, with just one phone per 2,000 persons!

New York is far and away the world's top-ranking city in sheer numbers of phones, but the municipality with the most phones per capita is Washington, D.C., with 1,358 phones per 1,000 persons. Incidentally, the state with the least phones per capita is Mississippi, with about 500 phones per 1,000 persons—but the nation ranking second in telephone use, Japan, can claim only 320 phones per 1,000 persons.

Surely, you've often wondered where the world's busiest telephone might be found. Well, at last glance, that honor belongs to a phone in the Greyhound bus terminal in Chicago, whose bell ting-a-lings about 270 times each day!

The word *phony*, by the way, may or may not owe something to Bell's invention. A New York paper once reported that "phony implies that a thing so qualified has no more substance than a telephone talk with a supposititious friend." But most dictionaries trace the word to the expression *fawney rig*, British slang for a valueless ring.

The first commercial transatlantic telephone service was inaugurated between New York and London in 1927—with a charge of seventy-five dollars for the first three minutes—but the first round- the-world telephone conversation did not take place until 1935. Round the world? Well, the call was placed in New York, routed via San Francisco, Java, Amsterdam, and London, and received in an office only fifty feet from the caller's!

Not surprisingly, there was only one person in the world capable of such telephone extravagance—the president of the American Telephone & Telegraph Corporation.

Why is it that the wrong number on a telephone is never busy?

The latest word in telephones is the single-level Touch-a-matic telephone with Touch-Tone dialing.

TOBACCO

Sir Walter Raleigh has been
credited with introducing
tobacco to the English.

"The pipe draws wisdom from the lips of the philosopher, and shuts up the mouth of the foolish," wrote W.M. Thackeray a hundred years ago; and to this day, pipe smoking retains a certain connotation of sophistication. The hoi polloi may take their tobacco by cigarette or cigar, but a true connoisseur of the brown leaf wouldn't think of any means of fumigation aside from the pipe. Perhaps the veneration of pipe smoking stems partly from its long popularity, for centuries in Europe, the pipe was virtually the only means of tobacco smoking.

The common myth about the introduction of tobacco in Europe credits Sir Walter Raleigh with bringing the leaf from Virginia to England in the late sixteenth century. True, Raleigh's tobacco created an immediate sensation at the court of Elizabeth I, but tobacco smoking actually first came to Europe by quite another means, involving neither the English nor the North American Indian.

Christopher Columbus observed the Indians of the Caribbean smoking tobacco, writing of "men with half-burnt wood in their hands." According to one story, the first European to smoke was Rodrigo de Jerez, one of Columbus's crew members, who sampled tobacco in the West Indies and brought a pinch home with him to Spain. Jerez's wife, so the tale goes, later denounced him to the Inquisition as a man who "swallows fire, exhales smoke, and is surely possessed by the devil."

Spanish explorers in Mexico found the Aztecs smoking crushed tobacco leaves in corn husks. Tobacco reached the European continent at least as early as 1558, when a Spanish physician named Francisco Fernandes, sent to the New World by King Philip II to report on its products, brought back some plants and seeds. The following year, Jean Nicot, the French ambassador to Portugal, sent tobacco seeds to the French court of Catherine de Medici. The queen reported that tobacco cured her of crippling headaches, and she immortalized Nicot by proclaiming the new plant *Nicotiana*, a name recognizable in our word for tobacco's most baleful element, nicotine.

Sir Walter Raleigh may not have been the first to introduce tobacco in England. Some historians claim that one John Hawkins brought back the leaf in 1565 after a voyage to Florida. In any case, we know that Sir Walter had a large hand in popularizing tobacco smoking in Europe.

At Myrtle Grove, Sir Walter Raleigh was soothing his mind with the tobacco he had brought from Virginia, when his Irish servant, thinking his master was on fire, dashed water on him.

Raleigh sent Sir Francis Drake on an expedition to colonize Roanoke Island, North Carolina, in 1585. When the expedition failed, Drake returned to Europe. He brought some tobacco and smoking implements to Sir Walter, who soon became the most notorious smoker in Renaissance England. According to one story, Raleigh lit a pipe before Queen Elizabeth and was promptly rewarded with a dousing by a member of the court who thought Sir Walter was on fire. A die-hard smoker indeed, Raleigh even "tooke a pipe of tobacco a little before he went to the scaffolde."

By 1600, the "dry drink" was fashionable in much of Europe. Many pipe smokers of the time carried hand-carved tobacco rammers, used to press the shredded leaf into the pipe bowl. Some of the more ornate rammers doubled as large finger rings. Smokers also had to carry ember tongs to hold the burning embers of juniper wood used to light their pipes.

Cigarettes were little known at the time. It was the beggars of Seville who get credit for creating the first paper-wrapped smokes.

Seventeenth-century doctors prescribed tobacco as a cure-all, fashioning the leaf into pills, plasters, poultices, oils, salts, tinctures, and balms. During the London plague of the 1660's, many people smoked tobacco as a preventive. Even in the later part of the century, doctors continued to prescribe the leaf for such disparate ailments as hiccoughs, imbecility, jaundice, corpulence, syphilis, and "general lousiness,"—for everything except a bad cough.

Some physicians even recommended a tobacco-smoke enema for various ailments. The enema—administered with a device known as the Clyster pipe—was said by one doctor to be "excellent good against colic." And James I of England proclaimed that the Clyster pipe was the only way to take one's tobacco. Well, different smokes for different folks.

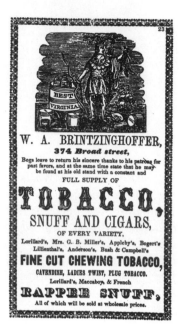
Philip Morris's "Marlboro" remains the most popular cigarette on earth, the 136 billion sold annually making the entire world "Marlboro Country."

It's odd that James would comment favorably on tobacco, in any form or guise, since the monarch had always been a bitter foe of the leaf. In his *Counterblast to Tobacco*, James described smoking as "a custom loathsome to the eye, hateful to the nose, harmful to the brain, dangerous to the lungs, and the black stinking fume thereof nearest resembling the horrible Stygian smoke of the pit that is bottomless." And you thought the Surgeon General was harsh on tobacco!

Tobacco cultivation was important in the American colonies from their earliest history. In fact, before the Revolution, tobacco was legal tender in several Southern colonies with large plantations. Virginia enacted a law ordaining that taxes be paid in tobacco. George Washington, you'll remember, was reported to have written from Valley Forge: "If you can't send men, send tobacco."

American cigarette manufacture dates from the Civil War, when Greek and Turkish tobacconists in New York City began hand-rolling expensive imported tobaccos. By that time, the cigarette—from the Spanish *cigarito*—was already the favored tobacco product in some parts of Europe. It wasn't until the 1880's, when natural leaf cigarettes made from domestic tobaccos began to dominate the market

Photo courtesy of Philip Morris.

Courtesy of Philip Morris.

and machine-rolled butts first replaced the hand-rolled varieties that cigarettes became affordable by all. Yet cigars and pipes remained more popular until 1920. By the 1950's, cigarettes accounted for over 80 percent of all American tobacco consumption.

In the early days of cigarette manufacture, a factory worker could hand-roll about 18,000 cigarettes per week. Crude machines for cigarette-rolling began to appear in the mid-1870's. In the following decade, the machines replaced hand-rollers almost completely, with one machine doing the job of fifty workers. A modern machine can turn out about 1,500 cigarettes per minute, or 36,000 packs in an eight-hour day.

In 1880, American cigarette production stood at a mere half billion. By 1895, the figure had soared to 4 billion. A large increase following World War I pushed the figure up to 124 billion. Another big rise after World War II brought the total to 400 billion. In 1975, cancer not withstanding, American cigarette consumption passed the 600-billion mark for the first time.

Has the increased awareness of the dangers of tobacco smoking lowered cigarette use to any great extent? In 1964, the year of the Sur-

From the 1850's, tobacco connoisseurs have shopped at the original Philip Morris store on Bond Street, London.

In 1933, a diminutive bellboy named Johnny immortalized Philip Morris cigarettes with his famous "Call for Phil-lip Mor-ress."

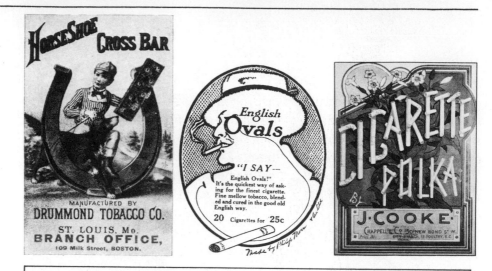

In the early days of the tobacco industry, as today, manufacturers vied with each other in creating eye-catching advertisements.

geon General's first warning regarding smoking, 52 percent of all men of presumed smoking age were regular smokers; by 1976, the figure stood at only 32 percent. But smoking among women showed an increase over the same period, and total consumption has risen since 1971. By 1975, there were an estimated 30 million former-smokers among the ranks of the non-smokers, with some 50 million persons still clinging to the habit.

Despite the Surgeon General's warning—repeated on every pack of American cigarettes—the United States still leads the world in per capita cigarette smoking. In 1973, the average American fifteen years of age or older smoked 3,812 cigarettes—that's about a half pack daily for each person, and well over a pack for each smoker. Japan is close behind with 3,270 cigarettes per capita annually, the United Kingdom third with 3,190, and Italy fourth with 2,774. West Germany, Denmark, and Sweden round out the top seven.

Cigarettes today are sold in three basic sizes—regular non-filter, regular filter, and 100-mm. king size—but in the past, butts have been sold in a wide range of sizes. In the 1930's, when cigarettes were taxed individually in some places, to save tax, one manufacturer brought out "Head Plays," each cigarette eleven inches long.

"Lilliput" cigarettes only one-and-a-quarter inches long appeared in England in the 1950's. And "English Ovals" are just that—oval in shape instead of round.

Philip Morris's *Marlboro* remains the most popular cigarette on earth, the 136 billion sold annually making the entire world "Marlboro Country."

Long before cigarettes became popular here, the pipe was well entrenched. Pipe smoking was common even among women for a time, and the wives of two American presidents—Andrew Jackson and Zachary Taylor—were wont to light up in the White House. Women pipe smokers are still numerous in China, where cigarettes are rarely encountered outside the major cities.

Speaking of female pipe smokers, perhaps you've heard the one about the young lady who retired to the cafeteria during her coffee break and lit up a pipe. "That's a despicable habit," remarked an elderly woman sitting nearby. "I would rather commit adultery than smoke!"

One day, Dr. Creighton, Bishop of London, was riding on a train with a meek curate. The Bishop who ardently loved his tobacco, took out his cigar case, turned to his companion, and said with a smile, "You don't mind my smoking, do you?"

The curate bowed, and answered humbly, "Not if Your Lordship doesn't mind my being sick."

IT TAKES AGE TO JUDGE

M&O CIGAR

Early cigar advertisements portrayed the stogie as the gentleman's smoke.

Thomas Edison once complained to his friends that his business acquaintances and associates would drop into his office, help themselves to his pure Havana cigars, and just take off. They would just take them by the handful, he said.

"Well," said his friend, "Why don't you lock them up in a humidor?"

"Well, I would find that rather inconvenient. As far as I'm concerned, I wouldn't fancy having them under lock and key. But a friend of mine thought of a clever trick. He knew a cigarmaker, and he had him make me a few boxes of cigars out of cabbage leaves and brown paper. My friend was sure that would fix the freeloaders.

"But that didn't seem to help either; and after my Havanas started disappearing again, I spoke to my secretary, and asked her what happened to those two new boxes of cabbage cheroots."

"Why, I sent those two boxes to your home," she said. When Edison asked his wife about the two new boxes of cigars, she said, "Well dear, when you went to California last month, I put them in your trunk."

"Well," confessed Edison, "you wouldn't believe it, but I smoked every one of those damned cigars."

Cheap, foul-smelling cigars burn much more evenly than expensive cigars. That's life.
—Douglas Yates

"So would I," answered the young lady, "but there just isn't enough time during a coffee break."

The first men—or women—to smoke probably managed without any implements at all, simply inhaling smoke billowing from a bonfire of burning leaves. The Greek historian Herodotus reported that certain Scythian tribes "drank smoke" from a fire, inhaling the fumes of what was most likely marijuana.

The first pipe fashioned by man was probably a tube pipe, a simple hollow cylinder of wood or bone. Tube pipes have been found in almost every cranny of civilization, some dating back as far as 200 B.C. And the use of a curled-up leaf as a makeshift tube pipe later led to the invention of the cigar.

In some cultures, the earliest pipe was the "mound pipe," a small mound of earth with a depression hollowed out on top to hold the tobacco, and hollow reeds protruding through the mound as rudimentary pipe stems. To make use of a mound pipe, the smoker had to lie on the ground on his belly and slip the reed through his lips. These primitive pipes were still being used by Indian soldiers in World War I.

The Indians of South America frequently built communal mound pipes, with as many as 150 people gathering around to share a smoke. When the first reed and clay pipes appeared among the Indian tribes, smoking was still regarded as a communal pastime. Thus arose the custom of passing the pipe around among the group.

Europeans exploring America in the sixteenth century found some Indians smoking a kind of tube pipe shaped like the letter "Y"—the smoker inserted the two upper prongs of the pipe into his nostrils and aimed the lower tube at a mound of burning leaves. Archaeologists in Africa have found tube pipes made of clay or reed measuring up to six feet long.

Indians of the Central United States carved stone pipes with either straight or curved stems. They smoked a blend they called *kinnikinnik*, made of tobacco, sumac leaves, and the bark of the willow tree. The Indians, who considered tobacco a sacred herb and regarded smoking as a sacred art, frequently shaped their pipe bowls in the form of animals and other totems. Historians have been unable to explain why some pipes found in the ruins of ancient Indian settlements were carved in the form of elephants and sea cows, two creatures the Indians had presumably never seen.

An African "earth smoker" fashions a pipe by pushing a stick through the soil to a pit in the ground that serves as the pipe-bowl. (Drawing after Henry Balfour, from The Pipe Book *by Alfred Dunhill).*

The Indian calumet, or peace pipe.

The hooka, an Oriental water pipe.

The calumet, or peace pipe, was usually a long, slender pipe with a wooden stem and a shorter stone end-piece containing the bowl. The calumet was considered a token of peace and friendship, and pioneers exploring the American West often took along calumets in the event they ran into hostile Indians. No instance has ever been recorded of an Indian violating the peace-pipe compact.

Incidentally, the word *tobacco* comes from the Indian word for the tube of the calumet, not from their name for the plant. When East Coast Indians introduced smoking to the Europeans, they presented their pipe and repeated the word *tobacco* to urge the stranger to put the calumet tube in his lips. The Europeans naturally assumed the Indians were referring to the substance they were smoking, and the leaf was forever after known as tobacco.

The water pipe, a popular means of smoking in the Near East for centuries, was probably invented by the Persians for smoking hashish. The earliest water pipes were called *nargeelehs*, from the Arabic word for coconut, since the coconut was used as the base for the first hydro-cooled fumigators. Later, the Arabs fashioned more elaborate pipes from glass crystal.

The *hookah* is a kind of water pipe with a number of flexible stems, called *narbeeshes*, each from six to thirty inches long. British officers in India often employed servants called *burdars*, whose sole duty was to attend to their master's *hookah*.

In a water pipe, smoke is drawn from the bowl into the base, where it is cooled by water vapor and then drawn through the stem. Some Persian men were so partial to the taste of smoke-flavored water that they regularly forced their wives to smoke four or five bowlfuls of tobacco or hashish in succession to produce a well-flavored drink.

The earliest pipes popular in Europe were made from clay. Clay pipes with small bowls were favored in England, the story goes, because in the first days of tobacco smoking the Englishman's desire for the leaf far outpaced the supply; to indulge frequently, then, the Englishman had to content himself with a small pinch at each light-up.

The clay pipe had the distinct disadvantage of heating up rapidly, which might also explain why its bowl was so small. The French, true to form, developed clay-pipe making to a fine art, molding their pipe bowls to depict religious, military, and domestic scenes.

There were two basic types of clay pipe popular in seventeenth-century England, the cutty and the churchwarden. The small cutty, equipped with a stem of about three inches, was the more popular among the general populace, selling for as little as three for a penny. But the cutty stem was often so short that a pipe took on the nickname of "nose warmer."

The churchwarden was fitted with a stem of some eight to ten inches, and a more decorated bowl. As a rule, the wealthy opted for the churchwarden, and frequently bought elegant cases in which to carry their prize pipes. When the lower classes began smoking church-wardens to emulate the rich, the case was still beyond their means, so

The Church Warden's pipe, made of clay, has an ultra-long stem to cool the smoke.

Contented I sit with my pint and my pipe,
 Puffing sorrow and care far away,
And surely the brow of grief nothing can wipe,
 Like smoking and moist'ning our clay; . . .
For tho' at my simile many may joke,
Man's but a pipe—and his life but smoke.
—Unknown

many an Englishman took to carrying his long pipe in a hole cut through his hat brim.

Washington Irving, in his *History of New York*, presents a tongue-in-cheek account of Dutch settlers in New Amsterdam who were ardent smokers of the long pipe until their leader, William the Testy, proclaimed smoking illegal. The furious populace refused to obey the edict, so William compromised by permitting smoking only from short-stemmed pipes. But the short pipes brought the bowl so close to the smoker's face that the fumes "befogged the cerebellum, dried up all the kindly moisture of the brain and rendered the people . . . as vaporish and testy as the governor himself."

The clay pipe is now but a curiosity piece. Only a handful of clay-pipe artisans remain to satisfy the smoker with a taste for the unusual.

Today, there are basically five kinds of pipe popular throughout the world. Many Alpine people prefer the porcelain pipe, usually fitted with a long, curving stem and two bowls, one for the tobacco and one for the residue of juices. Other smokers prefer cherrywood pipes. The most popular varieties by far are the meerschaum, briar, and corncob.

Meerschaum is a magnesium silicate compound mined extensively in Asia Minor. The Germans thought the substance in its raw form re-

This unique carved set of Meerschaum pipes depicting Queen Elizabeth II and Prince Philip of England is part of a collection of unusual pipes assembled by Alfred Dunhill of London.

Photo courtesy of Alfred Dunhill, New York.

sembled petrified sea foam, and dubbed it *meerschaum*—literally, "sea foam." Turkish craftsmen today still carve meerschaum pipe bowls by hand, favoring busts of Cleopatra, Bacchus, and other gods and notables.

The briar pipe owes its existence to a French smoker who journeyed to Corsica in the 1820's. Arriving on the island and discovering that his prized meerschaum pipe had been shattered in transit, the Frenchman asked a local artisan to carve a new pipe from the wood of the *bruyère*, or heath tree, which grows extensively on the island. The smoker was so delighted by the finished product that he sent heath wood and roots to France and began manufacturing the *bruyère*, or briar pipe. Today, the briar pipe is the most popular pipe in the world.

The corncob is an American invention. John Schranke, a Dutch immigrant farmer living in Washington, Missouri, first whittled pipes from corncobs as a hobby. In 1869, Schranke brought one of his creations to the shop of a friend, Henry Tibbe. Tibbe improved the pipe by filling in the uneven surfaces with plaster of paris, and then he began to market the pipes. A hundred years later, corncob pipe production stood at around 10 million per year. The president of the largest corncob pipe manufacturer in the world still uses Tibbe's workshop as his headquarters.

Corncob pipes have the overwhelming advantage of being dirt cheap. At the other end of the scale, the most expensive pipe in the world is the Charatan *Summa Cum Laude*, a straight-grain briar-root pipe that sells in the vicinity of $2,500!

But even such an expensive pipe won't guarantee a perfect smoke. To some tobacco connoisseurs, there's only one kind of pipe you can count on, as Henry Brown noted, in 1896, in a poem that begins:

> There's clay pipes an' briar pipes an' meerschaum pipes
>   as well;
> There's plain pipes an' fancy pipes—things just made
>   to sell:
> But any pipe that can be bought for marbles, chalk, or
>   pelf,
> Ain't ekal to the flavor of th' pipe you make yourself.

The Cobra Pipe, designed by the Danish artist Keo, has a lined bowl to prevent a wood taste in the smoke.

The odor-free Electra-Pipe reduces tar and nicotine and furnishes a cooler smoke.

TRUFFLES

Truffles make women
lovable and men
enamoured.
—*Brillat-Savarin*

The scene: winter in a wooded area of southern France. A group of farmers moves among the trees, following the meanderings of a half-dozen pigs. Suddenly, one of the pigs noses into the dirt, grunting and snorting in hungry anticipation, and begins to dig into the ground with its hooves. The farmers rush over and chase the animal, then complete the excavation job. Yes, they're searching for buried treasure—but what kind? They're hunting for the most expensive natural food in the world: truffles.

Caviar may be everyman's idea of gustatory luxury, but ounce for ounce the acme of epicurean opulence is the peculiar subterranean fungus known as the truffle. You may have eaten a deliciously sweet morsel of dark and light chocolate of the same name, but in terms of taste, origin, and price, the candied imitation bears no relation whatsoever to the real McCoy.

The truffle is a fungus of the class *ascomycetes*, found mainly in the temperate zones. There are about seventy species of truffles, of which only seven are edible. Truffles are usually black with warty surfaces, ranging in size from a pea to an orange, with the average truffle about the size of a golf ball. Most truffles grow close to the roots of trees, from one to three feet below the surface, and seem especially partial to the roots of the oak.

Like the mushroom, also a fungus, the truffle has almost no nutritive value. But its taste, aroma, and ability to heavily flavor anything it comes in contact with have made it a prized edible since classical

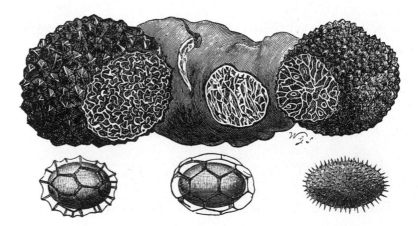

Three varieties of truffles are shown, with cross-sections.

A *truffle hunter and his specially trained rooting hog search for the precious mushrooms in Perigord, France.*

Photo courtesy of French Embassy Press and Information Division.

times. The Roman writers Juvenal and Plutarch both expressed the opinion that truffles were formed by lightning bolts that heated water and minerals in the ground where they struck.

After the fall of the Roman Empire, the truffle was virtually forgotten until the fourteenth century, but truffle hunting remained a hit-or-miss proposition until the nineteenth century. In 1810, a French peasant named Joseph Talon discovered a field of truffles in an area of Vaucluse heavily planted with acorns; he was the first to make the connection between the fungus and the oak. The enterprising Talon immediately went into the truffle business, and attempted to

---

The white truffle of the Piedmont district of Italy presently sells for over $200 a pound, making it the most expensive food in the world.

---

keep his discovery a secret, to no avail. But years of study have not revealed why the truffle prefers to grow in proximity to the oak, or why the planting of acorns will not necessarily assure the growth of truffles.

Over the centuries, truffles have become an integral part of many French dishes. The French satirist Rabelais's favorite snack was oysters with hot truffle-flavored sausages. Gastronomist Brillat-Savarin—born, appropriately enough, in the town of Belley—was convinced that the truffle is an effective aphrodisiac, proclaiming that "whoever says *truffle* utters a grand word, which awakens erotic and gastronomic ideas."

Today, the most valuable truffle fields, or *truffières*, are located in the Perigord district of France, near Bordeaux, and in the Vaucluse area north of Marseilles. The Perigord variety have been prized as the best since the fifteenth century. Truffles can be found in other areas, including North America, but are extremely rare outside of southern France.

Hunting the truffle is a difficult, delicate operation. Since the fungus grows underground, it's virtually impossible to tell where a crop of the delicacies might be found, but French farmers have developed a number of tricks. Some farmers with a nose for the trufffle claim they can locate their catch by examining the ground around oak trees. Others maintain that columns of small yellow flies hovering over truffle patches lead them to the buried treasure.

Most truffle hunting, however, is carried out with the aid of specially trained pigs or "rooting hogs." The pigs are better at scenting out the truffles, but they present the farmer with an additional problem. Once a pig locates a truffle, he's likely to gobble it right up before the farmer can chase him off. The pig's palate, it seems, is as partial to the truffle as man's. Farmers can train pigs to search for truffles in a matter of days—but it may take two or three years to teach them not to eat their find!

France exports about one-third of its truffles, so the French government is eager to encourage their growth. The French recently undertook a massive reforestry project in certain barren areas of the south in the hopes of increasing production. To begin a *truffière*, acorns or oak seedlings are planted with soil taken from truffle-growing areas. Truffles will appear, if at all, about five years after plant-

For a truly elegant brunch, serve omelettes trufflées, *filled with slices of black or white truffles, minced shallots, fresh parsley, and small cubes of Roquefort cheese or goose liver pate.*

SAUMON AU SANCERRE
(Makes about 4 servings)

4	salmon steaks	¼	cup butter
1	carrot, shredded	¼	cup flour
1	small onion, chopped	1	teaspoon grated lemon rind
½	cup chopped celery	2	tablespoons slivered French truffles
¼	teaspoon thyme		
1½	cup Sancerre, a dry white wine from the Loire Valley	1	cup (½ pint) heavy cream
			Salt and pepper
¼	cup Armagnac		

Place salmon steaks in large skillet. Add vegetables, thyme, Sancerre and Armagnac. Cover and simmer gently 20 to 25 minutes. Remove salmon steaks with spatula and keep warm on serving platter. Boil pan juices until 1 cup is left in skillet. In saucepan, heat butter and stir in flour. Stir in reserved pan juices, lemon rind, truffles, and heavy cream. Stir over low heat until sauce bubbles and thickens. Season to taste with salt and pepper. Drain off any juice that has accumulated on serving platter and discard. Spoon hot sauce over salmon. Serve with boiled new potatoes that have been drained, and rolled in a mixture of melted butter and Herbes de Provence.

Photo and recipe courtesy of Food and Wines from France.

ing. But hunting for the fungus doesn't become profitable until about ten years after planting; and in many cases, the maximum yield takes about twenty years to develop.

Sometimes even a twenty-year wait will fail to turn up any truffles, and no one is quite sure why. It's known that the delicate Perigord variety requires drought in mid-summer, or the winter harvest will frequently be sparse. Recently, many French truffle farms have failed completely, and gastronomists predict that if the next ten years doesn't see an increase in truffle finds, the delicacies may be priced right out of existence and disappear forever from our tables. But on the bright side, the attempt to encourage truffle growth has led to quite a boom in oak trees in some areas of France.

As you might imagine, thievery is a common problem in truffle-growing areas. A clever truffle-snatcher can become rich virtually overnight, since most varieties will sell for well above $100 a pound. The white truffle of the Piedmont district of Italy presently sells for over $200 a pound, making it the most expensive food in the world. On the streets of Milan, truffle vendors hawk this delicacy at the price of 5,000 lire (approximately $5.88) per truffle. An Italian law stipulating that any truffles found on leased property must be shared with the landlord has recently come under fire from Italian Communist politicians who have made the truffle law an important issue in the Piedmont area.

Truffles will probably be forevermore beyond the pocketbook of all but the rich. Gone are the days of the 1890's, when a Manhattan *bon vivant* could serve gallons of truffled ice cream at his dinner parties—leading to a custom that made that particular dessert *de rigueur* at fashionable New York parties for years.

The question in your mind might well be: could truffles possibly be worth their price? Well, the question can be answered only by your palate. For some gourmets, no price is too high for the pungent delicacy. For those who remain unconvinced, truffle fanciers propose a simple test. Taste any sauce requiring truffles, then sample the same sauce without the delicacy. The sauce without truffles, they're sure you'll agree, is simply not to be truffled with!

TULIPS

In the 1630's, a rage of tulip speculation, called tulipomania, gripped much of Holland, and farmers rich and poor began speculating in the tulip trade. Single bulbs of prized varieties sold for as much as $1,000—and one particular bulb sold for $4,000, a small fortune at the time.

To many minds, the tulip and the windmill are virtually synonymous with the Netherlands. Most historians would agree that the windmill in Europe made its first appearance in the Low Countries, sometime before the twelfth century. But you may be surprised to learn that the tulip is not a native of Holland, and was totally unknown in that country until the sixteenth century.

The colorful, cup-shaped flower, long popular among gardeners, is actually a native of the western Mediterranean and the steppes of Central Asia, and some species can be found growing wild in northern Africa, southern Europe, and in Japan. The empire of the Ottoman Turks once included much of the tulip's natural habitat, and it was through Turkey that most tulips reached western Europe and the Netherlands.

The Turks prized the tulip, and were cultivating that flower on a large scale by the mid-sixteenth century when the Austrian ambassador to the Turkish empire brought some tulip bulbs from Constantinople to his garden in Vienna. From Austria, the flower found its way to the Low Countries. In 1562, the first large shipment of Turkish tulips reached Antwerp, then part of the Dutch nation.

The tulip quickly became a favorite among European gardeners, and the Netherlands soon took the lead in producing prized specimens.

In the 1630's, a rage of tulip speculation, called tulipomania, gripped much of Holland, and farmers rich and poor began speculating in the tulip trade. Single bulbs of prized varieties sold for as much as $1,000—one particular bulb for $4,000, a small fortune at the time.

Alas, the tulip rage tapered off within a few years, leaving thousands of Dutchmen penniless. The economic scars of the tulipomania were felt in Holland for decades.

Still, the Dutch continued to raise their favorite flower. Today, the Netherlands remains the chief source of tulip bulbs for much of the world, with millions cultivated each year. The total value of Dutch horticulture approaches a quarter-billion dollars annually!

Tulips are also grown on a large scale in Belgium, the Channel Islands, and in parts of England, Ireland, and the United States.

The Turks, meanwhile, endured a period of tulipomania all their own. During the twelve years between the defeat of the Empire by Austria and Venice in 1718 and the revolution of 1730, the cultivation of tulip gardens became a craze in Constantinople.

The origins of most modern tulip varieties are untraceable, due to frequent hybridization and the plant's peculiar power of variation. Tulips grown from a single parent flower can change so greatly over the course of two or three generations that the relationship between the later specimens and their parents can be scarcely recognizable. It is this property—and not hybridization—that produces the prized variegated tulip.

New tulip varieties are raised from seeds. They produce flowers af-

Photo courtesy of Consulate General of the Netherlands.

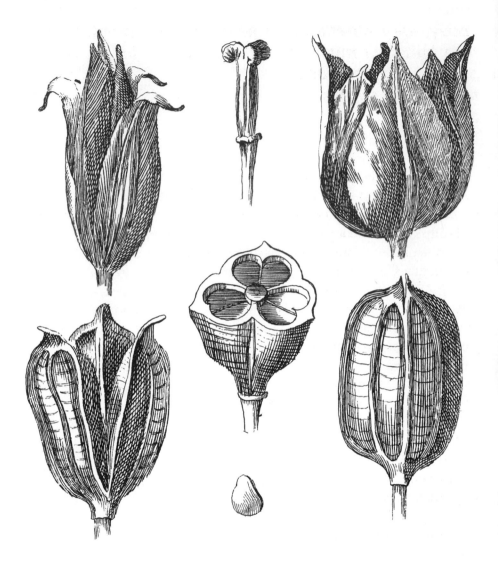

This cross-section of the tulip graced an 18th-century botanical guide.

ter about seven years of meticulous cultivation. At that stage, all tulips have but one color throughout. After the poorer specimens are weeded out, the good plants are saved as "breeder" tulips. A breeder tulip and its offspring may then grow for years without producing anything but flowers of the same hue.

But then, suddenly and unpredictably, some of the flowers "break," producing flowers with variegated colors. The so-called

Today, the Netherlands remains the chief source of tulip bulbs for much of the world, with millions of plants cultivated each year. The total value of Dutch horticulture approaches a quarter-billion dollars annually!

"rectified" tulip is then graded according to its coloring. If it is yellow, with purple or red markings, it is called a *bizarre*. If it is white with purple markings, it is called a *bybloemen*. If it is white with rose markings, it is called a *rose*.

Most tulips are raised from the shoots of a parent plant, not from seed. A shoot will begin producing flowers of its own in about three years. Most bulbs require a period of darkness and a thorough winter chill to bloom in spring; thus, many commercially grown tulips are produced in darkened bulb cellars. If you plant tulips in your garden, you can expect most species to bear blossoms for several seasons.

Among the many thousands of tulip varieties, we might mention the colorfully named *Rising Sun*, *White Hawk*, *Couleur de Cardinal*, *Pride of Haarlem*, and *Prince of Austria*.

But the tulip tree is not related to the tulip. It owes its name to its tulip-like green-yellow flowers. This tree is also known as the canary whitewood in England and the yellow poplar in the United States. Tulipwood, a white or yellow wood prized by cabinet makers, is, as you might expect, not a product of the tulip, but rather of the tulip tree.

Tulips have been the subject of at least two popular songs: *Tiptoe Through the Tulips*, and *When I Wore a Tulip, and You Wore a Big Red Rose*.

The word *tulip* has a rather odd origin. When the tulip was introduced to Europe, many gardeners saw a resemblance between the flower's shape and Turkish headwear, and they dubbed the flower *tulipan*, from *tülbend*, a Turkish word for "turban." From *tulipan* came the French word *tulipe* and the English word *tulip*. There is, as you can see, only a whimsical connection between *tulips* and *two lips*.

Clean as a lady, cool as glass, fresh without fragrance the tulip was.
—Humbert Wolfe, Tulip

TYPEWRITERS

At the 1876 Philadelphia Centennial Exposition, two recent American inventions were placed on public display for the first time. One, a certain voice-transmission apparatus invented by a man named Alexander Graham Bell attracted widespread attention among the fairgoers. The second, called the typewriter, attracted almost none. Yet by the time of the American Bicentennial Celebration, the typewriter had become such an integral part of American life that it's hard to imagine how business was carried on without it—just 100 years ago.

The fact is, more people are trained for the operation of the typewriter than for any other machine on earth—any machine requiring specialized training, that is. The typewriter has indeed come a long way. The early models resulted in machine writing being slower than handwriting. Today's modern machines are capable of speeds faster than speech, fulfilling the prediction of the Remington Company, the typewriter's first manufacturer, that the machine would "free the world from pen slavery and complete the economic emancipation of womankind."

The first recorded attempt to invent a typewriter actually took place in 1714, when an Englishman named Henry Mill filed a patent for what he rather longwindedly described as "An Artificial Machine or Method for the Impressing or Transcribing of Letters, Singly or Progressively one after another, as in Writing, whereby all Writing whatsoever may be Engrossed in Paper or Parchment so Neat and Exact as not to be distinguished from Print." If Mr. Mill was as verbose as this description suggests, it's no wonder he saw the advantages of a typewriting machine. In any case, Mill's typewriter was apparently never constructed, and no drawings of his project were ever found.

The earliest typewriting machines in America were crude attempts to mechanize the printing of Braille so that the blind could write as well as read. A machine called the "typographer," capable of printing ordinary letters, was patented in 1829. The type was set on a semicircular frame that had to be turned by hand, so that only one letter at a time could be shifted into position and printed. Needless to say, the machine was much slower than writing, as were most early typewriters. And many typewriting machines were as large as a piano, with keyboards resembling black and white ivories!

What this country needs is a typewriter that will strike an indefinite letter when you aren't sure of the spelling.

As late as 1881, Remington was selling only 1,200 machines a year.

In the 1860's, two Milwaukee inventors were busy developing a machine for consecutively numbering the pages of a book. One of the men, Carlos Glidden, came across an article describing a new British machine capable of printing typed letters, and he brought the article to the attention of his partner, Christopher Latham Sholes. If our machine could print page numbers, Sholes wondered, why couldn't it also print regular letters? By 1867, Sholes had constructed the first practical typewriter in his Milwaukee shop.

Sholes's first typewriter was a cumbersome machine with a piano keyboard, little improvement over other models then in existence. But in 1868, Sholes and Glidden turned out a second model, the first typewriter capable of printing faster than the pen.

Sholes's major innovation was an arrangement of keys that allowed two letters to be typed in rapid succession. With other early models, the typist had to wait until the type bar of the first letter had returned to the carriage before striking the second key, or risk locking the two bars together and bringing the machine to a halt. Thus, Sholes's keyboard, identical to today's except in minor details, was designed so that letters that combine frequently in our language would be separated on the keyboard—hardly the ideal arrangement for the typist, as proponents of the new Dvorak keyboard point out.

In 1873, Sholes signed a contract for the manufacture of his machine with E. Remington and Sons, gunsmiths of Ilion, New York, and the following year, the first model, called the "Remington," was placed on the market. You may imagine that the first Remingtons were scooped up by clever businessmen as fast as they could be manufactured. Not true. Most businessmen couldn't see the advantage of a machine only slightly faster than handwriting that cost, in the words of one, "a thousand times as much as a pen." As late as 1881, Remington was selling only 1,200 machines a year. It took almost a decade after the first Remington was manufactured that typewriter sales began a steady climb upwards.

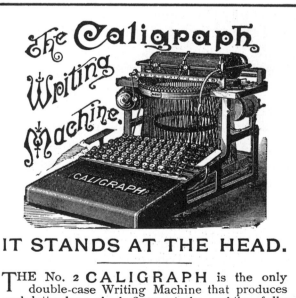
Typewriters of the 19th century varied widely in design.

This picture, executed in 1894, shows performers on the North Typewriter Company's machines.

One drawback of the early machines was their extremely slow speed. For one thing, upper and lower case letters were contained on separate keyboards, necessitating continual movement from one keyboard to the other; at the time, more words were capitalized than are today. It wasn't until 1878 that the first machine with a double keyboard (upper and lower cases on the same keyboard, with a shift key) was placed on the market, but even then the two systems remained in competition until 1888. In that year, a typing contest was held in Cincinnati between a Mr. Traub, one of the leading exponents of the separate keyboard system, and a Mr. McGurrin, who'd taught himself touchtyping on a double keyboard machine. McGurrin won the speed contest easily, and the separate keyboard typewriter became a museum piece.

The earliest typewriters were more cumbersome than today's models. At right is the first commercial typewriter, developed by Christopher Latham Sholes for Remington in 1873. The models on the left were popular in the 1890's.

Another drawback presented by early machines was the inability of the typist to view the paper until it was removed from the typewriter. In 1883, the first typewriter with visible printing was marketed, and Correcto-Type became a practical though distant reality.

There were few inventions of the late nineteenth century that Thomas Edison didn't at least dabble with, and the typewriter was no exception. In fact, Edison constructed the first electric typewriter, which printed letters on a moving roll of paper. Edison's device eventually became the ticker-tape machine, with the first electric machine perfected by James Smathers in 1920.

The first portable typewriter had been manufactured in 1909. In 1956, the two inventions came together to form the electric portable, the term-paper writer's best friend.

The IBM Corporation broke new ground in 1959 with the development of the Executive Electric, the first typewriter capable of line justification (the printing of lines flush with one another on the right side as well as the left) and differential spacing. In machines without differential spacing, letters as narrow as an "i" and as wide as an "m" are allotted the same amount of space on the page. With differential spacing, letters are allotted space in accordance with their width, making possible line justification and a much neater, printlike page.

In 1961, IBM developed the first typewriter with a spherical type carrier, the "the type ball," eliminating the nuisance of interlocking type bars.

Today's typewriters can print in almost any language including computer code. A New York linguist claims he can, in one hour, adapt a typewriter to print in any of 146 languages.

The first commercially successful electric typewriter was put on the market by IBM in 1933.

There's a Chinese typewriter called the Hoang with 5,850 characters on a keyboard two feet long and seventeen inches wide. Top speed on the Hoang is about ten words per minute.

There's also a musical notation typewriter capable of printing fifty different notes and symbols. And a shorthand typewriter—invented in 1910—that can record up to 200 words per minute. Modern versions of the latter are used today by court stenographers.

If you've ever lived in an apartment next door to a budding writer, you might be pleased to learn that a noiseless typewriter was invented more than fifty years ago. The machine used heavier type bars that moved with lower velocity but carried the same momentum as regular bars. Alas, the model proved to be poor for producing carbon copies.

If you're a practitioner of the "hunt-and-peck" school of typing, you may be encouraged by the development of the Dvorak keyboard, patented in 1936. The Dvorak keyboard is arranged so that the letters most common in English are most easily and comfortably reached by the touch typist. The Dvorak keyboard looks much like the universal keyboard, with three rows of letter keys. But on the Dvorak, 70 percent of all letters in almost any given passage can be found on the middle row, with the most common letters placed under the strongest fingers.

The typewriter will never achieve maximum utility until it stops making mistakes in spelling.

Proponents of the new system claim that the increased speed of the Dvorak method and the lessening of typist fatigue could result in a savings of $20 million a year in business expenses throughout the coun-

Everything works well on paper, except a broken typewriter.

try. However, the machine is a costly investment—an Olympia typewriter with a Dvorak keyboard costs an extra $300 above the regular price. It is not surprising then that as of April 1978, Olympia has sold no Dvorak keyboard machines for two years.

The first touch typist in the world was, not surprisingly, Sholes's daughter Lillian. In those days, incidentally, the typist as well as the machine was referred to as the "typewriter."

Candidates for typing instruction—both male and female—were chosen on the basis of physical strength rather than intelligence or dexterity, since operating the heavy keys of early typewriters was arduous work.

The first author to submit a typewritten manuscript was Mark Twain. But there's some disagreement as to which of Twain's manuscripts earned the honor. In his *Autobiography*, Twain maintained that *The Adventures of Tom Sawyer* was the first book he typed. But in a letter to a friend, Twain claimed that the earlier *Life on the Mississippi* was also submitted in typescript. In any case, Twain bought his Remington for $125. Later, when he attempted to give the machine away, he found it extremely difficult to find a taker.

In case you were wondering: Pope Pius X11 was the first pontiff to use the typewriter. He was an excellent touch typist. And George Bernard Shaw was the first playwright to use a typewriter as a stage—prop—in *Candida* (1898).

What's the fastest typing speed ever recorded? The top speed ever achieved by a typist, 216 words per minute stands as the record, set by one Stella Pajunas in 1946 on an IBM electric. To give you an idea of

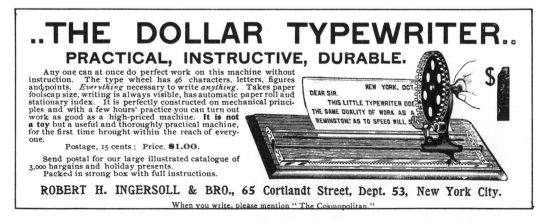

her accomplishment, sixty words per minute is considered good professional speed. The record for top speed for over an hour of nonstop typing is 149 words per minute, also set on an IBM machine.

Perhaps the most remarkable typing record is held by Albert Tangora, who during a 1923 business show in New York, ran off a total of 8,840 correctly spelled words in one hour of nonstop typing, a rate of 147 words per minute. Incredibly, Tangora achieved his record on a cumbersome old *manual* typewriter that would seem crude in comparison with modern models. Judges estimated that Tangora executed an average of twelve-and-a-half strokes per second!

The Dvorak Simplified Keyboard, or DSK, attempts to combat the tyranny of QWERTY through a logical arrangement of keys. The DSK places the most frequently used letters (70%) on the middle line or "home row" of the typewriter. On the top line letters used 22% of the time; on the bottom row, letters used only 8% of the time.

The record for sustained speed on a Dvorak keyboard is 170 words per minute.

The longest nonstop typing stint was 162 hours, one minute, set by California high school teacher Robin Heil in 1976. A blind English office worker named Mike Howell holds the duration record for a manual machine: 120¼ hours.

But the world's greatest typing buff must certainly be Mrs. Marva Drew of Waterloo, Iowa. Over a six-year span, Marva exercised her skills by typing the numbers one to one million on a manual typewriter—a feat requiring 2,473 pages!

UMBRELLAS

The rain it raineth on the just
  And also on the unjust fella:
But chiefly on the just because
  The unjust steals the just's umbrella.

Let us now turn to the subject of brolliology. What is brolliology? Why, it's the study of the brolly, of course—the gamp, the parasol, the parapluie, the bumbershoot, the bumbersoll—to you, the umbrella.

If you think the ribbed, collapsible umbrella was the invention of some clever eighteenth- or nineteenth-century Englishman determined to fight back against the soggy weather of London town—you're all wet. The fact is, the umbrella is one of the oldest artifacts in man's history, already a familiar item in many cultures by the time man began to write.

This bas-relief from the Palace of Persepolis shows Xerxes under the royal parasol.

Courtesy of Editions Albin Michel and Professor Laignel-Lavastine.

The early Greeks used the umbrella as a symbol of productivity and sexual aggression.

The umbrella is so old that brolliologists can't agree on its origin, or decide whether it was first used for protection from the rain or the sun. They do know that it was employed as an item of religious and ceremonial regalia from the earliest days of ancient Egypt. Egyptian mythology held that the visible sky was actually the underbelly of a god stretched from one end of the earth to the other like an immense umbrella. Hence, in contemporary art, priests and Pharoahs were often placed in the shade of an umbrella to symbolize royal and religious power.

Assyrian tablets dating from 1350 B.C. depict a king leading his retinue while servants shade the royal head with a long-handled parasol. In India, a religious group known as the Jains called their ultimate heaven of perfected souls by a name that translates as "The Slightly Tilted Umbrella."

This Greek vase depicts an original-looking parasol-bonnet—and the slave carrying it is an even greater original!

This Roman Fresco, "Woman With an Umbrella," is now in the Louvre, in Paris.

The early Greeks used the umbrella as a symbol of productivity and sexual aggression, usually associated with the god Bacchus, and they carried umbrellas in many of their parades and festivals. In later centuries, the Greeks put the umbrella to a more utilitarian use as a sunshade, and developed sunshade hats similar to the sombrero.

The Romans, too, used parasols against the sun. Women attending chariot races in the amphitheatre sometimes dyed their parasols to denote their favorite chariot team. If you've ever attended a football game in drizzly weather and have been annoyed to no end by umbrellas blocking your line of vision, you may find it comforting to know that the Romans had a similar problem at their games, with a hot dispute over parasol use finally decided by the emperor Domitian—in favor of the sunshade.

Brolliologists are divided over the origin of the Chinese umbrella. Some say the Chinese developed their contraption independently of the West. Others claim that the umbrella spread from Egypt eastward to China; still others maintain that the Egyptians owe the brolly to the Chinese. In any case, the use of the umbrella was well established in China at a very early date. Oiled paper or bamboo were the favored materials. A Korean tomb dating from 25 B.C. contained a collapsible umbrella complete with rib supports.

Europe was introduced to the bumbershoot through ancient Byzantium. In the eighth century, Pope Paul I gave Frankish King Pepin the Short a jewel-handled umbrella as a token of Papal support for his reign.

In the fifteenth century, Portuguese seamen bound for the East Indies brought along umbrellas as fit gifts for native royalty. Upon landing on a strange island, the seamen immediately opened an umbrella over their captain's head, to demonstrate his authority.

The Normans brought a twelve-ribbed umbrella to England in the eleventh century. But the first contextual use of the word "umbrella" (from *umbra*, Latin for "shade") does not appear in English literature until 1609, in the work of John Donne. The spelling was not finalized until much later, and *umbrellow*, *umbrello*, and *umbrillo* were common as late as the nineteenth century.

A fair-weather friend lends you an umbrella when the weather is fair, and takes it back when it rains.

The man usually credited with popularizing the umbrella in London was one John Hanway, a seventeenth-century traveler who brought the brolly to England from Portugal. Hanway created quite a stir by strolling through London under the strange contraption. He perambulated about in all kinds of weather, and was often greeted by jokes from passersby. He was likely to suffer abuse from coachmen, who feared the popularity of such a device would cut into their trade.

Religious Londoners objected to the umbrella on moral grounds—after all, the purpose of heavenly rain was to make people wet. But despite these objectors, the use of the umbrella spread steadily in the showery city. For some time, they were called Hanways in honor of their eccentric pioneer. The word *gamp*, incidentally, comes from Charles Dickens's novel *Martin Chuzzlewit*, in which a large cotton umbrella is the trademark of one Sairy Gamp.

The English didn't invent the umbrella, but they did develop the first *practical* waterproof bumbershoot. This happened in the late seventeenth century. By 1700, umbrellas were in regular commercial production, with whalebone the favored material for the ribs.

Early English umbrellas were hardly perfect, though. They were large and cumbersome, frequently they leaked, and they broke easily in a strong wind. They were most in evidence in coffee houses, where a supply was kept by the door for patrons who might dash from the coffee house to a carriage. Like the ancient Romans, the English for many years considered the gamp too effeminate for use by men.

Some wily Londoners put the brolly to another curious employment: orators frequently held an umbrella above their head while addressing a crowd, to protect themselves from missiles tossed by less-than-approving listeners.

You may think that at least the fold-up or transparent umbrella is a recent invention. Not true! An enterprising gentleman by the name of Gosselin of Amiens constructed a fold-up "pocket" model with four interjoined steel tubes in 1785! In fact, the construction of the umbrella hasn't changed very much since 1760, when most bumbershoots were already being built with eight ribs, a sliding brace, and a curved handle. As for the transparent umbrella, an apocryphal English tale attributes its invention to a Russian prince who wanted to keep a wary eye out for mad dogs!

Listen to this one: a group of British soldiers carried umbrellas into battle during the Napoleonic wars, until the British military decided the gamp was hardly a fitting implement for a fighting man. The Boers also used the umbrella on rain-drenched battlefields. Even the U.S. Cavalry carried brollies on occasion, particularly during the Indian wars in the rainy northern states.

By 1820, the umbrella had fallen out of fashion in Europe, and the parasol had arrived. Aristocratic English women imported fancy models from Paris made of silk or chantilly lace, with elaborate enameled handles. Some handles were fitted to carry perfume or writing materials, or even a dagger. And believe it or not, there was a model designed with one protruding side to offer protection for the bustle that most women wore in those days.

Bartine's Sunshade Hat was the rage in 1895.

The use of the umbrella in courtship dates back to the ancient Greeks. In the eighteenth and nineteenth centuries, young maidens frequently sat for their portrait with a delicate parasol in hand as a symbol of their class.

The umbrella or parasol has figured prominently in paintings by Degas, Monet, Goya, Delacroix, Seurat, and Renoir. In Brittany, custom still dictates that a young man can express his interest in a favored maiden by offering to carry her umbrella at the fair. Carrying

Close to 75,000 umbrellas are lost each year on the bus and subway system of London.

her umbrella along the road is considered a sure sign of engagement.

Brolliologists are reluctant to estimate the number of umbrellas in use throughout the world, but the country with the highest per capita use of the gamp is definitely England. As late as 1954, 300,000 umbrellas were produced in the British Isles each *month!* Today, most umbrellas are imported from Hong Kong and Japan. The Japanese, incidentally, cornered the American umbrella market in the 50's, by exporting almost 12 million bumbershoots to us within a twelve-month period.

Modern umbrella makers contend that today's models are so well constructed that the average person needn't go through more than two in his lifetime. But they make no mention of the phenomenon of the lost umbrella, which more often than not is the reason for a new purchase. To suggest the scope of this problem, it may help to note that close to 75,000 umbrellas are lost each year on the bus and subway systems of London alone!

This 100% windproof umbrella pops in and out in an instant from inside its walking stick.

In the eighth century B.C., *this substantial-looking brolly was in vogue.*

And the number of yearly umbrella thefts is anyone's guess. Which brings to mind the one about the man who left his brolly in the umbrella stand in a London pub with the following note: *"This umbrella is owned by the champion boxer of England, and he's coming back in two minutes."* The man then went to the bar for a drink. When he returned, the umbrella stand was empty, and in place of his brolly, he found a note that read: *"This umbrella was taken by the champion runner of England. He's never coming back."*

There's the widespread superstition that opening a bumbershoot indoors brings bad luck. Then, of course, there's the age-old belief that the easiest way to assure a rainy day is to leave your umbrella at home. Robert Louis Stevenson seemed aware of this peculiar meteorlogical wisdom when he wrote: "There is no act in meteorology better established . . . than that the carriage of the umbrella produces dessication of the air; while if it be left at home, aqueous vapor is largely produced, and is soon deposited in the form of rain."

VANILLA

Vanilla is unique among the 20,000-odd species of orchid known throughout the world, for it is the only orchid that produces a commercially useful commodity.

Vanilla beans ripen on the vine over a period of six weeks.

The vast legions of American ice cream-lovers fall basically into two camps: those who favor chocolate, and those who champion its chromatic antithesis, vanilla. Although vanilla and chocolate—long the most popular ice cream flavors in the United States—may be diametrically opposed on the color scale, they share more in common than you might imagine. Both cocoa and vanilla come from a bean. Both are natives of Mexico and Central America. Both are used primarily as a confectionary flavoring. In fact, for many years *chocolate* and *vanilla* were not thought of as opposites at all—they were almost always used *together*!

When the Spanish explorer Cortés arrived at the court of the Aztec king Montezuma in 1519, the Aztecs offered their guests bowls of a frothy black liquid chilled with snow. Chocolate, which Cortés had already heard of, was the primary ingredient of the beverage; but Cortés learned through court gossip that the Aztecs sweetened their drink with a secret ingredient, an extract from a wild orchid called *thilxochitl.* The Spaniards dubbed the white bean of the orchid with a diminutive of the word *vaina—vainilla—*or "little pod."

When cocoa from the New World reached Spain, vanilla came with it, for the two beans do have one important difference: chocolate in its unadulterated form is bitter tasting; vanilla is sweet. Wealthy Spaniards began enjoying a chocolate beverage sweetened with vanilla decades before coffee and tea became popular in Europe. The Spaniards guarded the secrets of their preparation for years, and it was almost a century before the two beans were widely enjoyed elsewhere in Europe.

Vanillla and chocolate reached France in 1660, when Maria Theresa of Spain arrived at the French court, with her maids and cooks, to become the bride of Louis XIV. The new queen enjoyed a vanilla-flavored chocolate beverage prepared by a maid each morning, and other members of the court were soon clamoring for vanilla. The clergy then decried the beverage as "provocative of immorality"—it was rumored that vanilla, like chocolate, was an aphrodisiac.

Queen Elizabeth of England, the owner of a notorious sweet tooth, was wont to fill her pockets with candies; she would nibble on the sweets throughout the day. Many of the candies were made from chocolate or from vanilla, or from a mixture of both. English confectioners vied to create new specialties to delight the queen, and one apothecary struck on the idea of using the juice of the vanilla bean as a flavoring for *marchpane*, almond paste. The occasion marked the first time that vanilla was used to flavor anything but chocolate, and Elizabeth loved the results.

By the late seventeenth century, chocolate was popular as a beverage throughout much of Europe, and chocolate houses—the forerunners of coffee houses—were common in many cities. But sugar gradually replaced vanilla as a sweetener for chocolate, and vanilla struck out on its own as a flavoring.

It wasn't until 1836, however, that scientists found a way of growing vanilla outside Mexico. Charles Morren, a Belgian botanist, discovered that the vanilla plant was pollinated by the Melipone bee, a tiny insect that lives only in Mexico. Thus, the plant could not be naturally pollinated in other country. Morren found a method for artificially pollinating the plant, and vanilla plantations soon began appearing in many of France's colonial possessions.

Rumor has it that Thomas Jefferson, credited with introducing spaghetti, french fries, and a number of other foods to America, was also the first to use vanilla as a flavoring agent. During the last 200 years, vanilla has become one of the most popular confectionary flavorings in the United States, and is now widely used in candies, baked goods, ice cream, carbonated beverages (cream soda is made from vanilla), sauces, and surprisingly, perfume.

The vanilla plant that the Aztecs harvested is the *Vanilla planifolia*, but another species native to Oceania is called, appropriately enough, *Vanilla tahitensis*. Vanilla is a climbing orchid that attaches itself to trees with aerial rootlets, though the plant does possess ordinary soil roots. The fruit, or pod, is long and thin, measuring from six to ten inches in length and a half inch in diameter. The pods of the

The vanilla plant flowers in the second year of growth, producing a lovely yellow orchid, which lasts but part of a day unless fertilized.

Photo courtesy of The Vanilla Growers of Madagascar.

Vanilla cultivation and production.
(LEFT) *Only the finest blossoms are fertilized, by hand pollination, to produce the best vanilla pods.*
(CENTER) *In Madagascar, ripe vanilla beans are harvested primarily by women and children. Harvested beans are stored until the pods begin to shrivel; then immersed in hot water, drained, exposed to the hot sun, and boxed or covered with blankets at night. This process is called sweating.*
(RIGHT) *Green vanilla beans are sold in the marketplace, primarily for the production of vanilla extract.*

Photos courtesy of The Vanilla Growers of Madagascar.

best varieties are, strangely enough, chocolate-colored, and are flecked with a crystalline substance called *givre*, or vanillin, a fragrant chemical secreted by the pod lining that gives vanilla its characteristic flavor. Vanilla, is unique among the twenty-thousand-odd species of orchid known throughout the world, for it is the only orchid that produces a commercially useful commodity.

Unripe vanilla is green; it turns yellow when ripe. Harvested vanilla beans are cured by immersion in hot water, stored for several months to develop the full bouquet. The beans are then shipped to factories for the production of vanilla extract. At the factory, the beans are first chopped, then steeped in a solvent to extract the vanilla essence. At some factories, the vanilla extract is aged for six months to a year before shipment to confectioners and retail stores.

Though a native of Mexico and Central America, and a favorite flavoring in Europe and the United States, vanilla is today almost en-

tirely a product of various Indian Ocean islands, where it was brought for plantation cultivation by French colonists. The Malagasy Republic (formerly Madagascar), Reunion, and the Comoro Islands now account for about 75 percent of the world's vanilla supply. Quantities are also produced in Tahiti, Indonesia, Mexico, and the Seychelles Islands.

Artificial vanilla flavoring can be produced from the sapwood of fir trees; and vanilla flavoring, synthesized from chemicals, is becoming increasingly popular as the cost of the raw vanilla bean rises.

Now chocolate, too, is being synthetically produced; it's possible that the dish of vanilla and chocolate ice cream you just enjoyed owned nothing to either bean. The next time you buy a vanilla or chocolate product, check the list of ingredients to find out if you were given the real McCoy—you'll find it all printed there in black and white.

INDEX